THE ENVIRONMENTAL IMPERATIVE

Eco-Social Concerns For Australian Agriculture

Frank Vanclay & Geoffrey Lawrence

First published by
Central Queensland University Press
PO Box 1615
Rockhampton Q 4702

Vanclay, F. M. (Francis M.)

The environmental imperative: eco-social
concerns for Australian agriculture.

Includes index.
ISBN 1 875998 00 4

1. Agriculture - Environmental aspects - Australia.
2. Agriculture - Social Aspects - Australia. I. Lawrence,
G. A. (Geoffrey A.). II. Title.

Cover Design by Jason Tweedie
Cover Photographs by Doug Steley

Designed & Typeset by Anne Camilleri,
CQU Press, Rockhampton.

Printed by Watson-Ferguson Co. Ltd.
Brisbane, Qld.

THE ENVIRONMENTAL IMPERATIVE

Eco-Social Concerns For Australian Agriculture

CONTENTS

ACKNOWLEDGMENTS

Many of the ideas contained in this book were generated during the early 1990s when we were colleagues at the Centre for Rural Social Research at Charles Sturt University, in Wagga Wagga. Centre members have assisted us in many ways, but Ian Gray and Perry Share deserve special mention. The Centre's postgraduate students were an important part of the intellectual community in which many of the ideas in this book were first developed. These students included: Hugh Campbell, Scott Glyde, Stewart Lockie, Helen McKenzie, Luciano Mesiti, and Emily Phillips.

Since Geoff Lawrence has been at the Central Queensland University, he has benefited from discussions with Richard Clark and Wal Taylor from the Queensland Department of Primary Industries; Jim McAllister, Dani Stehlik and other members of the Rural Social and Economic Research Centre; and Jane Gray, Linda Hungerford, Kristen Lyons, Patrick Morrisey and Janet Norton, postgraduate students attached to the Rural Social and Economic Research Centre at CQU. Discussions with Richard Hindmarsh, David Burch and Roy Rickson, from Griffith University have also been of great value, and Fred Buttel of the University of Wisconsin-Madison is thanked for his continued advice and encouragement.

Frank Vanclay spent a sabbatical in the Department of Communication and Innovation Studies at Wageningen Agricultural University, The Netherlands, in 1993. This time was very insightful and rewarding for him, and some of this book was written there. Special mention must be made of the assistance provided by Cees Leeuwis, Niels Röling and Cees van Woerkum, and Norman Long (now at the University of Bath).

The rapid publication of this book, together with the setting of a reasonably inexpensive purchase price, was made possible through grants from the Vice Chancellor of Central Queensland University, Professor Geoff Wilson and the Vice Chancellor of Charles Sturt University, Professor Cliff Blake. Thanks goes, as well, to Central Queensland University's Pro Vice Chancellor (Research) Professor John Coll and to the Dean of the Faculty of Arts, Dr Wally Woods, for supporting this project, as well as to Professor Seumas Miller and Associate Professor Ross Chambers at CSU.

Throughout the book, we have sought to update and extend materials which have been previously published. We wish to thank the editors and publishers of the *European Journal of Agricultural Education and Extension, the International Journal of Sociology of Agriculture and Food, Prometheus,* and *Rural Society.*

Chapter 2 is an updated version of a chapter in *The Global Restructuring of Agro-Food Systems,* edited by Philip D. McMichael. Copyright © 1994 by Cornell University. Used by permission of the publisher, Cornell University Press.

Chapter 5 is an updated version of a chapter in *Agriculture, Environment and Society,* edited by Geoffrey Lawrence, Frank Vanclay and Brian Furze. Copyright 1992 by Geoffrey Lawrence, Frank Vanclay and Brian Furze. Used by permission of the editors and publisher, Macmillan (Australia).

Anne Camilleri of CQU Press is thanked for her considerable effort in typesetting and constructing the index for the book.

The Australian Research Council, the Land and Water Resources R & D Corporation and the Rural Industries R & D provided funding for studies, the findings from which sections of this book have been based.

Our greatest debt goes to our families. We thank our partners, Jackie Walsh and Dimity Lawrence, for their encouragement, assistance and support, and our children for their forbearance. We hope that they might eventually reap the benefits of a less environmentally and socially exploitative Australian agriculture.

AUTHORS' PREFACE

Australian agriculture, in the mid 1990s, remains in crisis. The terms of trade for agriculture are falling, many farmers have negative incomes, and there are ineluctable pressures for structural adjustment -- with government policy assisting the exit of marginal farmers out of agriculture. Australian governments have been guided by philosophies which justify fiscal restraint. This has created a policy environment of reduced commitment to public funding for agriculture, a reduction in agricultural extension services, and opposition, in principle, to regulatory and incentive-based approaches to environmental management. The decade of the nineties has been a period of considerable change in agricultural extension services as they attempt to deal with these altered circumstances. The crisis in agriculture has become matched by what we have now come to recognise as a 'crisis' in agricultural extension. Yet, because of the socio-economic problems of family farm-based agriculture and the increasingly severe impacts of current production strategies on the environment, there remains a need for effective agricultural extension in Australia. Increasing levels of salinity, acidity, soil structure decline, soil nutrient decline, erosion by wind and water, destruction of native habitat and wildlife, invasion of rangelands by woody weeds, and other environmental problems are occurring on an unprecedented scale. The severity of environmental problems creates an environmental imperative for social action and government policy to address those problems.

To date, the debate about environmental degradation in agriculture has been dominated by technical discussion of the physical aspects of the problem -- of the physical causes and of the physical solutions. In agricultural extension circles, the debate has been restricted to a discussion of how to induce farmers to adopt environmental management practices. There has been little consideration of the social foundation of agriculture, of the socio-economic and political processes that have shaped Australian agriculture, or of the social bases of environmental problems within agriculture. Agricultural extension agencies, despite the various 'crises' in which Australian agriculture and extension services exist, have tended to maintain a commitment to traditional paradigms. Current thinking appears inadequate to the task of understanding the real nature of environmental problems within Australian agriculture.

This book addresses, from a critical sociological perspective, the issue of environmental degradation within agriculture. This perspective is applied at three levels of analysis: international, national, and local. The international level applies to the consideration of the position of the Australian agricultural economy in terms of the world political economy and how this affects farming practices and the environment. The national level applies to the ways extension agencies have responded to the issue of environmental management within a changing policy context. Finally, the book considers the role of individual farmers in the management of the agricultural environment and how they are affected by both international and national processes.

It is hoped that this book will contribute to a better sociological understanding of agricultural degradation, and to the formulation of strategies which assist in the implementation of more sustainable farming systems, in Australia.

AGRO-ECOLOGICAL CONCERNS IN AUSTRALIAN AGRICULTURE

There is strong evidence to suggest that the 'crisis' which Australian agriculture experienced in the mid 1980s has re-emerged in a somewhat different form in the 1990s. In the middle of this decade, drought, increasing input costs and sluggish markets have combined to place enormous pressures for adjustment on the farm sector. According to some assessments, up to 20 percent of Australian farmers are expected to leave agriculture over the next few years (*Australian*, 2 February 1994: 36). This will occur despite any benefits which changes to the General Agreements on Tariffs and Trade, Australia's continued integration with the Asia-Pacific, or commodity price increases might bring. Australia has developed as a producer of bulk agricultural commodities, particularly grains, sugar, meat and fibre. The value of these commodities has been steadily falling in real terms, while the cost of agricultural inputs has been increasing. Up until quite recently, agriculture has been one of the most important industries for the Australian economy. Because it is export oriented, Australia's agricultural economy is very vulnerable to world market fluctuations. With increasing world overproduction of most agricultural commodities, and the development of regional trading blocks, Australia faces the prospect of being progressively marginalised and peripheralised. Not only during the recent times of crisis in agriculture, but steadily since initial European settlement of Australia, agriculture has had a significant effect on the natural environment, so much so that the future of agriculture itself is threatened.

With the deteriorating economic position of farmers, with governments removing subsidies and concessions from farming, and banks unwilling to lend monies to what are increasingly viewed as risky farm businesses, many farmers cannot afford to invest in more environmentally friendly forms of production, nor can they willingly reduce the extent of their production. Changes in government (and grower) ideologies have contributed to a diminution in government support for, and underwriting of, agriculture. At a time in which farmers have been eager to receive increased information about how they can increase their productivity and efficiency, there has been a reduction in the commitment by many State governments to agricultural extension. If the future for many farmers looks bleak, the future of the environment looks bleaker still. How is this situation to be understood? What has caused, in such short time, the profound -- and in some cases irreversible -- degradation of the agricultural environment? What can be done to improve the situation? These are crucial questions which this book addresses.

This book examines the socio-political processes affecting the structure of agriculture in Australia, and the impacts of those processes on farmers and the agricultural environment. It also examines the responses of Australian governments (Federal and State) and government agricultural extension agencies to those processes, and the effect of those responses on farmers and the environment.

In order to achieve this, a multi-faceted approach is taken. First, critical political economy perspectives are used to analyse Australia's position in the world agricultural economy (Chapters 1 and 2). Attention is then focused upon the ways in which biotechnology -- heralded as the technological 'saviour' for farmers -- is being developed and applied in Australia (Chapters 3 and 4). Processes of farmer adoption are highlighted in Chapter 5. A critical sociological approach is again employed to analyse the deficiencies of traditional public agricultural extension agencies and the basis of farmer decision making with respect to environmental management (Chapters 6, 7 and 8). Finally, the book seeks to evaluate the extent to which the agricultural environment might be improved through the infusion of sociology into agricultural extension. It is argued, in Chapter 9, that there are beneficial aspects of traditional extension which should not be overlooked when governments make decisions about both the funding of new technologies and of the sorts of extension services which help farmers adopt new technologies and management practices. It is also argued that as extension becomes more group focussed there is a consequent need for the training of extension agents in aspects of social process -- group composition, power relations, leadership, gender considerations, decision making, political interests, attitude formation and behaviour. The further development of Australian rural sociology would seem to hold the key to better extension practice.

Although the book is directly concerned with the Australian situation, it utilises international literature and experiences. While the concern for Australia is paramount, it is likely that much of the analysis presented here is directly relevant to other countries and cultures, particularly those of the so-called 'semi-periphery' (countries such as Australia, Aotearoa (New Zealand), and Canada). Nevertheless, there are some important unique characteristics about the Australian situation.

It must constantly be kept in mind that Australia's agricultural environment is different from that of other countries, especially those in Europe. The geological nature of its soils, particularly the extreme age of the continent, has meant that its soils are much more vulnerable to land degradation than European agricultural lands (Watson, 1992).

Despite a very long geological history, and a very long prehistory, Australia's experience of European-style agriculture (especially cultivation, fertilisation and cropping) is quite short, at most 200 years, and is considerably less in the more remote parts of Australia. In some parts of Australia, the land is being farmed by those whose families undertook the original clearing, fencing and stocking.

European occupation of Australia was on the legal basis of *terra nullius*, a self-serving colonial concept that implied that if the land was not, in effect, being cultivated by the nation's indigenous inhabitants, it did not belong to them. And since the Aborigines did not defend the territory in the ways the Europeans expected, the white settlers considered that they had sufficient right to agricultural development of what appeared to them to be vacant lands. The direct assaults as well as the guerilla activities of Aborigines and Torres Strait Islanders -- that is, the resistance which was shown to white invasion of the continent -- is now understood to have been widespread and violent. But guns were always superior to spears. And European cultural tradition justified the use of force to contain what the early governments believed to be the unjustifiable, oppositional, behaviour of 'savages'. This led to a situation where acquisition of Australia was made without any consideration of the needs of local inhabitants or any appreciation of the ways in which they had managed the environment for some 40,000 years (see Reeve, 1988). In terms of compensation for Aborigines and Torres Strait Islanders, the first two centuries of white rule were characterised by forced resettlement on reserves, and the insertion of the ideologies of church and para-state authorities whose role was to 'civilise' the native population. There were no treaties or other negotiations like those which took place in places such as Aotearoa (New Zealand) and the USA.

Some conservationists have persisted with the Roussean-influenced view that the Aboriginal population did not impact upon the environment. However, in academic circles, this is now substantially rejected. There is clear evidence that the Aboriginal population modified the environment in many aspects, particularly by the use of fire (Reeve, 1988; Barr and Cary, 1992; Cary and Barr, 1992; Dovers, 1992). Furthermore, the legal basis of *terra nullius* has been successfully challenged in the High Court of Australia in what is known as the Mabo case. The implications of this for Australia are not yet clear, but it could potentially have enormous implications for land tenure, particularly on pastoral leases.

Land degradation, of one form or another, has been a major problem affecting agricultural land in Australia for at least the majority of this century. Land degradation had become so severe by the 1930s, that many Australian States enacted soil conservation legislation at that time. This has meant that, unlike Europe (see Röling, 1993), the promotion of conservation measures, as well as the provision of information upon which farmers can make production decisions, has been an important part of the work of agricultural extension agencies in Australia.

SETTING THE SCENE
MAJOR FORMS OF LAND DEGRADATION IN AUSTRALIA

Salinity

There are two main categories of salting, irrigation-induced salinity and dryland salinity. Soil salting or salinisation was initially experienced in irrigation areas where excessive irrigation and poor water management caused rising watertables which brought naturally occurring subsurface salt to the surface (see Barr and Cary, 1984). Dryland salinity is more complex and there are several types of dryland salinity. For our purposes, two will be identified. Salt scalds refers to those now salted areas which previously had been covered with topsoil and had been productive (in an agricultural or ecological sense), but through erosion or other physical process (such as logging operations), the topsoil had been removed leaving bare salty areas. In salt scalding, the erosion of the topsoil is the activity that lead to the salt layer being exposed.

Saline seepage, on the other hand, is similar to irrigation-induced salinity, in that it relates to rising watertables. Because of historical land-use patterns of land clearing and modern agricultural processes of cropping and grazing, a situation has arisen where less water is used by the agricultural ecosystem than was used by the pre-existing natural ecosystem. The excess water not only increases surface runoff, causing erosion problems, but also results in greater accessions to the underground watertable. For a variety of geological reasons (including the fact that much of the continent was under sea water during its early formation), the watertable in many parts of Australia is naturally salty. Rising salt watertables increase the salt in the soil profile. Through capillary action, salt is concentrated in the top metre or so of the soil profile whenever the watertable is less than two metres below ground surface. The process is accelerated by the increased evaporation due to the reduced vegetative cover which results from increased salinity. Areas that are affected by increased salting are known as discharge areas.

Accessions to the watertable are not uniform over a catchment area. The underlying geology of the terrain can profoundly affect the potential for the watertable to rise. Generally, bare hilltops -- particularly those formed by movements in the earth's crust which have produced hills displaying vertical or oblique rock strata (known as preferential pathways), contribute most to watertable accessions. However, the upper slopes used for pasture and cropping can also contribute to watertable accessions. All areas that contribute to rises in watertable levels are known as recharge areas.

In some locations, recharge and discharge areas can occur in close proximity, with localised salting being caused by water percolation from nearby hills. These areas are known as Province A recharge zones. However, in other situations, known as Province B zones, discharge areas can be far removed from their corresponding recharge areas, with the underground flow of water through aquifers and deep leads. Often the direction of these aquifers may be independent of surface topography making identification of the recharge areas for the respective discharge areas difficult.

The final outcome of soil salting is bare land covered with a salt crust, but there is a considerable lead-up to this situation. The first signs of soil salting are reduced yields in crops, or reduced biomass in pasture species, although this can be due to other factors. The composition of pasture species changes, with the less salt tolerant species -- such as subterranean clover -- giving way to the more salt tolerant species, such as strawberry clover. As the salting worsens (the concentration of salt increases) other, less palatable, salt indicator species such as barley grass and sea barley grass (*Hordeum maritium*) become prominent. With higher concentrations of salt only very salt tolerant species, such as salt bush, grow (see discussions in Squires and Tow, 1991).

Because salting is associated with high watertables, seepage of groundwater and resultant waterlogging can occur. A number of rushes such as spiney rush (*Juncus acutus*) and some other species, may indicate the presence of waterlogging by salty seepage. While these species are not restricted to salty environments the 'prolific establishment [of spiney rush] is usually associated with high groundwater salinity' (Jenkin and Morris, 1982). The seepage of groundwater, and increased surface runoff due to reduced ground cover, can lead to severe water erosion and gullying particularly in areas where ground cover has already declined as a consequence of salting.

Salinity is a major problem for Australia. Estimates of damage and potential damage vary widely, and may be impossible to calculate, but one estimate suggests that some 4.4 million hectares of land are affected, with approximately 3.8 million hectares experiencing salt scalds and another 639,000 hectares affected by seepage salting. The cost to Australia each year is estimated to be over $100 million (see Poulter and Chaffer, 1992;158). While salt scalding affects a greater area of land, much of the land affected, or potentially affected, is not prime agricultural land. Saline seepage is of greater concern because of its potential to affect all agricultural land in Australia. Saline seepage is also directly attributable to human activity. In the discussion that follows, unless explicitly stated otherwise, salinity refers only to saline seepage.

Agronomists are aware of the ways problems of salting can be addressed. In discharge areas, the salt-affected land should be fenced off to keep stock out; salt tolerant species, such as tall wheat grass (*Agropyron elongata*) should be sown. Protection against further evaporation should be made by increasing ground cover by spreading hay, for example. Trees can be planted around the perimeter of salt-affected areas to provide a windbreak which shelters the newly sown plants, to lower the watertable in the immediate vicinity and to reduce evaporation. However, the best form of control minimises further accessions to the watertable by preventing the percolation of water through the soil. This can be achieved by reforesting the recharge areas, particularly on the non-productive hilltops with preferential pathways, and by growing deep rooted pasture species such as lucerne and phalaris. Deep rooted pasture species and trees are both high in water use -- have high evapotranspiration potential -- and, because of their longer root systems, are able to utilise the available water. Rain falling onto paddocks of deep rooted species has less chance of entering the watertable than rain falling onto other pasture species or crops. A range of farm management practices such as stubble retention and minimum tillage can also be employed to reduce watertable accessions.

Rises in the watertable have occurred as a result of the European farming practices during virtually the whole period of white settlement (Reeve, 1988; Dovers, 1992). Reduction in future accessions to the watertable will only have minimal short term impact on watertable levels, particularly in Province B situations. The movement of groundwater through the aquifers and particularly the deep leads is extremely slow and, even if all percolation of water was stopped, it is likely that watertables will continue rising for some time.

The effects of salting are widespread. Quite apart from the loss of productivity, reduced profit levels, and reduced land value experienced by individual farmers, every section of a rural community experiences the consequences of widespread salting. Farm and town water supplies are affected, household and farm equipment can be damaged by salt water, the biological integrity of creeks and rivers is threatened, wildlife habitats are threatened, and road foundations are undermined -- causing deteriorating road surfaces. The need for expenditures to address these problems may reduce the capacity of local councils to provide other services, ruin the appeal of the area to those pursuing recreation or tourism, and reduce the amenity value of the area. In such circumstances, the consequences of salting affect the whole community. Yet, the community consequences of salting are less tangible than the direct loss in productivity experienced by individual farmers in discharge zones. For this reason, salinisation has often been seen as a 'farming' problem rather than a 'community' problem. The private ownership of farmlands is also a factor which limits the vision of both communities and authorities: salinisation seems to be an issue which farmers, alone, must address. And if they fail to, they are often viewed as the only ones to suffer.

While it is apparent that inaction on the part of farmers results in major (if yet unquantified) costs for the Australian community, this is not to attribute blame to the entire farming community. It has been suggested, for example, that a good deal of the land degradation in Australia has occurred because farmers have had poor information when they have made land management decisions and that, in past years, governments have formulated policies without concern for environmental impacts (Chisholm, 1987). Poulter and Chaffer (1992: 161) have argued that, in terms of dryland salinity:

> [information] appears to be difficult and costly to obtain, which will deter investment in gathering information by individual farmers. Because of the lack of information and the difficulty in obtaining it, salinity may exceed the socially optimal level. Thus, because of the existence of external effects and the difficulties involved in obtaining information, government intervention ... may be justified.

As with many land degradation issues, the problem of soil salting is one of externalities. The farmers who experience soil salting -- those who are in discharge areas -- are rarely the farmers whose properties extend into recharge areas. Strategies to reduce watertable levels, or even to prevent further increases in the watertable level, require that farmers in the recharge areas modify their farming practices. Since they are not the farmers who are experiencing the soil salting there is little incentive for them to adopt salting control practices. Salting control techniques, particularly tree planting, can be costly, and the use of deep rooted perennials, even though they may be profitable, limits the farmer's flexibility (Oram, 1987).

Salting is a form of non-point pollution. Not just a few individual farmers are responsible; all landholders in recharge areas, and the government, with crown land in those areas, are responsible. However, the specific identification of recharge areas and therefore the specific identification of those responsible for soil salting is very difficult (because of the inability to identify specific recharge zones). Furthermore, salting is also a form of non-temporal pollution. It is not just today's farmers who are responsible. Salting has occurred because of land management practices over the duration of European settlement. Current land management practices are not just the result of farmers' actions; as suggested earlier, they are the result of the philosophy of land management derived from European culture and which has been present both in farmers' attitudes and in government policy.

Because of the externality problem, a simple solution to soil salting, involving the action of farmers on an individual basis, would seem to be a partial solution at best. A community approach encouraging the widespread adoption of salinity control techniques is recommended (see Wilkinson and Barr, 1993). Yet, while local community support and local peer pressure may influence farmers in recharge areas to engage in salinity control, it is likely that this will only encourage adoption in Province A situations. A much more concerted effort will be required to encourage adoption of salinity control techniques on a widespread basis. This may involve the whole Australian community and quite possibly require some financial support to farmers who participate. Sociologists must seek to understand which farmers (and under which circumstances) adopt strategies to address salinisation, which communities act (and in what ways and for what reasons), how governments intervene, and whether the means for limiting the spread of salinisation conflicts with an ethos of land ownership and of productivity/efficiency. In other words, if it can be demonstrated that salinisation is a nationally important problem and that reducing salinity will lead to a more sustainable agriculture, how will it be possible -- in the context of entrenched attitudes and likely economic costs -- to bring about changes to agricultural practices? Economists have some important insights (see Hodge, 1982; Poulter and Chaffer, 1992) but have not, we would suggest, understood the social bases of farm decision making or the likely social impacts of some of their recommendations.

Acidity

Acidity is a major problem where mixed cropping and grazing practices have been undertaken, and is typically associated with the long term use of so-called 'improved pastures' -- pastures sown with clovers, often subterranean clover, and heavily fertilised, especially with superphosphate. Acidity, like salinity, is an insidious process -- one potentially affecting 8 million hectares in the southeastern corner of Australia (Watson, 1992); and costing $100 million in lost production (Smiles, 1989: 127).

Acidification refers to the chemical processes in the soil which result in the pH dropping to such a low level that crops can no longer grow (generally considered as being less than pH 5.5). Soils become more acidic because residual nitrogen and phosphorous are not 'bound up' in ways which prevent their free movement. Excess nitrogen and phosphorous occurs as a result of the over application of fertilisers (notably superphosphate) and through the extensive use of clovers and other legumes, which 'fix' nitrogen through their root nodules. The nitrogen, ammonia, urea and uric acid in the urine of stock can also lead to acidification particularly in the more intensively utilised areas of the paddock, such as near the watering trough and under the trees.

Apart from the loss of productive land as soil becomes too acid to support crops, the other major problem with excess nitrogen and phosphorous is their contribution to algae blooms should they enter the watercourses (see Chapter 2).

The management practice utilising subterranean clover and superphosphate (the 'sub and super' strategy) was heavily promoted by extension agencies and by a government superphosphate bounty that helped to subsidise the purchase of fertilisers. The 'sub and super' option was widely adopted by farmers because it led to large increases in yield. It is estimated that between 35 and 40 percent of Australia's cropping soils now have levels of phosphorous over that which is required to provide maximum growth to plants (Grierson *et al.*, 1991). Watson (1992) argues that the agronomists who undertook the work that led to the technological innovation of 'sub and super' were too narrowly focussed on yield-response curves to evaluate properly the chemical imbalances such practices would induce.

The temporary solution to the problem is to grow acid resistant plants, and/or to apply lime -- an expensive practice which is non-sustainable in the longer term. Ultimately, a new cropping and pasture rotation must be introduced so that there is much more careful management of nitrogen in the soil.

There are many reasons why farmers might be reluctant to adopt the new crop rotations. Although some of these claims are contested by the extension agencies, difficulties given by some farmers are that these so called 'sustainable crop rotations': require greater skill by farmers with a wider range of crops; require new and/or different machinery; increase workloads at already peak workload times; create increased difficulties for farmers in the marketing of an increased range of crops; require more inputs; require a greater use of chemicals (for weed control); and are not profitable (see Lockie and Vanclay, 1992; Vanclay and Lockie, 1993). Here, then, we revisit the problem of how to move to a more sustainable agriculture. What might be viewed as sustainable in agronomic terms may not be 'sustainable' in economic terms. And for the community, what will eventually manifest itself as a *community* problem requires the cooperation of those who own and control the means of production and who make decisions on the basis of individual interests, not the 'long term' interests of the community. Farmers have been quite keen to vocalise where they see much of the 'blame' lying. Governments gave incentives for the adoption of practices which are now viewed as non-sustainable; it is governments which should be asked to provide the necessary means to overcome the problem which they helped to cause.

Erosion by water and wind

Soil erosion has long been recognised as a major problem in Australia, and was the land degradation problem that prompted the establishment of extension agencies to promote better environmental management practices. The erosion of soil is a fairly simple process relating to the transportation of soil particles from one place to another. This transportation can occur by wind or by water. Soil loss occurs when the soil is not adequately protected from erosive forces.

The primary problem with soil loss is that it is normally the top layer of the soil profile -- the most fertile soil -- which is blown or washed away. The second problem relates to where the eroded soil travels -- silting up dams, muddying creeks and creating other problems for rivers and the plant, fish and animal life within them. To the extent that pesticide and fertiliser ions are tied to the soil colloids, they are also transported, usually to the nearest creek, causing water pollution and contributing to algal blooms (see Johnson and Rix, 1993). Wind erosion causes dust pollution in cities and towns. Even when eroded soil remains on the farm, such as piled against a contour bank, the act of it being eroded changes the structure and friability of the remaining soil so that it is no longer as productive. Fields that have been eroded suffer loss of fertility and may have the very unproductive B Horizon soil exposed. Finally, large areas can be rendered useless to agriculture because of extensive gullying, thus preventing access by agricultural machinery.

There are two major forms of water erosion, gully erosion and rill (or sheet) erosion (Johnson and Rix, 1993). Gully erosion is the most obvious and generally occurs when unprotected soil is exposed during a period of particularly heavy rainfall. Rill erosion is the erosion that occurs along rills (cultivation furrows) in a paddock. Such erosion has been found, in some districts, to average 5 mm per year (50 tonnes per hectare per year) over the whole paddock (Vanclay, 1986). While gully erosion is easy to see, rill erosion is an insidious process and easily disregarded by farmers. There are strong social norms encouraging farmers not to have prominent gullies on their farm. However, some gullying is unavoidable as it can occur as a result of a freak storm. Unfortunately, there is little social concern governing rill erosion.

Erosion can be prevented by both structural and management techniques. Structural techniques are the use of contour banks, grassed waterways, grass filter strips, and contour cultivation, in order to reduce the erosion risk by, for example, stopping the flow of water across the paddock. Rows of trees as windbreaks can also serve as a structural barrier against wind erosion. Conservation cropping practices (zero or minimum tillage, stubble mulching, managing the cropping cycle so that the paddock is never bare at high risk times, and using agricultural implements that are less destructive of the soil) are highly desirable (see Squires and Tow, 1991) but are not always adopted by farmers.

In past decades, extension agencies heavily promoted contour banks and were inclined to measure their own performance in terms of the number of miles of banks -- in the days before

Australia adopted the metric system -- which had been graded in any district. In some cases, the contour banks were not appropriate, or were incorrectly designed so that they would pond runoff, rather than directing runoff away to the watercourse. And, if the bank ever broke as a result of excess ponding, the resulting torrent would often cause more damage than if the bank had not been there. A further problem -- one which continues to be experienced today -- is that banks increase the accession of water into the watertable thus contributing to the problem of salinity.

Erosion has been a very serious problem in the past, with massive erosion gullies (sometimes over 10 metres deep) being evident throughout Australia as a relic of a bygone age. Memories of large dust storms blowing Australian soil to Aotearoa (New Zealand) are vivid and widespread. The last major dust storm of note caused severe disturbance in Melbourne in the early 1980s. This event aside, wind erosion is now viewed as less of a problem -- largely because of farmers' adoption of more appropriate land use practices.

Erosion of river and creek banks remains, however, a major concern. In many regions, the clearing of native vegetation has resulted in accelerated run-off, increasing the incidence of flash-flooding. Public works-related clearing of vegetation and changes brought about by road and railway development are also important contributing factors. Near creeks and rivers where tree removal has occurred, flash flooding can lead to considerable erosion of banks and surrounding farm land. Not surprisingly, one of the major concerns of Landcare groups in many catchments is river and creek bank protection.

Soil Structural Decline

Soil structure deteriorates as a consequence of excessive cultivation, and cultivation with certain types of disc blades. Good soil structure is important for the vitality of the soil. Structural breakdown leads to reduced yields and the increased erodibility of soil. In order to prevent structural breakdown, farmers are advised to reduce the number of cultivations they make, and to use less destructive implements. However, there are reasons for farmers' persistence with agricultural practices likely to induce structure decline. Farmers use cultivation as a form of weed control, and are reluctant to adopt zero-tillage techniques because they require a different management philosophy, new equipment, and use chemicals intensively. Zero tillage or conservation farming replaces cultivation with chemicals (the 'plough in the drum'). Another reason is cultural and historical, there has been a perception that a good farmer was one with a well-prepared seedbed, heavily cultivated and with perfectly straight furrows. Conservation farming requires farmers to plant seeds in what some regard as a weedbed.

Nutrient Decline

Plants absorb nutrients from the ground, which together with water and sunlight, produce the vegetative cover desired by the farmer. Over time there is a consequent reduction in soil nutrients, not only by their loss through exported produce, but also by accelerated erosion. In the past, nutrients have been replaced through the addition of artificial fertilisers, particularly by superphosphate, but such a practice is expensive and, ultimately, not sustainable. To counteract the problem of nutrient decline, farmers need to adopt crop rotation practices which are much more sensitive to the processes of nutrient cycling in the soil.

Other Problems of the Agricultural Environment

There are many other environmental problems that affect, or are caused by, agriculture. The five main problems that are of concern to cropping agriculture have been presented above. Other problems include infestation of rangelands by woody weeds, and plagues of pests. Rabbits have been a major problem -- with burrowing causing extensive erosion. In rangeland areas, populations of feral animals, especially goats, donkeys, and horses can lead to many forms of environmental damage including overgrazing. While infestations of prickly pear have been biologically controlled with the introduction of the cactoblastis caterpillar, other attempts at biological control, such as the introduction of the cane toad (*Bufo marinus*) to rid sugar producing regions of the cane beetle, have been disastrous. Cane toad populations are spreading south and west from Queensland, leading to the death of native animals and reptiles which feed upon them. Other introduced species, both plant (lantana, groundsel, blackberry) and animal (rabbit, fox, European carp) have been major problems in various areas and/or at various times. Loss of habitat for native species, and contamination of habitats, especially from water pollution has also had considerable environmental impact.

Apart from Australia's particular susceptibility to land degradation and its relatively short history of European-style settlement and land management strategies, there are other features of Australian agriculture which form a background to any discussion of the agricultural environment. The extensive (broadacre) nature of Australian agriculture, the vast distances within the country, and distances from Australia to potential markets, have meant that the degree of intensification of agriculture that has occurred elsewhere, in Europe for example, has not occurred to the same extent in Australia. In fact, despite considerable resources being devoted to agricultural research and extension, and despite adoption of new management practices, average yields of basic crops have not changed significantly during the course of the history of Australian agriculture. While, after the Second World War, the adoption of new management practices had an immediate effect on yield, in the longer run, yields have either improved very slowly, or have fallen. Declining yields have been largely due to environmental degradation as Australian agriculture has continued to 'mine' the soil.

Reeve (1988: 72) identified the factors contributing to the problems which have beset Australia:

> Agricultural development has moved into increasingly unsuitable or fragile marginal lands ... New technology has brought the means of inflicting environmental disturbance more rapidly, over greater areas and over a wider range of environments ... Substantial land use changes, driven by economic or political forces have taken place at a rate that exceeds the capacity and/or capability of soil conservation agencies to assess the effects of these chances, and to make recommendations on management practices ... Degradation problems appear to be becoming more complex. More time and resources

are needed to study processes and causes, new kinds of expertise are needed to formulate solutions and a greater degree of co-operation and co-ordination is required to implement these solutions.

As he noted, in 1987 the amount of money allocated to the National Soil Conservation Program was about the same as that allocated to landscaping the grounds of the new Parliament House. The Federal and State governments have, since that time, introduced a plethora of programs to address the problem of environmental degradation -- indicating the degree to which so-called 'brown' issues have been politicised (and often by urban-based green groups). Landcare aside, governments remain primarily interested in discovering technical solutions to environmental problems. While the biophysical nature of the Australian environment is an important part of understanding the causes of environmental degradation, policy makers have been excessively influenced by physical/biological scientists who have, at least in past years, seen the problem as one which can be 'fixed' by science. While poor landuse practices (overploughing, overstocking, overirrigating, poor crop rotation and excessive use of chemicals) do contribute to land degradation, they are only one aspect of the tension between agricultural production and environmental quality (Lawrence, Vanclay and Furze, 1992).

LIMITATIONS OF A TECHNICAL UNDERSTANDING

A narrow technical perspective is invariably based upon an uncritical acceptance of the social, political and economic status quo. In such a situation, solutions to environmental problems are narrowly conceived. Some of the assumptions which generally underlie the orthodox approach to environmental management are:

- Agriculture can and should maintain its present 'productionist' trajectory;
- The innovation diffusion model best explains farmer adoption behaviour;
- The provision of information about environmental and production issues will change farmer behaviour;
- The state has only a limited role in promoting change.

Environmental issues need to be examined in a broader context, one that includes an analysis of the social construction of agriculture, and the social structure of agricultural systems. Narrow technical analysis and the solutions posed within these views, often based on vested interests, need to be avoided. If Australia is to move toward a more economically and ecological sustainable future (one based on rural social development, agricultural sustainability and broader ecological sustainability) then the many views about what might constitute such a future need to be carefully analysed.

Given that environmental management -- including agricultural production -- is a human activity, one driven by the socio-political and economic demands of different groups within the community, it stands to reason that the human dimension must be brought to the fore in any evaluation of the agricultural environment.

Agricultural environmental problems are unambiguously social in origin, and it is in the long-term interests of all Australians that this is recognised and acted upon accordingly.

GOVERNMENT POLICY AND RURAL SETTLEMENT:
IMPLICATIONS FOR AGRICULTURE AND THE ENVIRONMENT

Many features of the history of Australia have set the stage for inevitable land degradation. These features tend to relate to government policies to develop the countryside and to deal with population and unemployment problems.

The most important of these, in environmental terms, were the Selection Acts which allowed 'selectors' to purchase and farm largely virgin lands. Following the gold rush era of the 1850s, a land tenure system was developed which confiscated part of the illegally held land of the 'squatters' and sold this to ex-gold diggers and others who had come to the colonies to make their fortune. The 'selectors' were families which were given formal title to small parcels of land under favourable financial conditions (Dovers, 1992). The amount of land available to individual farmers under this scheme was well below what was required for them to survive. Their attempt at survival produced considerable soil erosion, led to clearing of trees from vast tracts of land (which has contributed to salinity problems today), yet produced a people who were fiercely self-reliant and proud of the 'development' which they brought to inland Australia. They were often innovative and a series of inventions was forthcoming which improved their ability to farm the inland. These developments -- such as the stump-jump plough, and better harvesting equipment -- allowed the opening up of more lands. 'Closer Settlement' schemes were another feature of the development of agriculture in Australia (see Bolton, 1981; Davidson, 1981; Lake, 1987; Dovers, 1992; Share, 1994).

Following each of the two World Wars, the Australian government opened up new areas of land for soldier resettlement. These schemes were implemented to restore full employment and to develop further the countryside. These schemes saw many soldiers with no previous farming experience taking up small rural holdings. This created a widespread demand for practical information among the new farming population and, as a consequence of popular opinion that such farmers were 'deserving' of public assistance, helped to justify the proliferation of agricultural extension throughout the entire farming community. During the 1960s and 1970s, government development of new agricultural regions in Western Australia (for example, the Ord River Scheme and much of the wheat belt), the Northern Territory (around Katherine) and Queensland (especially in brigalow areas) led to the entry into farming of people largely unfamiliar with agricultural practice.

In other locations, 'back to the land' movements (Munro-Clarke, 1986; Metcalf and Vanclay, 1987), part time or hobby farming, and early retirement schemes have led to the situation where people devoid of an agricultural background (and, in most cases, any form of agricultural training) becoming involved in land management. These people may or may not have production concerns, but are by virtue of their occupation of rural lands, land users. Many are environmentally conscious and have Green sympathies. But this is not to say that they manage their lands any better than the farmers who have been implicated in past rounds of environmental degradation. There is evidence that hobby farming increases the incidence of pests and noxious weeds, for example. Clearly, if they reside in rural catchments, they need to be involved in any conservation programs, especially because of the social and off-site considerations of their own, and others', environmental practices.

THE STRUCTURE OF AUSTRALIAN AGRICULTURE

Due to Australia's geographical position in the world, its own internal geography, its colonial history, and its links to the world economy, Australia has been, and appears likely to continue to be, a supplier of bulk agricultural commodities, particularly grains (specifically wheat and rice), sugar, meats (specifically mutton, lamb, live sheep export, rangeland beef, and feedlot beef), and fibres (specifically wool and cotton). Bulk agricultural commodities constitute approximately 70 percent of all agricultural products exported from the nation (*Australian Farm Journal,* June 1991) and this is expected to be the case for the remaining years of this decade (Department of Primary Industries and Energy, 1989).

While individual farmers will diversify and produce new crops, such as tropical fruits, these are unlikely to be a major aspect of Australian agriculture, partly because of the scale of the production of the bulk commodities and also because of marketing difficulties of specialist crops. As is argued in Chapter 1, opportunities for value adding of agricultural produce are likely to be limited.

Faced with declining yields due, among other things, to drought, to environmental degradation, and to lower world prices resulting from global overproduction, Australian farmers are experiencing reduced income (Lawrence, 1990; *Australian Farm Journal,* April, 1995). The effect of declining incomes is exacerbated by rising input costs. With increased industrialisation of agriculture, and increased reliance on ever-expensive chemical inputs, farmers are experiencing considerable cost-price pressures. In Australia, the average net income of broadacre farmers during the 1990s has been negative (farmers have received no income after costs have been deducted, and have usually been required to borrow to remain in agriculture). For example, the average farm business loss on 'broadacre' farms for 1995 is expected to be $22,000 (*Australian,* 21 December, 1994: 5). Continuous losses of this sort mean the farm is -- at least in economic terms -- unsustainable. The lack of cash surplus militates against the adoption by farmers of strategies to protect the environment. It has been estimated, for example, that the cost of making the average Western Australian mixed farm sustainable is in the order of $150,000 per year for 10 years (*Australian Farm Journal,* December 1994: 64). The vast majority of farmers will not be able to meet such costs.

THE SOCIOLOGICAL CONTRIBUTION TO ENVIRONMENTAL MANAGEMENT IN AGRICULTURE

We take, as a starting point, Bowler's (1992: 251) summation of the position taken by rural social researchers in North America and Europe:

> Most informed observers recognize that the agricultural sector in developed market economies has reached a crisis in its evolution. In summary form, the crisis contains the twin dimensions of 'production' and 'environment' ... The reaction has been to develop the concept of a 'sustainable' agriculture, recognizing that ecologically based farming systems offer the best option despite the confrontation with contemporary agroindustrial systems.

This book presents a broad sociological interpretation of the major issues relating to environmental degradation and Australian agriculture, including:

- the causes of land degradation,
- the social and economic processes that promote an exploitative agriculture,
- farmers' inability to adopt more environmentally sound management practices,
- why farmers' non-adoption of environmentally sound management practices may, in some circumstances, be rational from their point of view,
- the deficiencies within traditional state agricultural extension agencies,
- the problems of new extension methods and programs,
- the benefits of publicly-funded agricultural extension programs which service all farmers,
- the basis of farmer decision making about environmental management,
- the nature of farmers' attitudes on environmental management,
- the potential for agro-biotechnologies to aid in environmental protection, and
- possibilities for linking macro and micro sociological theories in a manner which contributes to the development of group theory and leads to better group practice in Australian agriculture.

A number of definitive arguments are developed in this analysis:

1. There are major economic, social and environmental consequences for Australia as a result of the processes of economic restructuring in the world political economy.

2. The process of structural change in the world agricultural economy will continue to disadvantage the farming sectors of countries such as Australia which are dependent upon the sale of bulk undifferentiated agricultural commodities.

3. By locating the least desirable agricultural activities in the less 'regulated' nations of the periphery and semi-periphery, transnational agribusiness is engaging in a form of environmental imperialism.

4. The globalisation of agriculture will integrate farmers into a world production system which will limit farmers' ability to alter production regimes on their own

farm -- and which may prevent them from becoming more environmentally responsible.

5.   The three strategies employed by governments and public extension agencies in dealing with the crisis in agriculture and the crisis in extension -- segmentation, privatisation, and utilisation of group extension and bottom up approaches -- will not resolve environmental problems in agriculture and may well worsen them.

6.   The changing conception of 'rural' in Europe, with the countryside becoming a place of consumption as much as a place of production, allowing pluriactivity and off-farm income opportunities for farmers as well as urban support for public spending in rural areas, will occur more slowly in Australia. This will limit opportunities for farmers' to earn off farm income and, in a situation of deteriorating terms of trade, will limit their ability to adopt new more efficient and more environmentally sound management practices.

7.   Extension agencies have been using unsatisfactory models of extension based on an unsatisfactory model of innovation and adoption behaviour.

8.   The adoption of environmental management practices is fundamentally different from the adoption of commercial innovations in agriculture. In the latter, farmers must make a choice about what is in their interests. In the former, the public might desire changes which the farmers reject or do not believe are their individual responsibility. Different 'signals' will result in different behaviours.

9.   Farmers' non-adoption of technology and of environmental management practices may be rational, in keeping with a desire to minimise costs.

10.   The failure of extension in promoting adoption of new innovations, especially of environmental management practices, is not because of characteristics of those farmers (age, education level, economic status, or 'cosmopolitanness'), but because of the failure of extension agencies adequately to address the needs of farmers.

11.   The vast majority of farmers do not have environmentally hostile views or attitudes. They are guided, in fact, by an ideology of 'stewardship' of the land.

12.   Attempts to change farmers' attitudes or to promote a land ethic among farmers will not necessarily increase the rate of adoption of environmentally sound management practices.

13.   Economically marginal farmers who are being structured out of agriculture are not necessarily managerially inept, unwilling to consider new knowledge and innovations, or unwilling to alter their current practices. Their marginality and inability to act to change their circumstances are based on their relationship to the international agricultural economy.

It is hoped that through greater insight into the issue of environmental management in agriculture that will be gained through a sociological understanding of the problem, a more economically and environmentally sound agriculture can be developed in Australia. This book attempts to make a small contribution to the movement toward a more sustainable Australian agriculture and rural society.

PART A

POLITICAL ECONOMY PERSPECTIVES
ON
AUSTRALIAN AGRICULTURE

THE RESTRUCTURING OF AGRICULTURE
ENVIRONMENTAL AND SOCIAL IMPLICATIONS

AGRICULTURAL RESTRUCTURING IN THE SEMI-PERIPHERY

To grasp the nature of change within rural society, it is necessary to understand the dynamics of capital accumulation and to recognise the practical manifestations of patterns of accumulation modified by state regulation.

Structural change impacts in certain ways and occurs at several levels. This chapter is concerned with identifying the socio-economic processes which are facilitating the increasing influence of transnational agribusiness in Australian agriculture and with the attendant social and environmental impacts of those processes.

The Demise of the Post-War US Hegemony

A socio-politically negotiated balance between accumulation and regulation is considered to have been a dominant feature of capitalism since the second World War. This has been described as 'fordism' and is a regime typified by Taylorist labour processes, the mass production and distribution of consumer goods, the promotion and consolidation of trade unionism, and the development of the welfare state (that is, a basically Keynesian solution to the contradictions inherent in class-based post war capitalism). For reasons associated with changes in the international arena (including the collapse of the Bretton Woods agreement and oil price rises in the 1970s), inflation, commodity price uncertainties in the 1980s, the world-wide recession and intensified competition in trade during the 1990s (see Buttel and Gillespie, 1991; Goe and Kenney, 1991), the fordist mode of accumulation and regulation is considered by some to have been superseded by a post-fordist regime, one characterised by new industries, production methods, organisational forms, class relations and state policies (see Mathews, 1989).

The extent to which a transition to a full-blown post-fordist economy is occurring or has occurred, together with what exactly characterises post-fordism, are issues of considerable debate. Nevertheless, a significant change is occurring in the organisation of transnational capital and in the organisation of society. Whether this represents a fundamentally different mode of production, or is a new form of organisation under essentially the same mode of production, is not yet clear. What is clear is that many post-fordist characteristics, such as niche marketing, product diversity, decentralised production, transformation of work, and global sourcing, are being adopted by companies - including large corporate firms. Despite post-fordist rhetoric about a resurgence of craft production and new consumption patterns influenced by 'green' attitudes (ones that might, seemingly, reduce the significance of transnational corporations), it is doubtful whether any move to a post-fordist economy represents a significant threat to the global power of these corporations. It is quite likely, in fact, that post-fordist patterns of production are being adopted by transnational corporations in order to enhance their operations.

Restructuring of the US economy has resulted in a major decline in traditional sectors of industry -- including steel manufacture, automobiles, farm machinery and electronics. Firms have responded to increasing global competition and reduced profitability by retrenching labour, by automating, and by moving to new areas of weaker, cheaper and often non-unionised labour. Another feature has been the merging of businesses, spurred on by the increased economic strength of finance capital (Green, 1988). Goe and Kenney (1991) have argued that the crisis in US agriculture has occurred later than that within the industrial sector. Nevertheless, because of agriculture's quite intimate connection with manufacturing industry and finance capital, it is experiencing the same sorts of restructuring pressures. Agriculture is being required to develop new and more productive, efficient and flexible food and fibre production and delivery systems. Information technologies and the application of agro-biotechnologies are viewed as the sorts of responses which will provide capital with opportunities for production flexibility and product diversity. It is perceived that, with the mass markets of the older fordist regime giving way to fragmented markets based on increasingly differentiated patterns of consumption, the area of greatest profit lies in 'niche marketing'.

The transition from fordism to post-fordism is not simply one influencing economic organisation. Buttel (1992), following Roobeek (1987), has insisted that economic change has been accompanied by a movement from social democratic to neo-conservative forms of social organisation. Trade unions and their influence in industrial relations and national politics have declined, the welfare state and the social wage are being selectively rolled back, economic inequality is increasing, political parties have declined relative to special interest groups and social movements, corporate activities as well as market transactions have become increasingly transnational in scope (and thus less amenable to nationally ordered regulation). As part of this change, political cultures have shifted from an emphasis on mitigating the impacts of private accumulation to that of ensuring the sanctity of entrepreneurship (Buttel, 1992).

For Buttel, the movement from the social democratic (fordist) regime to the emerging neo-conservative (post-fordist) regime, is represented by the development of a non interventionist state, whose policies support a growing corporate elite and an increasingly differentiated working/middle class comprising poorly paid service sector workers, informal sector workers, and a growing urban and rural underclass (those groups who were once protected by the welfare state) (Buttel, 1992).

In summary, there are three likely outcomes of this transition that are important for agriculture. First, the reduced significance of mass markets will greatly disadvantage those nations (such as Australia) producing bulk undifferentiated commodities, particularly in an era of global overproduction. Second, a reliance on new technologies is viewed as necessary in any advanced system of agricultural production. The extension of computing and biotechnologies are perceived as essential to increased production despite their potential to polarise agriculture (see Chapter 3). Third, the demise of the welfare state is likely to translate into even further reductions in support for rural social infrastructure, with impacts felt by farmers and other rural dwellers.

The Globalisation of Food Production

With the increasing internationalisation of industrial and finance capital, agriculture has become quite vulnerable to decisions made in distant locations. Finance capital has gained an ability to by-pass many of the strictures previously set in place by once protectionist nation states. Two examples of restructuring are first, in the food processing sector (characterised in the 1980s and 1990s by asset stripping, international linkages and buy outs) (see Marsden and Murdoch, 1990), and second, in farming (with credit being provided to transform production relations and to allow the purchase of new technologies).

According to Friedmann and McMichael (1989), Friedmann (1991) and McMichael (1994), the integration of world capitalism has blurred any previous distinction between 'agriculture' and 'industry', and that to grasp the changes occurring in farming and in farm-dominated rural regions, it is necessary to conceive of an 'agrifood sector' run by transnational corporations which links various elements of rural production to manufacturing and service industries. The agrifood sector has become an intermediary between agricultural producers and food consumers:

> Instead of crops destined for the kitchen pot, agriculture increasingly supplies raw materials to the food processing industry for the production of durable goods. These raw materials become subject to global sourcing and to technically developed substitutions ... Agrifood industries have grown up around two elements in the postwar diet of advanced capitalism: (1) manufactured foods -- composed of several agricultural (and/or chemical) raw materials, notably sugar and oils; and (2) livestock products, especially intensively produced poultry and cattle (Friedmann, 1991: 66-67).

The development of a mass diet via industrial food production processes has been one of the outcomes of the development of a global agrifood sector, a sector whose profits were able to grow enormously through their ability to convince consumers that the purchase of take-away, prepackaged and convenience foods were a necessary and desirable part of modern living.

With a durable food industry capable of disguising the ingredients of a final product -- it was a short step to replacing the costly or unreliably supplied or inferior natural substances with what Friedmann (1991) has labelled 'generic ingredients':

> What is wanted is not sugar, but sweeteners; not flour or cornstarch, but thickeners; not palm oil or butter, but fats; not beef or cod, but proteins. Interchangeable inputs, natural or chemically synthesized, augment control and reduce costs better than older mercantile strategies of diversifying sources of supply of specific crops (Friedmann, 1991: 74).

This so-called 'substitutionism' (Goodman *et al.*, 1987) allows a higher degree of control by corporate capital over agriculture because it can, through increased interchangeability of components, by-pass entire products and regions in 'sourcing' its industrial requirements (see Lawrence, 1995).

The production of beef has been altered from a largely extensive system to an intensive one. The integration became complete with intensive livestock production being linked with the grain (feedstuff) sector particularly in the USA. Since the production of 'global food' is no longer the province of national commodity groups, producers find economic advantage in linking with transnational capital (under its terms) to take full advantage of world demand for agricultural products. In some circumstances the food industry demands standardisation. Pressures are exerted via contracts for farmers to specialise in producing monocultures of controlled, and predictably grown and harvested, crops and animals (see Burch *et al.*, 1992). There are negative environmental implications for those countries into which this form of agricultural production penetrates (see discussions in Bonanno *et al.*, 1994). According to Friedmann -- who evokes the fordist/post-fordist dichotomy as the means of understanding changing patterns of production and consumption -- the durable food and livestock/feed complexes have reached their limit. Along with world over-production, farm crises and the spate of rationalisations and bankruptcies in the corporate food sector, there is an underlying trend within the advanced nations to class-based food differentiation with poorer groups required to purchase increasingly standardised foods, and with privileged consumers enjoying a more varied and healthier diet (Buttel, 1994).

There are two important elements in this analysis. First, it is anticipated that the earlier comparative advantage enjoyed by so-called settler states such as Australia has virtually disappeared with the emergence of a global food system after the Second World War. It is doubtful that settler nations such as Australia can exert much control in agricultural development either in terms of choice of commodities produced or in terms of agricultural production strategies utilised. If TNCs decide that Australia, or some other semi-peripheral or peripheral nation, will provide bulk undifferentiated products for mass markets, possibilities in those nations for value adding and for capturing higher priced niche markets will be greatly limited (see Lawrence, 1995). Producers in these countries will be required to conform to demands of companies which want the separation of livestock and crop growing (the continued movement towards specialised systems of production) and which are unconcerned about the environmental or social impacts of these developments. At the farm level, there are growing pressures for farmers to conform to the upstream and downstream components of transnational capital by utilising modern inputs and producing corporate-required outputs. By becoming increasingly subordinated to finance capital, producers will have little room to alter production regimes (see Campbell, 1994).

Second, given the continuation of the influence of corporations in supplying existing and new (especially Asian) markets with durable foods, it is likely that there will be increasing pressures on the environment. Ecological problems will invariably increase with any intensification of existing practices (see Lawrence and Vanclay, 1992; 1994). While there may be consumer demand for 'cleaner' (or 'greener') agricultural practices, many of these practices will translate into higher costs of production and so place greater pressure on farmers to increase output as a means of sustaining farm income. This, itself, may cause accelerated environmental degradation, but will also lead to the hastened exit from agriculture of now marginal farmers unable to bear any additional input costs. In conditions where nation states are reluctant to impose tighter regulations for fear of capital flight, it also may result in continued unacceptable levels of abuse of natural resources.

In the period before World War Two and up to the mid 1970s, the nation state largely organised agriculture and provided social stability via policies which encouraged the development of mass consumption and high wages. Since then, transnational capital has sought to by-pass state regulations in its organisation of new production arrangements. For Friedmann and McMichael (1989), two possibilities for future development present themselves: the growth of global institutions (such as a World Food Board) aimed at stabilising and regulating capital accumulation, or the reassertion of the 'local' and 'regional' aimed at counteracting the power of the TNCs. A globally coordinated system with localised (or regional) control over the use of resources is a distinct possibility under circumstances where local consumer groups have the power to influence developments. How producers and consumers in countries like Australia will act -- whether as 'victims' of transnational forces or as active players is the reorganisation of local patterns of production based on ecological and other concerns -- is at this time yet to be determined.

Contract Farming

In contrast to the conventional industrial model of vertical integration, agribusiness tends not to engage directly in on-farm production. Instead, the major means of control by agribusiness is contract farming, 'a system in which companies involved wholly or partly in the processing, marketing or retailing of agricultural goods enter into contractual arrangements with farmers for the supply of a particular commodity' (Burch et al., 1992: 260).

Contract farming results in a transfer of responsibility for many production and environmental management decisions from the farmers to the corporation -- with a consequent loss of autonomy for farmers. Corporate concern about profit and cash flow may result in lower investment in conservation activities than would be undertaken by farmers on their own. Furthermore, where environmental degradation occurs, corporations can, because of international sourcing, simply move to another location for their produce requirements. This creates a situation in which corporations need not be particularly concerned about environmental quality. At the same time, competition between farmers in the international marketplace creates a situation in which farmers may not have the financial wherewithal to invest in environmental management strategies.

Individually, farmers who are engaged in the production of produce for a corporation have little power in the relationship. Corporations maintain control over farmers by threatening not to accept their crop, a situation which would be disastrous for farmers because of the lack of alternative outlets for produce in a particular region. Consequently, growers are vulnerable to the whims of the corporation. Growers are forced by the logic of the contract system to cultivate intensively and, in order to ensure the quality of their produce to the satisfaction of the processing company, to apply agri-chemicals (see Burch *et al.*, 1992). The system also reduces the flexibility of the farmer in that the contract may specify certain practices that the farmer must adhere to, such as the use of specific chemicals. It also limits the choice of crop rotations and alternative commodities available to the farmer because of the monocultures which develop in locations where contracting occurs. Farmers become dependent on the infrastructure provided by the agribusiness corporation, and in semi-peripheral nations like Australia, with a small, geographically dispersed population, the corporations are able to monopolise the processing and handling of produce very easily.

Burch *et al.* (1992) argue that the complex nature of the agribusiness system is such that the activities involved in contact farming are not satisfactorily coordinated and this has implications not only for the farmer (in that there may be contradictory advice) but also for the consumer (in that there may be, for example, inadvertent but structurally built-in breaches of regulations relating to the withholding periods for certain agri-chemicals). A farmer may be directed by the field officer to spray a crop with a certain chemical, only to be told by the production control manager to harvest the crop. In some cases farmers may be given only 48 hours notice to harvest, whereas some agri-chemicals have withholding periods of up to 14 days (Burch *et al.*, 1992). The increasing power of supermarkets in the fresh fruit and vegetable industry is another factor which grower groups have become aware of. It is thought, for example, that Australia's three largest supermarket chains (Woolworths, Coles and Franklins) have gained enough market strength to dictate the terms of price and quality to growers (*Australian Farm Journal*, January, 1995: 26). The price reductions which come with near monopoly strength means fewer dollars reach the growers; their economic ability to undertake important land and water conservation works may be subsequently limited.

Value-Adding Activities

Another strategy being promoted in Australia is to 'value add' to products before they leave Australia's shores. At present, the $15 billion of agricultural goods Australia exports is currently converted into $80 billion abroad. It is argued that if this $15 billion worth of agricultural products which Australia exports in largely unprocessed form were to be further processed in

Australia, there would be higher levels of employment, higher levels of income, and enhanced foreign currency earnings (see Bureau of Rural Resources, 1991a).

According to the Department of Primary Industries and Energy (1989: 7):

> Value adding is the essence of economic growth. Value adding is the means by which individuals and businesses meet their objectives to prosper and grow ... if a country wants to trade for the purposes of economic growth without subsidies, it will only do so via industries, businesses and individuals who are able to compete successfully ... Hence, value adding and the competitiveness of agribusiness are inexorably linked.

The opportunities seen to be available to Australian producers currently producing largely undifferentiated food and fibre for world markets is to link with agribusiness in a manner beneficial to both parties (see National Farmers' Federation, 1993; Department of Foreign Affairs and Trade, 1994). For agribusiness, the markets abroad are well known and already penetrated by branch firms, providing an easy entrée for those producers who seek agribusiness affiliation. For farmers, the sale of specific product lines which can be readily distinguished from those of competing producers will allow consumer brand identification and it is presumed that this will result in increased profits. With extra income, once-struggling farmers will be able to overcome debt problems and begin to undertake much needed environmental repair work. In this scenario, the further integration of family-farm agriculture and international agribusiness will be a cornerstone to both improved environmental sustainability and the continuation of high export earnings -- not necessarily from any increased volume of exports, but the sale of higher value goods (National Farmers' Federation, 1993).

The positive environmental flow-on effects suggested above are viewed as part of a healthy and prosperous agricultural sector. Would family-farm agriculture be 'reinvigorated' by agribusiness? Agribusiness firms are renowned for their ability to organise their production and distribution activities in the input-supply and output-processing sectors without, as it were, getting their hands dirty on the farm (see Lawrence, 1987; Mooney, 1988; Burch *et al.*, 1992). Market strength and management strategies enable agribusiness to leave the production risks with the farmer, while purchasing raw materials from the farmer as cheaply as possible. It is not on the farm where value is likely to be added, but off the farm in food processing factories. The individual farmer has little opportunity for value adding and product differentiation on the farm and is therefore unlikely to receive profits received by those involved in the processing industries. The question that remains is -- can Australia benefit from value adding activities in circumstances where transnational agribusiness assists in the transformation of family-farming activities?

The answer would seem to be no. Foreign interests have determined that Australia is not the most appropriate location for value adding. For example, in 1988 five of Australia's top agricultural exporters were Japanese trading houses which sent abroad, in one year, approximately $7 billion of unprocessed food and fibre (*Financial Review*, 15 March 1988). While submissions to, and commissioned studies produced on behalf of, the Australian government have implored the nation to embark upon value adding -- particularly for foods destined for Asian markets -- most suggest that it is agribusiness which will be the key to such developments (see Instate, 1993). Agribusiness does not, however, appear willing to take up the challenge -- at least within Australia. It should be understood that of the top 47 world food companies, only one, Goodman Fielder, is Australian based. Others, such as Philip Morris, Unilever, Nestle and ConAgra, have quite large concerns in Australia and have been involved in the production of foods destined for overseas consumers. But they 'owe' nothing to Australia. If it is not economically feasible to value add in Australia, there will be little incentive for these corporations to do so. Like the Japanese trading houses, they may find it more profitable to export bulk materials for value adding in locations where labour is cheaper.

Attempts by successive Australian governments to diversify the economy and to have foreign capital invest in food, fibre (and wider) manufacturing have not resulted in the production of increasing volumes of value added products for export. In 1972, so-called 'elaborately transformed manufactures' (embodying high-tech processing and knowledge-intensive applications) comprised 13 percent of Australia's exports. However, this had fallen to 9 percent by 1986 (Fagan and Bryan, 1991: 15) and to 8 percent by 1989 (Kulkarni, 1991). For the 1980s, Australia imported value added imports at a rate faster than both domestic growth in GDP and the export earnings of food and materials (Jones, 1989). By the 1990s, Australia had reverted to its 1930s economic base selling 'simply transformed manufactures' (unprocessed or semi-processed raw materials) in exchange for manufactured goods. In relation to foods, for example, some 80 percent of exports by value are bulk commodities -- cereals, meats and sugar (Department of Prime Minister and Cabinet, 1991: 6). Importantly, there was an 'alarming' slowing of growth in the processed food export sector in the 1980s (see Department of Prime Minister and Cabinet, 1991: 7).

This has placed Australia in a difficult economic position. In terms of the export of fibres and foodstuffs, the nation continues to remain reliant upon those products which are suffering declining terms of trade. Australian agriculture is, at best, a slow growing sector which will continue to be susceptible to world oversupply. More importantly, Dunkley and Kulkarni (1990: 20) suggest:

> Trade in [simply transformed manufactures] is unlikely to revive in the near future because of technological change raising global productivity, agricultural subsidies in major countries, a trend to self-sufficiency in developing countries, the emergence of new primary suppliers and possible reduction in demand for [some rural] products for ecological reasons.

Australia's manufacturing industry primarily constitutes branch plants of foreign transnational companies. It is being progressively locked out of Asia-Pacific markets because of cheaper production costs overseas, particularly in South East Asia. There is no reason to believe that local or foreign agribusiness firms will discover advantages in food and fibre processing in Australia that they have been unable to obtain elsewhere. Labour in Asian countries is cheaper than in

Australia, so it is likely that raw materials will continue to be sent abroad in unprocessed form. This has been grudgingly admitted by the Federal Government and has been more-or-less accepted by the National Farmers' Federation (1993). According to the Department of Primary Industries and Energy (1989: 15):

> In considering the question of adding value to Australian agricultural products, it is reasonable to argue that the value adding activity will often take place outside Australia (by companies that may or may not be Australian owned), and that this activity will be initiated by companies positioned near the retail end of the channel rather than near the raw material end.

Without tariff protection which has provided support for Australia's 'infant industries', there are few incentives for firms to move beyond simple semi-processing activities. Significantly, the processed foods' area -- that described as providing the best opportunities for value adding (1991a) -- now forms a declining proportion of total food exports (Wettenhall, 1991).

ECONOMIC AND SOCIAL IMPACTS OF RURAL RESTRUCTURING

There have been different outcomes in different countries as the new forces of economic change have begun to impact upon regions within nation states. In countries of the European Economic Community, there has been a move from production strategies which have tended to endorse continued expansion of output to those which preserve rural communities and protect the environment (Commins, 1990; Lowe *et al.*, 1990; Berlan-Darque and Klaora, 1992; Glasbergen, 1992; Lowe, 1992). With agriculture gradually losing its status as the major form of enterprise in rural regions, policy is coming to reflect the variety of concerns of rural and urban dwellers. In the USA, where an increased diversity of economic activities (particularly the growth of decentralised service and light manufacturing industry) has helped to reduce rural community dependence on agriculture (see Swanson, 1988), new employment opportunities have arisen. There is evidence that changes are not necessarily beneficial for all regions or for all people within all regions experiencing change: labour market segmentation has been one outcome (Summers *et al.*, 1990).

Australian governments have responded to global restructuring in a number of ways. At the macro level they have been prepared to integrate their economies into international circuits of capital by deregulating banking, removing regulations on capital flow, orchestrating high interest rate policies as a means of limiting domestic demand and of attracting investment dollars, and seeking to reduce real wage levels to achieve labour competitiveness (Lawrence, 1987; Rees *et al.*, 1993; Fagan and Webber, 1994).

The changes have included measures to provide greater market determination to capital allocation, reducing the costs of and improving flexibility in relation to resource allocation, and encouraging greater economic competition (see Stilwell, 1993).

In Australia, the following measures have been applied as a means of integrating the Australian economy into that of the Asia-Pacific Basin:

- reduction of import tariff levels;
- freeing of interest rates;
- floating of the exchange rate and lifting of foreign exchange controls;
- deregulation of the finance and banking industries;
- conversion of traditional government departments into new state-owned enterprises;
- privatisation of state-owned enterprises;
- deregulation and privatisation of state monopoly control in primary industries;
- deregulation of the airline industry;
- forced competition in the telecommunications industry;
- reductions in public-sector and welfare spending.

In relation to agriculture, the vehicle for such integration is the agribusiness corporation. Statutory marketing authorities -- once the bastion of family-farm commodity marketing -- are viewed as standing in the way of the private corporations (National Farmers' Federation, 1993). As suggested earlier, it is the latter which, through strategic links and size advantages, are deemed to be capable of providing value-adding to food and fibre production and will help to reorganise farming to reduce inefficiencies (Department of Primary Industries and Energy, 1989).

The agribusiness model -- requiring high inputs to achieve high outputs -- is likely to alter the pattern of agricultural production in Australia with the effects being increased output, greater pressure on the environment and an increased need for adjustment of those farmers unable to compete under the new rules (Lawrence and Vanclay, 1992; Lawrence and Vanclay, 1994). Farmer stress -- another obvious consequence of the combination of forces 'rationalising' agriculture -- is one of the least well understood dimensions of the economic restructuring of farming (see Gray and Lawrence, forthcoming).

It would appear that the removal of the protective mantle of policies which supported and reproduced (albeit, allowing for appropriate structural adjustment of those deemed to be least efficient) family-farm based agriculture will expose producers to further economic stress. For example, any move to post-fordist agriculture will require producers to move from bulk commodity to 'niche' market production. This will require farmers to alter existing production regimes and grow new crops or animals using a variety of new inputs (including advanced information technologies). If, as might be expected, this results in the polarisation of agriculture -- with the more capital-intensive agribusiness-linked farmers increasing their share of commodity production and sector income -- what will be the fate of those unable to compete? Some of the likely options for this group may be:

- reducing farm expenditure to 'match' reduced farm income levels;
- further borrowing to allow expansion and/or change;
- 'pluriactivity' to provide new income sources as a means of supporting a farm-based lifestyle;
- short (and perhaps medium to long) term exploitation of the resource base of the farm as an attempt to improve farm-based income levels;
- selling the farm.

In the first case, the reduction in household expenditure has important social implications. With little money available for entertainment and other social activities, supportive networks may begin to deteriorate with a consequent loss of vitality in the farming district (Lawrence and Williams, 1990; Stone, 1992; Alston, 1995). With male farmers often being reluctant to seek assistance from counsellors (Fairweather, 1989), there is likely to be a hidden problem, which has, at times, manifested itself in stress-related behaviour including alcoholism, increased domestic violence and suicide. Australian farm women have been forced to take the brunt of the cost-price pressures on family-farming properties. According to Alston (1995) while many of the tasks allocated to women have remained 'invisible' their activities have been crucial to the overall well-being of the farm family and community. Yet, with economic pressures to undertake more on-farm work, more off-farm work, and yet maintain domestic responsibilities, women are caught in a triple bind. Their resilience is being tested, and they are gradually recognising the need to become more personally assertive and politically active (see Alston, 1995).

So-called belt-tightening (see Lawrence, 1987) was once an acceptable short-term response to price collapse. The rules of rural production have changed with the winding back of state supports for agriculture. Farmers, who might once have adopted belt-tightening as a short-term response (and might have been victims of periodic poverty), are likely to be trapped by continued low prices and may become part of a new rural poor -- unable to sell their farm and unable to trade their way out. While financial counsellors are likely to interpret this as an 'equity crisis', it is in reality a structural crisis affecting those producing traditional farm commodities in a world where such bulk products have lost their competitive edge. The future of the traditional family-farm producer in a post-fordist world system is one which needs greater attention.

Some producers will borrow to expand. Again, however, it is not likely to be in the expansion of output of traditional products where major economic benefits are likely to be achieved. While there will be a demand for grain and unfattened animals for the burgeoning feedlot beef industry, this will be with its own limitations (Lawrence and Vanclay, 1994). Other farmers may be able to link with agribusiness (and, perhaps, with local grower-owned marketing bodies) to produce for niche markets. Such 'opportunities' will be limited in a geographical sense and by the management skills of individual farmers. It is the traditional family farmer, producing bulk commodities, who will be isolated from recent developments, and who will be likely to find product diversification and farm expansion a major problem. Obtaining the capital to do either of these things will be difficult unless credit suppliers can be convinced of the long term suitability of such developments. And, where credit is obtained, the need for the farmer to 'perform' for the bank or credit agency is likely to intensify both social and psychological pressures on the farmer.

Pluriactivity is an important option for the smaller farmer within a post-fordist era. It is viewed as a survival strategy and as a means of integrating farm-based labour into new areas of capital accumulation (Le Heron, 1991). It is becoming a preferred option for those farmers (and family members) seeking alternative occupational opportunities and lifestyle options. With between one third and one half of farm households in Australia being pluriactive (Lawrence, 1987), it is obvious that job opportunities within regional economies become crucial to the general well-being of a large number of farmers.

There is evidence that the growth of tourism may provide the sorts of jobs which farm women (in particular) can successfully combine with farm work (see Share, Campbell and Lawrence, 1991; *Australian Farm Journal*, January 1995). Niche opportunities provided by ski field development -- in Aotearoa (New Zealand) -- or the farm holiday trade are providing flexibility to farming and so allow producers to remain in agriculture. However, not all regional areas are likely to experience new injections of capital (Stilwell, 1992). Much of the economic activity associated with tourism in Australia is coastal, while most of the farmers suffering economic problems are located in inland regions. Furthermore, opportunities for achieving work within country towns have declined because of the removal of government-based services (as part of rationalisation) (Lawrence and Williams, 1990; Stone, 1992). What remains to be done is to examine which, if any, opportunities are being provided to those farmers and farm members who are under stress as a result of global restructuring. Pluriactivity may be an excellent farm-based option to structural adjustment, but opportunities are likely to remain limited so long as regional economies are not provided with stimuli to attract industry.

Just as there is evidence of overwhelming farmer commitment to the local town and its future (Kidman, 1991), there is also evidence that the deepening recession is responsible for increasing industry closures and economic distress in rural economies. In this sense, the wishes of farm family members to take off-farm work are undermined by economic realities of lack of investment dollars. Of course, when development does occur, it is likely that it will be on terms of finance capital rather than of local need (see Share *et al.*, 1991).

One outcome of rural restructuring is further pressure on the environment as farmers seek to counteract falling commodity prices by reducing inputs, working the land harder, and reducing expenditure on conservation works. While this may allow farmers to reduce their personal stress over farm income, many are knowingly running down farm resources (usually perceived as a short term option) to remain in farming (Lawrence, Share and Campbell, 1992).

Much needs to be understood about resource-use behaviour in times of economic stress. What can be stated is that the Australian agricultural environment is under severe pressure as farms seek to employ past (and new) techniques aimed at boosting production. Financial constraints prevent farmers from spending money on needed works to redress land degradation, while overstocking and overcropping are a consequence of the need to sustain income levels -- particularly as a loan repayment strategy (Lawrence and Vanclay, 1992).

The final option for producers is to leave agriculture. While structural adjustment has been an option for unviable farmers and has proceeded reasonably smoothly (in Australia) from the 1960s, the stress farmers face leading up to and during the transition out of farming has yet to be fully studied. There are some estimates that the number of farms in Australia will have dropped from 174,000 in the early 1980s to about 70,000 early next century (see Lawrence, 1990). If this occurs, there is likely to be quite significant social disruption in rural areas. Yet, as stated earlier, in an era distinguished by reduced levels of government involvement in the rural economy, there is likely to be little support offered to those leaving agriculture. While, in Australia, there has been a quite significant increase in the number of rural counsellors, it appears that many assume the role of financial counsellors. Many of the growing social problems remain hidden from view and there is a certain 'denial' of the personal and family stresses which are occurring as a direct result of the unviability of family-farm agriculture (see Bryant, 1991,1992).

REGIONAL CHANGE

It has been argued by European and some US writers that a focus upon global networks and upon the structural aspects of agricultural production has tended to reduce the importance of 'the rural'. Some regions -- for reasons of natural resource endowments, local policies, labour availability and skill, or market proximity -- have managed to attract capital and to develop economically, while others -- particularly those where agriculture is the exclusive generator of wealth -- have faced pressures for contraction. It is possible to point to regions within Bavaria, Colorado, north east England, Ireland and Tuscany as new productive areas which have attracted population and capital, as well as to those which have become economic backwaters (see Marsden, Lowe and Whatmore, 1990). There is an argument that production flexibility -- something accompanying the move to niche markets -- will advantage rural regions (Urry, 1984; Lash and Urry, 1994). It is thought that through the use of new technologies and production regimes, manufacturing and service industries do not have to be large units. And the smaller the unit the more likely it is to be adaptable. In Urry's words, capital is becoming 'indifferent' to where it is located, something which provides opportunities for rural regions to take advantage of economic developments formerly -- and usually exclusively -- obtained by cities (Urry, 1984).

As rural areas become sites of consumption (in regard to leisure, tourism and recreation), rather than, as in the past, sites of production (agriculture), it is likely that new opportunities for economic development will arise (see Lash and Urry, 1994). The rural will be a site for the social production of meanings (Marsden *et al.*, 1990) where city-based individuals come to appreciate, as a cultural asset, the 'space' provided by the countryside. While there will be varied and competing meanings, this is indicative of the potential politicisation of the rural. An obvious example is the degree to which urban dwellers demand (and obtain) conservation works and 'clean food' rather than leaving agricultural production and resource use in the hands of farmers and agribusiness interests.

If rural society was once a distinctive entity seen as different from (that is, usually inferior to) that of the city, in the post war period the spatial division between rural and urban has become blurred (Mormont, 1990). While 'space' will continue to provide important insights into the development and reproduction of social relations (when 'localism' may become a key term in understanding local responses to global changes), the 'rural' will not be a self-evident category, but, rather, a term used by different groups in different combinations to attract different forms of economic development. For Mormont, those farmers tuned-in to the demands of the new middle classes, may use 'natural food' labels to obtain 'value-added' benefits, environmentalists might seek to shift agricultural policy to protect endangered species, tourist operators might appeal to visitors to experience the 'real' countryside, and so forth. The term 'rural' will be appropriated by those wishing to achieve some economic, social or political outcome.

People may achieve higher levels of 'cultural capital' by living in a rural village or by working from a small property in the bush -- something guided by lifestyle preference, but now made possible due to communications technology. Furthermore, space becomes attractive to those whose worklife occurs in urban settings (Mormont, 1990). New uses for rural space by new groups of users will ensure that conflicts arise. In some instances, farmers may find they have new allies in their attempts to remain in farming. Altered affiliations are possible. Their effect might be to redefine farming as 'land management' or to promote the countryside as the logical location for new industries. Whether the rural is viewed as something to be exploited, or as something to be preserved and nurtured, will be based largely on the collective assets of those making decisions about rural resource use. There is a specific opportunity for local coalitions of farmers, conservationists, professionals and so forth, to oppose particular global trends and to foster others. According to Lowe, Marsden and Munton (1990: 6):

> The balance and combinations of use and exchange values on land, homes and recreational space in the countryside is in a state of continual flux as different fractions of capital seek to exploit rural space, open up new markets and thereby produce new systems of exchange. [State policies of] deregulation [and] ... privatisation ... often lead to acute conflicts between, for instance, the protection of publicly-regulated use values and the attempted imposition of productivity-oriented exchange values. For many groups living in urban and rural areas, parts of the countryside thus represent pockets of space for the public consumption of use values in a world dominated by exchange and commodity values; and for this reason the retention of such use values may be vigorously defended.

The implications of these changes for rural regions of Australia are many. First, 'rural' will be a category employed by groups other than farmers whose meanings are broader than 'agriculture'. Farmers are likely to find themselves defending their version of what constitutes 'rural' and what are legitimate and desirable activities within that space against those with new definitions and with new priorities. Conflicts may arise which will not necessarily enforce current patterns of land use and production.

Second, with the possible growth of more flexible production not tied to coastal or other areas of high population, rural regions may attract new groups of people whose training and forms of employment will stimulate economic growth. They may help to shape social space according to their (usually gentrified) views of what constitutes modern life and actively defend their definitions against others. They may represent, at the local level, the articulate forces which can oppose inappropriate developments which seek to exploit unskilled labour or cause environmental havoc. That is, they may encourage certain forms of development while opposing others. This is certainly evident in the growth of the alternative lifestyle or multiple occupancy movement in Australia (Munro-Clarke, 1986; Lawrence, 1987; Metcalf and Vanclay, 1987).

Third, Massey (1984) argues that capital movement shapes regions by utilising and manipulating spatial differences to capture higher levels of profit. Changing circumstances in rural areas due to decreased farm viability result in the establishment of a supply of labour in non-metropolitan regions, and the increased potential for the exploitation of that labour by what might, in other language, be construed as 'growth' and 'development'. According to Massey, this results in a spatial division of labour.

Although the changing nature of regions will have definite impacts on Australian rural society, there are many uncertainties as to the full extent of these impacts. It is not altogether certain that the changing nature of regions will be as dramatic in Australia, with its vast land mass and relatively small population, as it will be in more densely populated nations of Europe and North America. Nevertheless, areas surrounding major centres of population and regions noted for their natural beauty already experience pressure to conform to urban demands, and rural communities in those regions have responded to the potential created by that demand in the form of altered forms of production. It is unlikely, however, that inland Australian agricultural areas -- which are not close to centres of population and not particularly aesthetically or otherwise attractive in terms of other demands that may be placed on these regions -- will be significantly affected by the changing concept of region.

There are also other concerns about the validity of the claims about the impact of the changing role of regions. If new industries do emerge, would farmers be capable of combining their usually less-viable on-farm activities with new work opportunities? Marginal farmers find themselves in a situation of 'agricultural involution' (Geertz, 1963), in which they cannot afford the capital outlay to invest in alternative forms of production, and where they have minimised their cash outlays by retrenching on-farm labour and adopting low-input agricultural systems which have low returns. This survival strategy locks them into a situation which they cannot change and which ultimately leads to decreasing equity. By reducing farm labour, the workload of the owner-operators increases to fill all their available time. Off-farm work by the farmer inevitably means sacrificing some farm-related production activities. Marginal farmers are also unlikely to have the skills that provide them with the potential to find off-farm work, or to adapt their farm to sites of pluriactivity. Changes in agricultural production and non-agricultural on-farm production are more likely to be undertaken by farmers in the higher socio-economic categories.

The final concern is that in a 'disorganised' and de-regulated post-fordist economic system, it may be difficult to establish what are realistic and beneficial local opportunities and what are attempts by the metropole, driven by capitalist pressures, to locate inappropriate and/or environmentally harmful industry in rural areas in order to relieve urban political pressure.

CONCLUSION

Global economic change is disadvantaging certain sections of Australian agriculture. It is essential to understand the nature of global developments and their likely impacts in any assessment of the opportunities for family farm survival and/or growth in Australia. There will continue to be a substitution of capital for labour in agriculture, the growth of agribusiness, greater farmer involvement with agribusiness, and pressure on farm units to adjust to a regime of decreasing commodity prices. Farmers will have some opportunities to expand their activities -- so long as they link with and conform to the production needs of corporate capital. One of the main effects of the changes now occurring will be further 'adjustment'. Some farmers will have the chance to supplement farm income with off-farm work. But in the context of reduced commitment to regional policy on the part of the state, only certain farmers and regions are expected to benefit. Farmer stress will quite possibly increase over the next decade, exacerbating already existing social and personal problems among farm family members.

Niche marketing will expand, but again, it would seem that TNCs rather than growers and their organisations will exploit these opportunities. With the state largely unwilling to intervene to support agriculture and inland rural communities, the fate of people living in rural areas will become progressively dependent on private investment decisions. It is unlikely in the context of declining business in rural towns that individuals and companies will readily invest in smaller towns. The move to a post-fordist or 'neo-conservative society' will quite probably create greater levels of social inequality in rural regions at the same time as it increases pressure on the environment.

Just as it would seem that the prognosis for the physical environment is bleak, so too the prognosis for the human environment. The outcomes for rural people living in an era of post-fordist state policies and economic development arising from supposed free market forces -- while admittedly difficult to predict -- are likely to be poor.

ENVIRONMENTAL DEGRADATION IN THE SEMI-PERIPHERY

PROBLEMS IN THE MURRAY-DARLING BASIN

INTRODUCTION

Australia occupies what is termed a 'semi-peripheral' position in the world economy (Armstrong, 1978; Clegg *et al.*, 1980). Semi-peripheral nations are neither major economic entities such as the USA, Japan and Germany (the 'metropoles'), nor are they underdeveloped regions of the world such as for example, Bangladesh, Peru or Angola (the 'periphery'). Semi-peripheral nations sit between those two extremes, obtaining few benefits when they trade with the metropoles, but receiving net benefits when they engage in exchange with the periphery (Arrighi, 1990). While living standards and economic processes may mirror those within the metropoles, the subordinate role of the semi-peripheral nations means that their economies are highly vulnerable to changes within the international marketplace. Nations such as Australia, Aotearoa (New Zealand) and Canada -- older settler states whose economic *raison d'etre* was to provide raw materials for the factories of Britain and cheap foods for its burgeoning eighteenth and nineteenth century working class -- have continued their earlier role, albeit with direction from new economic masters. As Martin (1990: 8) has emphasised, 'the semi-periphery bears the burden of the modern Janus: facing oligopolistic and political pressures from core zones and economic competition from the periphery below'. While some political economists believe that the globalisation of the world economy renders less than useful terms like 'core-periphery' (see Fagan and Webber, 1994), it nevertheless remains desirable to pin-point Australia's past growth in terms of its links with imperial powers.

An important feature of Australia's development, based historically on primary produce exports, has been the ability of successive federal governments simultaneously to appease labour (through high wages), local capitalists (via protectionist policies and justified by infant industry arguments), and farmers (through a mantle of subsidisation, technical support and marketing arrangements). As Australia has become increasingly integrated into global circuits of capital, the impacts of investment decisions by transnational capital -- and the state in its efforts to reduce balance-of-payments deficits -- appear to be leading to a deterioration in Australia's semi-peripheral status.

In the period of economic vitality from the Second World War to the early 1970s, environmental issues were rarely addressed in political debate. The prevailing ideology was one of economic and agricultural 'development' -- not only as a means of contributing to the reconstruction of a war-ravaged world, but also as a means of stimulating internal economic growth. Rural producers were encouraged to grow and to sell as much as possible, utilising the most advanced technologies. The price signals from the international market and the backing of the state overruled some of the more obvious manifestations of price instability and environmental degradation. The excesses of the development policies and practices of the post war years culminated in a number of rural economic crises from the early 1970s and quite profound environmental damage.

The breakdown of domestic protectionist policies, the reduction in international regulations, and the transnationalisation of the global economy, have created certain internal tensions in Australia. While political parties adopt an active stance in seeking domestic and international funding to stimulate industrialisation, the economy is actually being deindustrialised in line with its role in the Pacific Rim economy. As a high-cost labour region, Australia is seen to be more suited to raw material production. This has placed pressure on the primary industries -- agriculture and mining -- to attain the necessary overseas income to help sustain the nation's metropolitan-style standard of living. Australia is, however, continuing to import more higher-costs goods than it exports. Trade deficits have been one outcome. The message to the farm and mining sector is: become more efficient and more competitive.

The problem for Australia, however, is that any intensification of agricultural production is likely to have a major impact upon the environment. Yet the state -- diminished in power as integration with international markets and firms increases -- is structurally bound to support such intensification. It would appear that at the very time metropolitan nations are showing clear signs of a movement to post-fordist industrial strategies, Australia is being required to conform to the interests of transnational food processors by maintaining fordist strategies of production (see Lawrence, 1995). The growth of the hitherto unfamiliar beef feedlot industry serves as an example of the type of development required by international capital and accepted by a compliant Australian state -- seeking investment as a means of offsetting balance of payment difficulties. While the environment is now certainly on the political agenda in Australia, it is the forests and coastal waters which have received the greatest public concern. As was shown in the Introduction, agriculture continues to exploit the land. The decline of fordist agriculture in the metropoles and its re-location to semi-peripheral nations like Australia, might be best considered a form of environmental imperialism -- the exploitation of the resources of weaker nations in the world order as the core nations move towards 'clean', post-fordist agricultural development strategies.

In this chapter, the Murray-Darling Basin (MDB) -- Australia's most important agricultural region -- provides a case study allowing examination of the environmental impact of changes as the nation is integrated into the Pacific Rim economy.

THE AUSTRALIAN ECONOMY IN THE GLOBAL ORDER

Following white colonisation in 1788, Australia's economic development was linked closely to Britain's need for cheap raw materials as inputs to manufacturing industry (McMichael, 1987). Britain's intention was to ensure growth in its own manufacturing industry, and political and social stability in the colonies from which raw materials were obtained. The emergence in Australia in the early nineteenth century of a property-owning bourgeoisie utilising the labour of an agrarian proletariat provided the basis for capital accumulation in the pastoral industry. The state -- a representation of British social organisation -- was city-based and was both a seeker of, and a conduit for, British capital investment. Following population inflows during and after the gold rushes of the 1850s, the consolidation of pastoral holdings, and the continued growth of the urban labour market, Australia developed a small manufacturing sector (Boreham *et al.*, 1989). While labour was well organised and challenged capital for improved pay and working conditions, it was nevertheless largely compliant (Connell and Irving, 1980). It also identified with the nineteenth century bourgeois vision of progress.

'Development' was a motivating economic and political catchcry, associated with the Australian adage 'if it moves shoot it; if it doesn't chop it down' (see Smith and Finlayson, 1988). The clearing of native vegetation and the destruction of wildlife (categorised as 'vermin'), together with the widespread adoption of farming practices more suited to British than Australian conditions, had a major impact in the first 100 years of white occupation. By 1901, the federation year of the Australian States, land had been exploited to an extent that wheat yields were about half those recorded in earlier times, and native pastures had been extensively damaged through overgrazing (Heathcote and Mabbutt, 1988).

Australian staple exports continued to rise to meet the needs of Britain, while Europe -- particularly after the devastation of the First World War -- became an important market for Australian agricultural products. Declines in the terms of trade for wool and wheat meant that labour was progressively shed from agriculture and new machinery was harnessed as a means of achieving productivity gains. Pastoral and farming activities moved into the drier, less environmentally suitable regions of the continent (Catley and McFarlane, 1981). The state provided continued support for agriculture and initiated various scientific and organisational councils to both boost production and provide a basis for orderly marketing. It provided railways, electrical power, irrigation schemes and subsidised credit (Shaw, 1990).

Before the Second World War, some 79 percent of Australia's exports were farm products (Gruen, 1990). However, during and immediately after the war, Australia's traditional exports -- wool and wheat -- were either unable to be transported or were given a low priority status by importing countries. As a consequence, surpluses rose in Australia. Politicians perceived that future problems would no doubt occur if the nation relied too heavily on agriculture and the government implemented a number of measures including continued high protection for manufacturing industry, increased immigration, and the encouragement of foreign capital investment to provide a basis for 'balanced' economic development.

When conditions improved in the post-war years, there was a commitment from the British to purchase Australian agricultural products. Beef was to have a special priority and the Australian Government recognised the opportunity of developing a northern beef industry (Catley and McFarlane, 1981). Such a policy was seen to have the added advantage of leaving Australia's 'vulnerable' northern borders with Asia less exposed to potential aggressors (Davidson, 1966). 'Northern Development' received the unusually high status of a government portfolio. Agricultural development, particularly the substitution of labour by capital, continued alongside the growth of urban manufacturing industries.

By the late 1960s, Australia had moved away from Britain as a trading partner: the USA had become Australia's largest supplier of imported goods, and Japan its largest market for exports (Gruen, 1990). However, Australia's manufacturing industry was construed to have failed to develop successfully as an export sector. It was mineral development spurred by Japanese and US capital which kept the Australian economy reasonably buoyant -- even during the world oil shocks of the 1970s.

The farmers have fared the worst since the beginning of the post war economic slump in the 1970s. Since that time, the contribution of agriculture to Gross Domestic Product, to employment, and to export earnings, has been deteriorating steadily. Efficiency and productivity goals have been imposed upon agriculture and rural reconstruction measures have supported farm amalgamation and the removal of smaller, less viable, producers (Lawrence, 1992). Farms have increased in size and decreased in numbers, with those farmers remaining harnessing the latest technologies in an attempt to achieve competitive advantage (Williams, 1990). Despite this, US and EC subsidisation, and price and market support has led to Australian producers experiencing quite severe terms of trade declines. Increased exposure to markets -- brought about through the policies of governments from the early 1970s -- has, in concert with deregulation and the removal of subsidies, placed Australian producers in a precarious position.

As suggested in Chapter 1, since the great bulk of Australia's output enters the world market as unprocessed foods and fibre, it faces the vagaries of price fluctuation associated with climatic variability, buyer resistance, changing industry and consumer demands, and tactics by competing countries. With economic conditions in farming considered to be as severe as they were in the 1930s and 1890s, and with farmers having experienced, due to the El Nino Effect, what is considered to be the worst drought in Australia's history (*Sydney Morning Herald,* 31 December 1994: 1), it is variously estimated that between one fifth and one third of Australian farmers are economically unviable (*Bulletin,* 16 July 1991; *Australian,* 2 February 1994: 36). Unable to obtain bank loans for expansion and facing declining markets and rising costs, it is expected that the majority of this group of producers will be forced from agriculture by the year 2000.

Since markets tend to produce 'minimum cost' solutions (Gruen, 1990), rather than optimal environmental-maintenance solutions, the response of farmers during the continuing crises of the 1980s and 90s has been to attempt to produce ever higher volumes for export -- thereby collectively exacerbating the very market and resource use problems producers seek, individually, to overcome (Lawrence, 1987). Importantly, the main spillover effects of short-term decision-making imposed upon farmers by the realities of the global market place have been declining rural incomes and quite severe ecological destruction (Lawrence, 1987; Cameron and Elix, 1991; Lawrence and Vanclay, 1992).

THE AUSTRALIAN RESPONSE

There was a series of major government inquiries during the 1970s and 1980s including: the Crawford Report on structural adjustment in Australian manufacturing industry; the Myer Report into technological change in Australia; the Campbell Inquiry into the financial system; the Jackson Report on the development of manufacturing; and, more recently, the Garnaut Report on Asian-Australian trade relations. These can be read together to provide a coherent theme: while heavily protected local manufacturing industries have fulfilled certain social goals, many industries -- particularly in areas where Australia must compete with countries of low wage labour -- are uncompetitive internationally. The key to the future for Australia is seen to be the development of industries based on the latest technologies and which provide opportunities for value-adding. Economic growth will be achieved by increasing exports from Australia's resource-rich primary sector and through development of a skill-based sector. In turn, it will import cheap manufactures from Asia and capital from the metropolitan 'core' nations (see Clegg *et al.*, 1980).

The Garnaut Report develops this theme more fully. Garnaut (1989) insists that Australia must attach itself to the 'ascending' economies of East Asia and develop new initiatives including trade liberalisation, greater Asian immigration and increased foreign investment (Garnaut, 1989; *Sydney Morning Herald*, 20 November 1989). Garnaut argues that during the 1965-86 period, Australia's share of world exports fell from 2.1 percent to 1.4 percent, while at the same time East Asia's contribution grew from 11 to 26 percent. This is seen to be reflected in per capita income levels which increased by as much as 40 (Taiwan) and 50 (Japan) times in roughly the same period (*Sydney Morning Herald*, 23 October 1989).

Australia is to be required to satisfy the demands of (that is, to produce goods for) Asian markets. Since wage levels are much higher in Australia than overseas, the necessary liberalisation of the economy may result in industrial restructuring, with East Asian investors providing capital and direction. It is further argued that only by becoming more internationally competitive (via restructuring) will Australia advance its role in Asia.

The main recommendations of the Garnaut Report and of the previous trade-related inquiries have been accepted by Australian governments. They have progressively removed barriers to manufactured imports and capital on the basis that this will force Australian secondary industry to compete internationally. More flexible labour relations (a move from unionised collective bargaining to individual employer-employee contracts) are also viewed as essential to future economic prosperity (Thomas, 1991).

However, far from being 'successful', the emerging trend is that of Australia being deindustrialised (as economic activity in manufacturing declines), delabourised (in association with the introduction of labour-displacing technologies), and rationalised (through the centralisation -- merging -- of capital) (see Stilwell, 1986; Fagan and Webber, 1994). Over 80,000 jobs per year have been lost from the manufacturing sector since 1974. New imported technologies have reduced the workplace power of organised labour. Rationalisation has led to business mergers which favour international integration of key sectors of Australian industry (Stilwell, 1986). According to Bell (1994: 18):

> Essentially, the domestic industrial base is being eroded as global market forces sweep through the economy. The overall share of the domestic market taken by manufactured imports has risen from 17 percent in the late 1960s to 31 percent by the early 1990s ... a hollowing-out of manufacturing has (also) occurred.

In essence, the transnational capital 'Pacific Rim strategy' (Catley and McFarlane, 1981) has specific requirements: the Pacific-based center nations, Japan and the USA, are to provide capital and technology; Australia, Canada and Aotearoa (New Zealand) are to deindustrialise while concentrating on the delivery of cheap foodstuffs, fibre and energy; the newly emerging industrial powers, Taiwan, Singapore and South Korea are to produce manufactures (including items such as cars, clothing and footwear) with cheap labour.

What is of particular importance here is the extent to which the clearly defined role of Australia as a raw material provider for East-Asia runs counter to the development of environmentally sound domestic agricultural practices.

THE PRESENT STATE OF THE AGRICULTURAL ENVIRONMENT IN THE MURRAY-DARLING BASIN

Australia has a vast array of production regions and commodity types and therefore it is somewhat inappropriate to discuss environmental problems in the context of an homogeneous 'Australia'. However, one important 'natural' region is the Murray-Darling Basin (MDB). The MDB is Australia's most important agricultural region: it is also a region experiencing severe environmental degradation.

Basin agriculture, producing one third of the nation's output, is based predominantly on wheat cropping, the open grazing of sheep and cattle and intensive horticulture (confined to irrigation areas). The majority of farms are family owned-and-operated with annual production of Basin farms in the order of $10 billion (Crabb, 1988; MDB Ministerial Council, 1990).

This achievement has taken its toll. The soils of the Basin are nutrient deficient, thin, and are easily damaged by floods, droughts and agricultural practices such as continuous cultivation (Ockwell, 1990). Increasing acidity and rising salty watertables are also a severe problem. Yet the economic development of the Basin has required the clearing of native vegetation, the damming of rivers, the heavy irrigation of vast tracts of the semi-arid inland (areas which, for millennia, received an average annual rainfall of less than 250 mm), and the introduction of destructive foreign plants and animals.

Soil formation rates in the Basin are so low that the notion of an 'acceptable loss' is rejected by scientists (see Smith and Finlayson, 1988). At present, estimates of soil loss are that for each tonne of grain produced, some 13 tonnes are either blown or washed away (O'Reilly, 1988). Between 40 and 60 percent of farmers in the Basin are considered to employ inadequate on-farm measures to combat soil erosion on their properties (Vanclay, 1986).

Salinity is another major problem. Both irrigated and non-irrigated (dryland) areas of the Basin have experienced quite severe salting. Salinity in irrigation areas is associated with rising watertables due to excessive irrigation and inadequate drainage. Dryland salinity is also due to rising watertables, with modern pastures and crops using less water than the complex ecosystems they replaced. Dryland salting can also be caused by the eventual exposure of salty lower soil horizons arising from the erosion of topsoil by overgrazing and tree clearing (Vanclay and Cary, 1989). Dryland salting was only identified as an issue in the mid 1980s: now estimates are that it will become four to five times as bad within the next thirty years (*Australian*, December 1994: 4). The rising watertable in one of the Basin's largest cities, Wagga Wagga in south western NSW, is threatening homes, roads, bridges and sporting fields. The watertable was some 45 metres below ground level in 1913, but has been rising by half a metre every year and is presently close to the surface in many places (*Sunday Telegraph*, 25 September 1994: 21). Foundations of some homes in the city are beginning to be affected, road asphalt is being broken up, and some locals are concerned not only about the likely structural damage, but also the consequent decline in property values (see *Daily Advertiser*, 8 April, 1995: 14).

The outcomes of salinisation, in terms of agriculture, are productivity losses for the Basin which have been valued at $100 million per annum (Cook, 1988). Virtually the entire riverine plain around the Murray will experience rising watertables early next century and some 1.3 million hectares of prime irrigation land is expected to be waterlogged and salinised by the year 2040 (*Australian*, 7 December 1994: 4). It is predicted that at present rates of salting, many of the Basin's currently highly productive irrigated horticulture areas will be unable to grow fruit trees within 50 years (O'Reilly, 1988).

The total cost of land degradation is calculated to be hundreds of millions of dollars per annum (*Australian Farm Journal*, November 1991; Fray, 1991; MDB Ministerial Council, 1990), and it is acknowledged that farmers are economically incapable of paying for the measures necessary to prevent further environmental deterioration (see *Australian*, 7 December 1994: 4). Other problems, such as habitat destruction, the extinction of native plants and animals, as well as the loss of water quality because of turbidity, industrial effluent discharge, sewage, and agri-chemicals, are impossible to 'cost'. In total, it is estimated that over $1.5 billion will be required to address present environmental problems in the Basin (see Crabb, 1988). The Federal Government currently allocates some $87 million per annum (Australian, 7 December 1994: 4).

Tree planting schemes and other initiatives have begun, with the Federal Government providing funding for the so-called 'Decade of Landcare'. There are, today, some 2,000 Landcare groups Australia-wide (Campbell and Siepen, 1994: 252). Ironically, just as the Federal Government has begun to provide monies for environmental improvement, State governments have endorsed development strategies which act counter to the wider goal. For example, while the Federal Government has initiated and funded the Billion Trees Program (the planting of one billion trees by the year 2000), over a billion trees have been removed from a relatively small region of Queensland since 1985, in accordance with that State's land development strategy (Beale and Fray, 1990).

FUTURE OPTIONS: AGRICULTURAL SUSTAINABILITY OR FURTHER EXPLOITATION?

Views differ significantly on the precise causes of the environmental problems of the Basin and on the policies that might be implemented to address them. The favoured approach is to view past problems as occurring because of: inappropriate attitudes to the environment on the part of farmers; lack of knowledge about the damage caused by agricultural practices; and the policies of past governments which subsidised and fostered large-scale land clearing, ill-conceived irrigation developments, and excessive chemical applications (see Cameron and Elix, 1990; Dumsday, Edwards and Chisholm, 1990; MDB Ministerial Commission, 1990; Vanclay, 1992a; Johnson and Rix, 1993). It is generally believed that 'adaptive management' schemes, including remedial action initiated by farmers and governments, will be the key to environmental sustainability in the Basin (Mackay and Eastburn, 1990).

Another hope is that when 'user pays' principles are introduced into irrigation water charges, that water will be used with greater efficiency (Simmons, *et al.*, 1992). It is suggested that by making water entitlements transferable, there will be a potential return of some $40 million. What is very often not discussed is the likelihood that transferring water will mean that the bigger farmers will get bigger, that smaller farmers -- forced by economic circumstances to sell their entitlements -- will have little security in agriculture and will leave the industry. The state, which once subsidised irrigated agriculture, because of its ability to fulfil rural development objectives such as the spread of population and the creation of 'family farms', is now not prepared to do so. Just what this will mean for farming-dependent communities in the irrigation areas is not yet clear. One likelihood, in line with the 'Goldschmidt thesis' (Goldschmidt, 1947), is that as farm size and corporate involvement increases, the prosperity of surrounding rural towns will diminish. A more efficient agriculture may lead to community decline. If this were to occur, towns such as Griffith and Leeton in NSW -- once held to be shining examples of the benefits of decentralisation policy -- might experience a reduction in retail sales, job loss, as well as population decline. The result would be fewer people in fewer viable communities in inland Australia. However, there are some who suggest that this is not likely to occur (Simmons *et al.*, 1992).

There is a real dilemma for those attempting to manage irrigation agriculture in the Basin. If water remains subsidised, there is little incentive for producers to adopt the most appropriate strategy to overcome salinisation -- which is to reduce (or make more efficient) water applications. On the other hand, with water entitlement transferability, those holding the (increasingly costly) entitlements will have reason to get the most from them. And, where farm size increases as the larger farmers buy up entitlements, there will be a tendency for the intensification of agricultural production to occur. Larger farms use larger machinery and tend to use high levels of fertilisers and chemicals. Will this benefit the environment?

It is important not to forget the economic conditions under which market-oriented agricultural production takes place. The structural characteristics of Basin farming -- high production risks, a relatively fixed supply of available land, discontinuous applications of labour, input costs rising faster than prices received, and low income elasticities of demand for agricultural products (Williams, 1990; and see Buttel, Larson and Gillespie, 1990) -- when taken together, are likely to mean continuing low overall returns to producers. Furthermore, the global marketplace creates the structural tendency for farmers to over-produce, to have short term planning horizons, and to disregard the long-term returns from soil conservation (Buttel *et al.*, 1990; Redclift, 1987; Rickson *et al.*, 1987; Vanclay, 1992a).

In the current period of low returns which has extended from the early 1990s, Basin producers have knowingly made agronomically incorrect decisions as a means of ensuring short term economic survival (*Bulletin*, 31 July 1990; Share *et al.*, 1991). Increased production (overgrazing and the farming of marginal lands) and minimising the application of inputs (such as lime to prevent acidification) have direct crop yield and environmental implications. However, reduced farm income (due to low commodity prices), the lack of equity and the reluctance on the part of farmers to borrow (and banks to lend) in times of falling prices, means a shortage of capital. These factors prevent, or inhibit, the adoption of techniques considered necessary to improve the environment. Many farmers, compelled to work off the farm for additional income to service debts, find that they are neglecting their farms: they do not have the time to engage in the labour-intensive land-conserving activities that are required. With limited income, farmers lack the economic ability to change their situation or to take risks to experiment with new production strategies such as conservation farming techniques. Large-scale environmental degradation is a serious outcome of the present farm financial crisis. In a 1991 survey of 4000 Australian farmers, 30 percent indicated no money would be spent during the year to address environmental degradation on their farm, while a further 50 percent indicated that the poor economic outlook would limit what could be done (see Fray, 1991). The MDB Community Advisory Committee (1991: 23) has conceded that 'on-farm land management practices are expensive and their implementation, in this time of economic price problems, threatens the survival of the farms'.

When price levels improve, Australian farmers -- like their competitors abroad -- purchase inputs designed to increase production and/or lower unit costs, rather than invest in conservation technology. New mechanical, chemical and biological inputs drive the farm further towards specialisation, including the pursuit of fordist-style monocultural practices (which contribute to environmental degradation) (see Buttel *et al.*, 1990). Similarly, some consider that the 'new' solutions such as zero or minimum tillage create their own environmental problems resulting from the increased use of herbicides (Cameron and Elix, 1991; Barr and Cary, 1992). More disturbingly, most soil conservation practices, especially the planting of native trees, are not usually profitable for the individual farmer. This is especially so in times of high interest rates and when future discounting techniques are applied (Rickson *et al.*, 1987; Vanclay and Cary, 1989; Cameron and Elix, 1991; Vanclay, 1992a). Australian farmers do recognise soil degradation as a general problem, but the vast majority of producers reject the notion that their own soils are being degraded (Rickson *et al.*, 1987; Vanclay, 1992a).

The trends towards fewer and larger farms, greater reliance on technology, and increasing specialisation in production -- all in the context of world overproduction -- provide the foundations for the continuation of an environmentally exploitative agriculture, one which 'constrains' efforts to attain sustainability. Redclift (1987) goes further in condemning the present course of modern agriculture. He argues that sustainable systems are characterised by diversity and stability in achieving a high level of biomass. In contrast, in modern agricultural systems, large quantities of biomass are achieved by the applications of high levels of artificial inputs in less-mature and less-diverse ecosystems. For Redclift, sustainability and commercial agriculture are logically incompatible.

Rather than seeking reduced-input systems to provide a sustainable basis for farming in the Basin, there has been a growing interest on the part of capital and the state to introduce new (and potentially more damaging) forms of agriculture.

NEW STRATEGIES

Cotton Production

Cotton is an example of a crop which will, through advanced breeding programs and other experimental research, assist Australian farmers to improve market share. A new crop for Australia in the 1950s, cotton has become the fifth major export commodity and is the fastest growing of all agricultural industries. Australia has become the world's third largest exporter of raw cotton, and, in a 'good' season, the nation's 1,500 growers produce about one billion dollars in export earnings (*Australian Farm Journal*, October 1994: 50). The bulk of this -- some 80 percent -- is sold to the East Asia region. Farms are generally large agribusiness concerns and are heavily reliant upon extensive agri-chemical inputs. The industry is dominated by corporate interests. It has no statutory marketing boards and receives no subsidies or protection (Wormwell, 1990).

Some 209,000 hectares of Australian cotton farmlands (some 88 percent) is within the MDB. Expansion in cotton growing has been dramatic -- from some 40,000 hectares Australia wide to about 240,000 in 1994 in two decades (*Australian Farm Journal*, October 1994: 51). This growth has been reliant upon the damming of rivers which has required considerable public and private investment. Virtually every tributary of the Darling River is dammed (see Johnson and Rix, 1993). Moreover, much of the existing water resources are over-committed. Farmers in NSW are demanding more water, but upstream users in the St George and Macintyre (Queensland) regions are also eager to have increased allocations. NSW cotton farmers have been so desirous of reliable allocations, that their combined damming and water pumping activities have begun to interfere with wildlife habitats of international significance. It is perceived by some northern NSW cattle producers who have 'finished' their animals on the pastures surrounding the Gwydir river wetlands, that the volume of water necessary to maintain the wetlands is no longer being received. As the wetlands have begun to dry out, noxious weeds and other unsuitable grasses have taken over (*Australian Farm Journal*, October 1994: 52). Another undesirable outcome of cotton expansion has been an increase in the level of toxic chemicals in the ecosystem. As Johnson and Rix (1993: 117) have detailed:

> A typical cotton crop is sprayed with over a dozen different herbicides and insecticides with up to 25 different applications in a growing season ... Everything living, both plant and animal, is targeted in this chemically intensive agriculture. Pesticides and herbicides used in cotton farming are in many cases toxic to humans, animals and aquatic life. Endosulfan and other cotton pesticides can persist for several months in the sediments of dams, streams, and rivers. Pesticide and herbicide application methods are not capable of such accurate control as to entirely prevent their escape onto adjoining lands and into river systems.

Despite the negative environmental consequences of its production, cotton is heralded as Australian agriculture's success story with 'King Cotton' having become, in very short time, Australia's fourth largest rural export (*Australian Farm Journal*, October 1994: 50). Governments, eager to overcome balance of payments problems, and to support the development of products which will tie the nation's economy closer to that of Japan and Asia, have provided quite significant assistance to the industry. For example, the Federal Government has funded a Cooperative Research Centre for Sustainable Cotton Production based at Narrabri, NSW. Despite the problems of environmental degradation, the 'progressive' nature of the industry and government endorsement (as witnessed through state expenditure on dams) give growers a signal that cotton expansion is desirable. In NSW, for example, taxpayers are to pay half the cost of construction of the Pindari Dam near Moree, in the State's north central region. Growers are to pay via deferred payments over a 17 year period. As Johnson and Rix (1993) argue, this deferral is really a loan to cotton producers. They have also questioned the manner in which the State has allowed the dam to proceed:

> the same government agency, the NSW Department of Water Resources, is the proponent, the client and the assessor of the project. Objectivity is clearly compromised. Unless there are major reforms to institutional arrangements such as this, it is unlikely that the requisite reforms to water management in the country [will] occur (Johnson and Rix, 1993: 118).

Beef Feedlots

Feedlot beef enterprises provide another example of change with the Basin. Feedlot and abattoir complexes are appearing along the river systems of the Basin to take advantage of the reliable supply of water, grain and (unfattened) store cattle. Investment from Japan, Korea, Taiwan and Singapore has been used to develop vertically integrated complexes with direct links to Asian markets. The recent developments initiated by firms such as TKK, Mitsubishi, Marubini, Nippon Meats and Itoham have included feedlots of up to 60,000 head. In the Riverina region of the MDB, an area traditionally known for its broadacre cropping and extensive grazing, feedlots with a total annual production capacity of 250,000 head, have commenced operation (*Land*, 31 January 1991).

With liberalisation of the Japanese beef market, beef exports are growing dramatically. There has been a corresponding growth of some 56 percent in the feedlot industry in the four years since 1990 (*Australian Farm Journal*, November 1994: 58). It is presently growing by about 15 percent per annum and is expected that up to 50 percent of Australia's entire beef output will be occur through feedlots by the year 2000 (*Australian Farm Journal*, November 1994: 60). The industry is becoming concentrated in size and in export orientation. For example, there are currently about 1,500 feedlots in Australia, with about 20 percent carrying over 1,000 head. Those 20 percent are responsible for most of the economic activity within the industry (*Australian Farm Journal*, November 1994: 58). Japanese consumers believe that the great bulk of Australian meats which have previously been exported have been grass 'tainted' (*Australian Farm Journal*, October 1992: 53). The development of the feedlot beef industry has, in part, been a response to Japanese consumer resistance to pasture-grown meats.

One leading grower explained what the future might bring:

> Large feedlot 'food factories' will be located in the grainbelts where they can draw upon grain and cattle as well as by-products of sugar, cotton and rice growing such as rice hulls, cotton seed and molasses ... The feedlot industry is growing and here to stay because it meets our customers' requirements. We are an integral part of agribusiness and we will be the driving force in the cattle industry over the next few years (reported in *Australian Farm Journal*, November 1994: 60).

In the agribusiness model likely to evolve in the MDB, farmers will be issued with contracts to supply grain and unfattened animals to the new complexes. Like feedlotting, contract agriculture is new to the Basin (*Australian Farm Journal*, May 1991: 85) and farmers who have lost the protection of marketing boards and other support in industries such as dairying and wheat growing, are expected eagerly to seek involvement with the feedlots. According to the Executive Director of the Lotfeeders' Association: 'feedlots are going to change the face of the Riverina region, creating a new economy based on supplying grain and cattle to the feedlot industry' (*Land*, 17 January 1991: 10).

Labour relations in the agricultural sector are also being targeted for change. Workers in the feedlot/abattoir complexes are expected to accept 'more flexible and internationally competitive labour arrangements and awards' (DPIE, 1989: 67). The first non-union based contract working team has already been employed in an Australian meatworks (see *Stock and Land*, 5 September 1991) with the support of the farmers and the National Farmers' Federation. This is in contrast to the high levels of unionisation normally experienced in Australian workplaces. Furthermore, rural workers, in current times of financial distress for Australian agriculture, are being required to place rural community interests ahead of union loyalty (*Australian Farm Journal*, May 1991). There is large-scale retrenchment from rural-based industry with non-locals migrating to urban areas. The remaining workers tend to be farmers working off the farm, or those with a farming background. They often do not share traditional blue-collar union ideology, avoid union membership and are therefore vulnerable to structural adjustment in the industrial workplace.

Environmental Impact

While rural restructuring raises important questions about the effects of change on rural communities and about the overall structure of the newly emerging agricultural economy, what appears to have been ignored by those supporting change is the impact of restructuring on the environment.

Developments in the cotton industry (agronomic and biotechnological) are likely to intensify existing environmental problems. For example, while cotton may be one of the 'glamour' crops (Wormwell, 1990), it is heavily dependent on agri-chemicals and is known to have already caused quite serious downstream pollution (Lawrence, 1987).

Of perhaps greater significance is the development of feedlots. One estimate is that effluent from a feedlot of 40,000 head is equivalent to that produced by a city of 500,000 people (*Land*, 15 January 1989). Cities of this size require waste treatment works in the order of $100 million. In contrast, the traditional method of treatment of feedlot effluent in the Basin is the containment of liquid in holding ponds and the sun-drying of manure for sale to district farmers (*Land*, 17 January 1991). Expansion of feedlotting is likely to result in seepage and run-off that will eventually reach the already-polluted Murrumbidgee River (see *Narrandera Argus*, 21 August 1990), considered the 'lifeblood' of the Riverina. A State Pollution Control Commission's negative assessment of feedlot beef complexes along the inland waterways was ignored by the State Government which gave approval for their development (*Murrumbidgee Irrigator*, 22 February 1991). While problems of overgrazing and overcropping associated with conventional agriculture have caused havoc in the Basin, the removal of pastures and the replacement with grain to supply the feedlots may intensify current environmental problems. The potential for erosion is higher on cropping land than pasture land (see Heathcote and Mabbutt, 1988) and a greater volume of fertilisers and agri-chemicals will inevitably be employed. Pollution of the river system will bring its own problems.

A Case in Point: Blue-Green Algae

One of the major concerns is that the new forms of economic activity will lead to the proliferation of blue-green algae in the river systems of the Basin. Algal blooms are of serious concern because they are toxic to stock and humans. A major outbreak in the summer of 1991-92 is reported to have killed hundreds of cattle and sheep. The water cannot be treated by boiling, and conventional water purification plants in Australian towns do not adequately detoxify the water. Therefore, algal blooms pose a severe threat to town water supplies and the health of people living along inland rivers. Many towns have had to rely on expensive emergency measures such as the carting of freshwater from elsewhere. Blue-green algae tends to be the threat to human life which makes the problem newsworthy: what is often not acknowledged is that the presence of blue-green algae is symptomatic of widespread environmental deterioration.

Algal blooms develop only under certain environmental conditions: sunlight, still water, warm temperature and an ample (over-)supply of nutrients, particularly phosphorous (Johnson and Rix, 1993). While there are historical reports of algal blooms in the Murray River last century and in England as early as the 12th century, and acknowledgment that algal blooms can potentially occur naturally, their natural occurrence on a large scale is very unlikely. While blue-green algae organisms may be present in the water in small quantities, algal blooms indicate an environmental system that is exceeding normal equilibrium limits. That is, the high levels of nutrients required for a bloom do not occur normally. Large algal blooms are a human creation -- one symptomatic of land and water mismanagement.

The problem which occurred in late 1991 was a consequence of a number of factors: low water flow, high temperature and high nutrient levels -- all of which occurred simultaneously. If any of those conditions had not been present, the bloom may not have been quite as worrying to producers and authorities. However, its occurrence is no surprise as large scale toxic blooms of this kind have been predicted for the Murray-Darling for over 10 years. Despite the predictions over the years in government reports warning of high nutrient levels (with some identifying phosphorous levels up to 80 times those recommended for environmental safety), little action has been undertaken. Even the objective of the task force set up to investigate the algal bloom of 1991 was limited to understanding the implications for human health (Johnson and Rix, 1993).

It would be unfair to overlook the general physical constraints upon land and water use. For example, flow rates in the Basin are subject to enormous seasonal and annual variation and it would be difficult to quantify the exact impact of the extent of human activity on the rate of flow. Nevertheless, it is clear that flow rates are seriously affected by human activity especially in times of low flow. The numerous weirs and dams, and the enormous use of river water for stock watering and irrigation mean that in times of poor rainfall, when water levels in the river are low, there is an increased use of river water and a lack of river capacity to eliminate or disperse the algae.

In times of high rainfall, surplus unelected water is granted to irrigators and thus any regular flushing of the river system may not occur. In drought times, such as the Basin has been experiencing, overgrazing and loss of ground cover can lead to accelerated rates of erosion. Evaporation rates are also higher, further reducing the flow rate of the river. The rural crisis and low prices for stock, mean that when pasture growth is plentiful farmers tend to overstock. But continuing low farm incomes means little investment in environmental protection.

Consequently, both the drought and the rural crisis contribute to accelerated rates of erosion and to the growth of algal blooms.

Where the eroded soils have nutrient fertilisers embedded this will lead to enhanced prospects for algal blooms. Soil particles -- with phosphate attached -- eventually find their way to the river system. Scientists have grave concerns about the existing level of silting of the river systems. Phosphates which have accumulated in the silt will continue to act as a nutrient bank which will feed the algae for decades no matter what is done to address the problems in the short term. Much of the nutrient load is chemically locked up in the sediment. Under anaerobic conditions, sulphates are converted to sulphides, and phosphorous, stored in the sediment, is released (see Johnson and Rix, 1993) providing nutrients for algal growth. Superphosphate was heavily applied on Australian farms over the last 50 or so years, particularly on the Darling Downs, the headwaters on the Darling River, and considerable amounts of nutrient could be present in the silt at the bottom of the river. Agricultural chemicals (pesticides, weedicides and defoliants) also kill zooplankton which feed on blue-green algae. Chemicals that are sulphur based may have the effect of assisting bacteria to release phosphorous entrapped in the silt.

There may be things that can be done to try to reduce the level of nutrient in the river. Sewage treatment plants along the river can be upgraded to remove nutrients from the discharge. Ideally they should not discharge into the river but into local wetlands where vegetation can extract any residual nutrients. Urban (and rural town) runoff is a major cause of water pollution in rural areas with storm water drains typically leading directly to the nearest watercourse. While farmers may use high quantities of agricultural chemicals, their application rate is far lower than that of urban (and town) people in their backyards and recreational facilities such as golf courses. People in rural towns (and cities) need to be educated about the environmental impacts of their seemingly benign gardening activities.

Similarly, river banks can be fenced to prevent stock from watering -- and therefore defecating -- directly into rivers and their tributaries. This would also prevent riverbank erosion and so reduce the amount of silt and any entrapped nutrients from entering the river. By revegetating river banks, erosion can be further prevented with the vegetation itself serving as a buffer to capture and utilise the nutrient-containing runoff from nearby cultivation.

Agricultural inputs (at least their loss from the agricultural system) need to be reduced. This will be achieved by lowering the quantity of inputs applied, changing the types of inputs used to more environmentally friendly forms, changing the form of agriculture to a production system that is less dependent on and/or more efficient in the use of these inputs, and minimising the loss of these chemicals from the agricultural system into the environment by reducing erosion and runoff. By improving the agricultural management practices of farmers -- especially in terms of conservation farming, particularly stubble retention (to reduce erosion and runoff), and appropriate rotations (to maintain high yields and soil fertility without the use of artificial inputs) -- much less nutrient is likely to enter the river systems.

Immediate adoption of these suggestions is not likely. Nor is medium term adoption. While the suggestions above may seem obvious and harmless enough, there is enormous cost involved. Many of the farms affected are marginal -- marginally viable farmers on marginally viable farmland. The cost of the required changes such as fencing off the river and installing pumps and water troughs (which have their own environmental problems) would be beyond the means of these farmers and would mean that they were altogether unviable. Rural shires often have a small rates base largely based on these marginal farmers. These shires are unlikely to be able to afford to upgrade their sewage systems. The rural crisis means declining population and wealth in rural areas making these rural shires even less likely to invest in large scale capital infrastructural works. The widespread adoption of environmentally sound agricultural practices by farmers is unlikely for a myriad of reasons largely related to farmers' economic and social situation.

In a fragile environment where drought is always a threat, land and water management is a real problem. Commercial farmers can stay in business only by improving productivity and efficiency -- something which translates, in most cases, to increasing the stocking rate of animals, clearing more land, extending monocropping systems and employing potent agri-chemicals and fertilisers. The MDB Commission has, in its own research, identified intensive animal industries such as piggeries, cattle feedlots, and dairies as the main culprits in environmental pollution of the Basin (see Johnson and Rix, 1993: 116). Yet individual economic logic dictates that farmers, if they are to survive and take advantage of the new overseas demand for agricultural products, become increasingly involved in intensive activities. To stay in business, the latest techniques and methods must be employed. Undesirable 'externalities', such as nutrient-rich runoff, are exported downstream. The real cost of modern agriculture is never fully established because the environmental effects of poor agronomic practices rarely show up on the balance sheets of the individual farmer. It is the widespread incremental decline of farmlands together with the incremental pollution of water systems which are the real concerns for rural Australia. They occur because of a failure of the marketplace to 'cost' the environmental degradation of capitalist agriculture and the reluctance of governments to employ a tighter system of regulation for land and water users in the MDB.

The MDB Ministerial Commission is virtually unable to change current practices. It has no legal authority to impose fines, or to plan for water use. In essence, the States have been simply unwilling to cede powers to a body which may (and should) overrule the policies of both State and local governments. As Walker (1992: 12) has emphasised in regard to the issue of salinisation:

> Responses to problems often remain short-sighted and expedient. In August 1988 the Murray-Darling Basin Ministerial Council adopted a 'new' policy for salination reduction which, although a step forward in interstate cooperation depended largely on short-term, engineering measures: in effect, 'throwing money at the problem'. Land retirement, favoured strongly in some quarters, was not adopted as a major strategy ... The new policy not only fails to work with the ecosystem, but displaces the problem further into the future.

The same criticism might be applied to the problem of algal blooms. Although there is a group led by representatives of the MDB Commission looking of ways of reducing nutrients, Australia neither has a national water policy nor a nationwide system of regulation to deal with those polluting the environment. It is highly likely that future blooms -- greater in impact and size than those which have occurred previously -- will occur in the remaining years of this century, and, if the above assessment proves to be correct, well into the next century.

FORDISM, POST-FORDISM AND THE PACIFIC RIM

It would appear from the foregoing analysis that new options for Basin agriculture have the capacity to stimulate higher levels of production -- but at the further expense of an already seriously degraded environment. This is despite assurances from the Federal Government and scientists that some of the new technologies and management regimes have the capacity to produce a more sustainable agriculture (see Begg and Peacock, 1990; Bureau of Rural Resources, 1991b).

The question is, how is it possible to explain, theoretically, Australia's acceptance of potentially more harmful agricultural strategies for regions, such as the Basin, which are already greatly disadvantaged by existing capital-intensive agricultural practices? Why, in other words, has Australia so readily adopted a role in Pacific Rim development which seems to ensure that its economic growth is contingent upon acceptance of further environmental degradation?

The answer appears to be in the movement towards a post-fordist economic structure in metropolitan nations and the 'exporting' of environmentally harmful fordist production strategies to the semi-periphery and periphery as the metropolitan nations adopt more strict environmental regulation. In an attempt to maintain their position in the world economy, semi-peripheral nations are driven by the need to balance trade deficits. To achieve this, they usually rely upon external capital investment and are therefore compliant in the acceptance of environmentally damaging fordist production methods. The net effect of this is to worsen lifestyle conditions in the semi-periphery and to increase economic dependency.

Fordism has been associated with a system of mass production based on the development and sale of standardised commodities to undifferentiated national markets. Motor vehicles, petroleum and electronics were the key elements of a system which fostered productivity increases in industry as well providing a social-democratic system of regulation which ensured widespread consumption of mass produced items. Full employment was a social goal of the trade union movement -- a powerful agent in the fordist regime and responsible for shaping the welfare state (see Roobeek, 1987; Buttel and Gillespie, 1991; Hampson, 1991). Rising wage levels which occurred in tandem with productivity increases mitigated tendencies towards underconsumption and falling profits (Hampson, 1991).

According to French regulation school proponents (see, for example, Lipietz, 1987), the regime of capital accumulation which produced the 'golden age' of fordism after the Second World War began to founder in the 1970s (Sauer, 1990). The causes of instability during this time were significant oil price increases, the collapse of the once-stable Bretton Woods agreement, growing levels of inflation and the transnationalisation of the economies of nation states -- associated with global domination by the corporate sector (see Marsden, Lowe and Whatmore, 1990).

The technological opportunity for reorganising production was, from the 1970s, based largely on the computerisation of industry. Instead of requiring large factories with relatively unskilled workers using heavy machinery, computerised systems provided opportunities for production flexibility. For example, shorter production runs became possible and improved the capacity for firms to move quickly from one product to another. Skilled workers using sophisticated computerised equipment provided a competitive base for new industries which could identify and readily serve 'niche markets' (see Piore and Sabel, 1984).

Although the mass production (fordist) and flexible specialisation (post-fordist) dichotomy has been viewed critically by theorists (see Williams *et al.*, 1987; Foster, 1988; Sayer, 1989; Gartman, 1991; Hampson, 1991), it has nevertheless become an important distinction in the understanding of contemporary agrarian social change (Kenney *et al.*, 1989; Goe and Kenney, 1991; Friedmann, 1991).

From as early as the 1930s, but particularly in the three decades since the Second World War, farmers in the advanced economies -- producing largely undifferentiated products for national and later world markets and 'consuming' industrial inputs -- have been progressively integrated into the circuits of international capital (Kenney *et al.*, 1989). Commercial family-farm agriculture became dependent upon the products of mass production such as the tractor and other agricultural machinery as well as fertilisers and chemicals. Price supports and a variety of other 'welfare state' initiatives (including taxation concessions, input subsidies and commodity disposal mechanisms) provided farmers with conditions for stable production. The working classes of the advanced economies were advantaged by cheaper foods which were mass produced in much the same manner as industrial household goods. New forms of management and distribution, as embodied in 'fast food' restaurants, enabled agricultural products to be commoditised in ways which ensured uniform quality and competitive pricing (see Kenney *et al.*, 1991).

According to Friedmann (1991), the fordist food regime enabled a series of commodity chains -- particularly those uniting farmers to consumers -- to develop and link into one of three agri-food complexes: wheat; livestock/feed; and durable foods. The livestock/feed complex is the one of greatest significance in the fordist diet. In the USA, extensive livestock production had been replaced by intensive methods designed to standardise meat production while taking advantage of increasingly cheaper grain feeds (Friedmann, 1991). Pigs, cattle and poultry were enclosed in increasingly smaller areas and fed grains and supplements which were standardised to produce the highest possible grain-to-meat conversion ratios. The cattle feedlot and associated abattoir became a prototypical example of 'factory farming' in the metropolitan countries such as the USA, Britain and Germany. Meanwhile, nations such as Australia and Argentina -- areas of cheap grazing lands -- continued to produce meat for the growing global mass market in hamburgers, frankfurters and canned-meat products (Friedmann, 1991). The growth of intensive livestock production in centre countries was premised on extension of the 'American diet' -- first to Europe and later to Japan and the newly industrialising countries of the Pacific Rim (Kenney *et al.*, 1989).

With the quite significant structural problems which the US economy faced in the 1970s, the fordist production regime in agriculture was undermined. Kenney *et al.* (1989) explain that the marketplace for foods has become fractured as mass consumption diets have given way to middle-class interests in ethnic foods, chemical-free foods and 'healthy' foods. Friedmann (1991: 86) notes also that there is a growing class differentiation in the diets of the advanced nations: 'While privileged consumers eat free-range chickens prepared through handicraft methods in food shops, restaurants or by domestic servants, mass consumers eat reconstituted chicken foods from supermarket freezers or fast food restaurants'. Although standardised and highly processed foods remain a key element in global food distribution, the metropolitan nations are experiencing -- as part of the crisis in fordism -- rejection of the very techniques, methods and products which so successfully tied food production to consumption in the post-war years.

Capital no longer supplies integrated national markets. It operates globally to supply regional and enclave markets using a mixture of fordist and post-fordist production regimes. With transnational capital having the overall say in the form and location of production, it is capable of orchestrating global production to take account of new consumer demands or profit-making opportunities (see Lawrence, 1995).

Another essential, but inadequately discussed, part of the story is the growth of 'green' movements in metropolitan nations. There is an emerging consensus in these nations that past agricultural practices are incompatible with food quality and environmental safety. For example, Hirsh and Roth (quoted in Sauer, 1990: 269) have argued that 'the dynamics of the fordist reproduction process leave in their wake a progressive scale of ecological destruction'. This, in addition to animal rights arguments, is one of the main reasons for European resentment of factory-farming methods. Environmentalists in Germany, for example, have introduced both ethical and cultural arguments in questioning 'high tech' agriculture and its future. Thus, animal husbandry is no longer something to be left to farmers -- it must be guided by ethical principles and allow the interests of consumers and environmentalists to be placed alongside those of the producer (Sauer, 1990). In rejecting factory farming, German consumers are providing direct and explicit support for family-farm based reproduction strategies and environmental security (Sauer, 1990).

Sweden, too, has initiated moves to strengthen environmental protection legislation and to provide financial support for family-farm units. This has been interpreted as both a challenge to mass production agriculture, and evidence of the 'greening' of agricultural policy in Europe (see Vail, 1991). Moves are afoot to assist producers to convert cropland to pasture, and there is an associated move to grass-fed beef, away from intensive forms of meat production.

Buttel (1992) has described the process of incorporating 'green' considerations into the economic, social and political policies of the state as 'environmentalization'. He anticipates that the process of environmentalization -- which embodies resource conservation, sustainable development and social justice elements -- will have the capacity to challenge the bases of technocratic productivist methods and ideologies.

In the USA, agriculture has been central in the debates about environmental pollution (see Kenney *et al.*, 1989). As in the case of feedlotting, where there is a growing awareness of ecological damage and of undesirable animal husbandry practices, there is likely to be capital flight to regions of the world less prepared or able to impose rigid environmental constraints on production. In addition to Goe and Kenney's (1991: 152) assertion that 'large scale production of any commodity will be a low-value business, always threatening to move to places with low land values and low labour costs', regional and national regimes of environmental regulation will guide decisions about industry location.

In the EC, especially Britain, where new residents are helping to redefine the social meaning of the countryside (see Munton, Marsden and Whatmore, 1990), those whose economic and social interests are in tourism, retirement or recreation are forcing farmers both to conserve and preserve the landscape. The new dual-income 'gentry', ever-conscious of the advantages of rural living, are capable of mobilising and organising the community in an effort to 'protect' village and community life (Cloke and Thrift, 1990). Environmental pollution is very much an issue of concern for these groups.

Lipietz (1987) argues that environmental problems arising from fordist production strategies have been highlighted by the groups who have lobbied for better work practices and for the realignment of business interests to issues of environmental safety. And, for Goe and Kenney (1991: 152), 'as long as a lack of environmental restrictions ... permit an adequate rate of return for mass produced commodities, [fordism] will continue'. The irony is that while the environmental degradation of Australian farmlands would seem to necessitate radical changes in production methods, what Australia appears to be gaining are the discarded fordist production methods of the metropolitan nations.

Capital is seeking new ways of extracting economic surplus in an increasingly competitive global economy, with the impacts of change being uneven and usually socially disruptive (Redclift and Whatmore, 1990). New arrangements between finance and industrial capital have tended to undermine decisions made by national governments. Credit finance -- upon which the transnational economy is reliant -- is notoriously mobile between regions and industries (see Marsden, Lowe and Whatmore, 1990). In Australia, it has facilitated most of the mergers and rationalisations which have taken place in agribusiness and has sought new products (such as cotton, feedlot beef and tropical fruits), new regions (such as the traditional broadacre farming areas), and new methods (vertically integrated production, direct contracts with growers, intensive animal production and biotechnological applications) to help to reorganise Australian agriculture along corporate lines.

The language of post-fordism is in fact that of finance capital and its transnational allies. Instead of specialising in broadacre cropping and grazing under a state-organised system of statutory marketing boards, Australian farmers are being told to adopt more 'flexible' production regimes and seek 'niche markets' for their 'value added' products. The irony here is that Australian farmers have been renowned for their diversified production regimes, at the farmer level if not the national level, and for the ability of their monopoly marketing bodies to find niche markets. Furthermore, value adding for products like meat, wheat and wool has been notoriously difficult because of market distance and labour costs. Because of overproduction in agriculture, effective strategies were necessary just to secure markets and often involved specialised markets and production. Examples of this are the live sheep trade and the kosher butchery, and certain types of fat-enhanced meat as well as lean meat. However, much of this has not resulted in value adding, but has served only to secure a market for certain goods in a situation of overproduction. Consequently, some of the possible means of value adding in agricultural commodities are excluded by overproduction. It is also becoming recognised that value-adding will take place closer to the retail, rather than the raw material, end of commodity chains (DPIE, 1989). With the removal of tariff protection for 'infant' industries, there is little incentive for firms to move beyond simple semi-processing activities in Australia.

The post-fordist discourse is not all hollow rhetoric. There is evidence that those manufacturing industries which remain in Australia are exhibiting post-fordist characteristics, particularly new production strategies, new management strategies, new technologies, and production for niche markets (see Mathews, 1989, 1992; *Australian*, 14 November 1992). Agriculture, too, cannot be construed to be uniformly fordist. Biotechnological innovations and applications, providing opportunities for more varied production regimes and specific markets, might be viewed as post-fordist (see Goodman, Sorj and Wilkinson, 1987). Again, in post-fordist style, the new beef feedlot/abattoir complexes are seeking to use more 'flexible' labour arrangements and produce a specific product -- marbled beef so desired by the Asian restaurant trade. However, the fact that the Asian restaurant trade is itself a vast decentralised (mass) market for uniform marbled beef strips, makes it difficult to sustain the notion that this represents 'niche' production.

It is necessary to recognise that the movement from fordist to post-fordist strategies will be both regionally uneven and over-determined temporally by state policy and by existing and potential conditions of surplus extraction. There is little doubt that livestock producers in the MDB and in other regions of Australia are becoming enmeshed in corporate production relations aimed at forcing on-farm specialisation (of both crops and stock) and the integration of those producers into the fordist, transnational livestock/feed complex. Friedmann (1991: 71) concurs: 'food is no longer simply something produced by farmers and bought by consumers, but a profitable product of capitalist enterprise, transnationally sourced, processed and marketed'.

CONCLUSION

Foreign capital is poised to dictate the form Australian agriculture will take. Banking interests have usually helped to reorganise agriculture to fulfil short term profit making goals and have endorsed intensification of farming. Transnational agribusiness -- pressed by overseas governments, consumers and environmental lobby groups to initiate more ecologically sound practices -- has turned to Australia as a location for investment. This is being encouraged as Federal and State regulations disappear and as the nation seeks foreign capital investment to overcome balance of payments deficits (Lawrence and Campbell, 1991).

As Buttel (1992, following Redclift, 1987) has argued, 'debt stress' is one of the major forces driving countries (particularly those in the periphery and semi-periphery) to introduce production-boosting technologies and practices, which result, inevitably, in environmental degradation. Farm debt has burgeoned and, at some $18 billion, is at the highest level ever recorded (*Australian Farm Journal*, April 1995). Martin (1990) has stressed that historical analyses of the nations within the semi-periphery have tended to indicate a failure to move towards core status. Even if we accept, as Niosi (1990) argues, that Australia has been closer to the metropole than the periphery, it might be assumed that the current combined trajectories of deindustrialisation and the agribusiness domination of family-farm agriculture is likely to push Australia closer to the periphery.

The present pattern of capital accumulation is one which Australia, as a recipient of production regimes abandoned by the centre, may be forced to accept if it hopes to become part of the Pacific Rim economy. The danger is that the relationship of Australia and the Pacific Rim will come to resemble that of Mexico and the USA. Like Australia, Mexico is well suited to range-fed beef, and as Sanderson (1989: 227) has commented 'technological and capital investments in ... [beef production] would be better spent in ecologically sustainable, low technology range management'. Instead, the beef industry in Mexico has been made to conform to US demands for grain-fed animals, irrespective of Mexico's traditional practices.

By locating the least desirable agricultural activities (and toxic industries generally) in less regulated countries of the periphery (see Piore and Sabel, 1984) and semi-periphery, the metropolitan nations -- through the transnational corporations originating from those nations -- are engaging in a form of 'environmental imperialism' -- specifically, the formal or informal control over economic resources in a manner which advantages the metropolitan power, at the expense of the local economy (see O'Connor, 1971). Notwithstanding the obvious and well-focused criticisms levelled at attempts to explore 'peripheral fordism' (see Cataife, 1989), this analysis has sought to provide an explanation for regional changes in a nation whose self-determination is being progressively compromised.

In Australia, the MDB is being restructured as a food factory and effluent disposal system for the increasingly wealthy consumers of the Pacific Rim. Importantly, but not surprisingly, the state in Australia is unwilling to impose tighter controls for fear of driving away much needed capital investment. Indeed, many of the State and local governments have a vested interest in ensuring that growth is not hampered by the imposition of tighter controls. Embedded within the changing structure of world capitalism, Australia is hostage to decisions made by those whose international economic power not only influences -- but also effectively determines -- the structural character of local agriculture. At present, there is little evidence to counter the view that farming will be considered as a convenient means of obtaining cheap inputs to the Pacific Rim's burgeoning consumer market for meats and for inputs to the food and fibre processing industries. The increasing level of subsumption of Australian farms with respect to agribusiness parallels the increasing level of subservience of the entire Australian economy to transnational capital (see Jones, 1992). For Australian agriculture, the effect is economic marginalisation for many farmers and the continued degradation of the environment.

THE SEARCH FOR NEW TECHNOLOGIES
IS BIOTECHNOLOGY THE ANSWER TO ENVIRONMENTAL DEGRADATION?

INTRODUCTION

Biotechnology is being heralded in Australia and elsewhere (see Lowe, 1992; Peacock, 1993; Lawrence and Norton, 1994) as the most appropriate mechanism for both increasing agricultural productivity and overcoming many of the environmental problems associated with modern agriculture (such as the heavy use of pesticides and weedicides). Some consider biotechnologies will create the best opportunities for a sustainable future (Department of Primary Industries and Energy, 1989; Begg and Peacock, 1990; Bureau of Rural Resources, 1991a).

Biotechnologies are expected to allow producers to reduce their levels of inputs (and hence costs) while achieving higher levels of output. Embryo technology, for example, may provide opportunities for transferring superior genes to existing cattle herds and sheep flocks at a lower per unit cost than normal breeding techniques. Vaccines created through biotechnology are considered to be superior to those obtained in conventional ways. Bovine somatotropin -- a hormone manufactured in laboratories through recombinant DNA technology -- will allow more milk to be produced by dairy cattle from the same level of feed, thereby (potentially) increasing profits by lowering milk production costs (see Begg and Peacock, 1990; Baumgardt and Martin, 1991). Experiments in Australian laboratories are designed to confer pest resistance on plants and so reduce or eliminate the need for chemical applications on Australian croplands. The creation of insect-resistant plant species may not only mean that fewer dangerous chemicals will be used in farming but also that the costs to farmers will be reduced. Biotechnologists are also working on ways to 'mop up' chemical pollution and to convert what are now waste materials from food manufacturing into new products (see further details below). Proponents estimate that biotechnologies may reduce the use of natural resources by between 40 and 60 percent -- allowing farmers to move rapidly towards sustainable production (Begg and Peacock, 1990). Threats to the further degradation of lands are expected to be averted through new genetic manipulations and applications which reduce input use and allow output increases without soil loss (Bureau of Rural Resources, 1991a).

Since biotechnologies are 'enabling technologies', they are likely to have different outcomes according to the purpose of their application. For Redclift (1990) biotechnology will fulfil its promise if it can encourage the development of a low-input, high-tech system of sustainable agriculture in which there are reduced applications of proprietary inputs. The hope then, is that in line with growing public concerns for the environment, scientists will develop plants and animals with pest and disease resistance, salt tolerance and productivity-enhancing qualities which will overcome many of the problems associated with current agricultural practices (see Lowe *et al.*, 1990; Baumgardt and Martin, 1991). However, evidence from Australia (Hindmarsh, 1994) and abroad (Lacy *et al.*, 1988; Busch *et al.*, 1991; Goodman and Redclift, 1991) indicates that the biotechnological promise is, in the context of existing social arrangements, unlikely to be fully realised.

There are a number of concerns. First, environmentalists point out that if corporate capital is involved in the production and distribution of biotechnologies, the profit motive will distort both the basis of experimentation and the likelihood of benefits being distributed evenly amongst producers (Hindmarsh, 1994). Thus, the production of herbicide-tolerant plant species is not designed to free agriculture from chemicals but to have farmers purchase a proprietary package of herbicide and herbicide-tolerant seeds (Kloppenburg, 1988; Busch *et al.*, 1991) -- something which will ensure the dependence of farmers on the agri-chemical industry and increase input costs for producers. Furthermore, with herbicide use continuing at high levels, the possibility of chemical resistance amongst weeds is increased and there is a greater likelihood of groundwater pollution (Otero, 1991).

Secondly, there is also no proof that genetically modified organisms will be environmentally benign. They may proliferate to occupy 'niches' in ecosystems thus displacing other organisms, or produce substances toxic to other organisms. Here, the use of supposedly environmentally friendly genetically modified organisms may result in environmental destruction. Ironically, the new products may be even more dangerous than the dangerous chemicals they have been designed to replace (see Busch *et al.*, 1991).

Thirdly, if costs of biotechnological inputs are reasonably high -- which they are expected to be given that they will be corporate, rather than state-released, products -- the adoption of the new biotechnologies will be limited to the well-financed and usually larger farmers. That is, many of the possible environmental benefits (of reduced chemical applications) would not, in any case, be available to often-struggling middle 'family' farmers. The very people who might have been most advantaged will inevitably fall behind, concentrating food production among those in the wealthier sectors of farming.

In the USA, employment in farming is declining faster than virtually all other occupations. With existing trends heightened by biotechnology, there will be fewer farmers (Lacy *et al.*, 1991). There is evidence that, in terms of environmental management, corporate-linked agriculture is no better, and is perhaps worse, than family-farm agriculture (see Lawrence, 1987; Strange, 1988; Lawrence and Vanclay, 1992, 1994).

Byman (1990) considers it to be somewhat worrying that new technologies are being advanced as the answer to the problems of environmental pollution and over-supplied markets, when the past applications of technologies have helped to cause those problems in the first place. Redclift (1987) too, has argued that the future of the advanced societies -- such as the USA, UK and Australia -- is premised upon the transformation of the environment, yet the transformation of the natural environment is occurring in a manner which reduces sustainability and long-term productivity. The 'environmental contradiction' is viewed as the central contradiction of advanced capitalism (Redclift, 1987; and see O'Connor, 1990).

The global economy is dominated by transnational capital and it is the large, transnational, agribusiness firms which are controlling biotechnological development in agriculture (Goodman *et al.*, 1987; Kloppenburg, 1988; Otero, 1991). Farming will exist, in its present form, only for as long as it can conform to the profit-making requirements of firms supplying agricultural inputs and of firms involved in the food processing industry -- those using either the direct products from farming or farming products converted for use for industrially produced 'biomass'.

AGRO-BIOTECHNOLOGIES -- A BRIEF OVERVIEW

There are several ways of categorising the new biotechnologies which are beginning to have an effect on Australian and world agriculture. One is to divide them into those which will have impacts upon the performance of plants or animals or bacteria. Another is to consider which ones will have on-farm effects (for example, providing producers with new inputs) and which ones will have industrial applications (for example, allowing firms to increase the production efficiencies of food processing and fermentation through the use of bacteria or enzymes). Another highlights the type of biotechnology under analysis (for example, fermentation, cell culture and fusion, genetic engineering and diagnostic probes) and then seeks to assess the application of this technology to specific industries. Yet another is to classify them according to outcomes -- improving efficiency, increasing resistance to pests, or improving the quality of farm or food industry products (see for examples, Tait, 1990; Baumgardt and Martin, 1991; House of Representatives Standing Committee, 1992). The latter approach will be used here as a way of presenting the main developments in Australian agro-biotechnology under the broad headings of improving production efficiencies and improving the quality of the environment.

Improving Production Efficiencies

Some of the most important work being undertaken in Australia is aimed at improving the level of efficiency in crops and animals. Examples are provided below.

Nitrogen Fixation: The aim of research in this field is to allow non leguminous plants to fix their own nitrogen and to allow those plants which already have a symbiotic relationship with

Rhizobia species to improve their nitrogen uptake. Were nodule formation and function to be improved -- and, particularly where commercial crops like wheat and barley might be altered so as to require no external nitrogen applications -- it might be possible for farmers not only to save money on fertiliser inputs, but also to produce crops which, through enhanced 'nitrogen economy,' will be higher yielding. Another advantage would be that these crops could be grown in longer rotations, with less need for less productive fallow periods. This research is long term and there appears to be no more than three or four groups of researchers working on this area in Australia.

Pest Resistance in Plants: Traditional breeding programs involved the transfer of resistant genes from a species of plant into new generations of the same species as a means of conferring resistance in those plants. Genetic engineering takes this one step further by allowing resistance to be transferred between species. Australian researchers are looking for ways to make commercial crops resistant to herbicides. This is achieved by either altering the level of the enzyme in the commercial plant which is affected by a proprietary herbicide, or inserting a gene which will detoxify the herbicide. Proponents claim that if plants can be made to resist chemicals which destroy weeds, farmers will be able to use chemicals in a way which improves efficiency. Work is being conducted in the CSIRO's Division of Plant Industry, and in several university departments throughout Australia. The most recent example of success in this area is that of the Calgene Pacific scientists who have genetically engineered lupin plants to express genes from a soil bacterium. The lupins are now able to resist herbicides. It is anticipated that about $15 million will be added to the $200 million lupin industry because of the increased output through more effective weed control (see *Australian,* 22 May 1993: 9).

Another important piece of research concerns the imparting of insect resistance in plants through the introduction of *Bacillus thuringiensis* (Bt) genes. This bacterium produces proteins which are toxic to various moths, butterflies and beetles. If Bt genes can be inserted into and expressed by plants, those plants will be able to resist insect attack, saving farmers the cost of insecticides, and should increase production. Less insecticides in the environment is also seen to be a desirable outcome.

Plants are also being developed which can tolerate saline soils, temperature stress, and water stress. This research has the potential to increase productivity by preventing losses relating to environmentally unfavourable situations and would allow farmers to grow crops in new regions, including degraded areas. A sugar cane variety has been developed, for example, which can tolerate quite low temperatures. It has the potential to be grown in inland, rather than in coastal, areas of Australia.

Photosynthetic Improvement: Possibly as a consequence of the past interest of Australian plant scientists in photosynthesis, there is a great deal of work being conducted into genetically induced improvements in photosynthetic ability of commercial crops. In a series of semi-structured interviews conducted as part of an Australian Research Council study (see details in Chapter 4), the majority of scientists identified improvements in plant development as perhaps the most important field of research in Australian agro-biotechnology, and gains through photosynthesis were highlighted as especially significant. The reason? If plants were able to convert sunlight to energy in a more efficient manner, and to grow faster, the productivity of farmers would be increased (especially if more crops could be grown per year).

Animal Production: Research in the area of animal production includes improved nutrient digestibility in ruminants, and in the development of transgenic animals which have the capacity to resist disease and to utilise more effectively their food intake. Research is being undertaken to identify new or improved metabolic pathways, to increase animals' production of endogenous hormones, to alter immune response, and to improve fecundity. Cloning will allow an increased output of animals which are deemed to have superior genetic characteristics, while sex determination and DNA fingerprinting will assist breeders further to control the growth and reproduction of farm animals (see Bureau of Rural Resources, 1991b). Some brief examples will suggest the array of work being undertaken. At the University of New England, for example, research is underway to enhance the capacity of bacteria in the rumen of grazing animals to convert the grasses which have been ingested. It is also thought that bacteria can be altered so as to detoxify naturally occurring plant poisons. Productivity gains are the expected outcomes in both cases. In Adelaide, university researchers have inserted genes from *Salmonella typhimurium* into sheep. These genes code the two enzymes which produce cysteine -- an amino acid that sheep need but which, through evolutionary history, have lost the capacity to produce. CSIRO's team of animal geneticists at Prospect NSW, is also attempting to introduce cysteine production in sheep, in this case by the introduction of genes from *E. coli*. An increase in the volume of wool production of between 20 and 50 percent is expected without any need to increase the food intake of the sheep (Nancarrow *et al.*, 1988). The production of milk in dairy animals is anticipated to rise by some 20 to 30 percent if bovine somatotropin -- a bacterially synthesised exogenous hormone -- is approved for use in Australia. Finally, the recent patent granted to the Adelaide firm, Bresatec, which has developed the transgenic pig indicates the speed with which the new developments in biotechnology have been able to reach the marketplace. The so-called superpig is larger than existing commercial pigs, but is a lean animal which grows about 20 percent faster than normal pigs and does so on less food (see *Sydney Morning Herald*, 1 April 1993: 3). Industry is very supportive of transgenic animals because of their improved growth performance, efficiency in feed conversion, and carcass quality (House of Representatives Standing Committee, 1992: 69). It is argued that such features will save farmers money, and through its nutritional advantages, such as reduced fat, will boost sales.

Improving the Quality of the Environment

Many of the developments above are seen to produce positive environmental outcomes. Transgenic, pest resistant, animals are not expected to require anything like the amounts of environmentally damaging chemical applications which are deemed to be required at present. The prospect of reduced chemical run-off has impressed those who recognise the current problems associated with watercourse pollution and the longer term effects of bioaccumulation by various species along the food chain. The development of herbicide resistant plants is considered to be desirable because it could result in reduced amounts of herbicide application, and in reduced need for ploughing (thereby assisting producers in minimum tillage strategies) (see House of Representatives Standing Committee, 1992).

Biological control of pests like the fox and rabbit is considered a possibility. The idea is to inject into a virus which only affects the target species, a gene for a protein to stimulate production of antibodies which will attack the animal's reproductive chemistry. Quite simply, the species targeted would have a severely reduced reproductive ability. Losses farmers currently experience as a result of the presence of the introduced pests would be minimised, thereby increasing output from the more commercially desirable species.

Bioremediation is an especially important development from an environmental perspective. According to proponents, genetically modified organisms will be able to break down toxic chemicals which may remain as residues in the soil, eliminate the problems associated with contaminated sites, and may counter the damage which grazing animals cause to soil structure through compaction. The logic is that bacteria could be produced which would thrive in soils which have been compressed by hoof footed animals -- soils which traditionally lack high levels of the bacteria which exude polysaccharides which, in turn, bind soil particles and improve soil structure (House of Representatives Standing Committee, 1992: 80).

Environmental benefits are expected to arise from the land-releasing effects of developments in crop protection, feed conversion, nitrogen fixation and stress reduction (see Tait, 1990). What is being suggested here, is that when farmers are able to increase productivity and output, there will be less need to use the same amount of land in production. Industrial applications, including enzyme technology (such as in the production of high fructose corn syrup) and microbial production (such as production of foods from non agricultural substrates), may also result in the release of land from agricultural production, thereby reducing pressures on the ecosystem.

AGRICULTURE, BIOTECHNOLOGY AND SUSTAINABILITY

The debate about the possibilities for a sustainable trajectory for modern agriculture is one which has been conducted over many years. This is not the place to restate the arguments which various groups and individuals have advanced in support of their positions. Nor is it necessary to discuss the challenges made by those concerned with the possible negative outcomes of biotechnological applications (see Baumgardt and Martin, 1991; Busch *et al.*, 1991; Hindmarsh *et al.*, 1991; Hindmarsh, 1992, 1994). However, it is useful to highlight the place of biotechnology in any future sustainable agriculture.

Contested Meanings of Sustainability

Sustainability is an ill-defined concept. There often seems to be uncertainty surrounding the question of what is to be sustained and at what level. One obvious reason is that we do not have the knowledge to determine how the human race might ensure a safe and productive future for generations to come. According to Reeve (1992), there seems to be two approaches taken at present. One suggests that since science and technology are generally viewed as having contributed massively to human progress, the answer to problems associated with the application of science and technology is to apply more of the same. The role of *Homo sapiens* is to seek to improve life via technical intervention -- we are seen to dominate nature and, in wanting to achieve environmentally desirable outcomes, we look favourably upon schemes to alter, in incremental ways, the negative 'externalities' of proven practices. In agriculture, this translates to replacing soil-damaging tillage methods with herbicide applications and addressing the declining productivity of plants growing on soils which are acidic or saline by altering the plants so they can tolerate those soils. Here, scientists and farmers conform to the existing patterns of production, rarely questioning the productivity drive which underlies modern farming practice.

The second approach, often referred to as 'alternative agriculture', is based upon a rejection of the assumptions of scientific agriculture. What is stressed here, is harmony with nature and opposition to the supposedly exploitative and damaging practices of 'high tech' agriculture, a desire to link production to local needs rather than to demands from distant marketplaces, and community self-reliance (see Reeve, 1992). Goodman and Redclift (1991) have suggested that the polarisation can be viewed as a clash between the Baconian positivist/rationalist tradition which links progress to production, and the spiritual/holistic approach which seeks to challenge, among other things, both the means and the ends of the genetic manipulation of plants and animals.

Given that the two approaches rest upon fundamentally different conceptions of the relationship between human society and the environment, it might be expected that there would be different beliefs about the ability of biotechnologies to improve the sustainability of agricultural systems. This was born out in a recent study. Farm leaders from all major farming industries in Australia were asked to assess the ability of biotechnology to aid agricultural sustainability. While the majority of respondents were favourably disposed to biotechnology -- with the majority agreeing that biotechnologies would increase agricultural productivity (77%), increase farm output (69%), protect crops and animals from pests (68%), reduce the level of inputs such as pesticides and fertilisers (62%), allow the development of new products for export (57%), and increase the sustainability of agriculture (65%) -- when the results were broken down further, it was revealed that those who disagreed or strongly disagreed with the above statements were virtually all from grower groups which endorsed organic agriculture (see Lawrence, McKenzie and Vanclay, 1992).

In other words, while it could be claimed that the majority of farm leaders believed in the benefits of biotechnology, there was a very sharp division between those who appeared to see the new products as simply an extension of existing practices (and therefore as desirable) and those who rejected existing practices -- and biotechnologies along with them. In a survey of farmers, the only one of the above claims about biotechnology with which the majority did *not* agree with, was that biotechnology would improve the sustainability of agriculture, some 44 percent agreed, 15 percent disagreed, and another 41 percent were not sure. The capacity of the new technologies *to assist the environment* is looked upon with a degree of scepticism by farmers -- even if their own grower organisations favour biotechnological applications.

Finally, it is worth mentioning that those charged with developing policies on ecologically sustainable development in Australia did not think it necessary to highlight the potential of biotechnologies to alter the ecosystem in damaging ways. The Ecologically Sustainable Development Steering Committee (1992) discussed pest management, biodiversity and chemical management without mentioning biotechnologies. Similarly, the Working Group on Sustainable Agriculture (1991) failed to discuss biotechnologies, the only references being in a table where it was claimed that biodegradable pesticides, selection of genetically resistant plants and animals, and biological control of pests, were considered to be appropriate ways of 'ameliorating' the present problems besetting agriculture.

In the House of Representatives Standing Committee's (1992) report on genetic manipulation in Australia, one of eight chapters was devoted to the evaluation of the environmental impacts of biotechnologies. The Committee reached the viewpoint that if legislation were tightened and scientists had to produce 'worst case scenarios' when applying for research grants from public bodies, the environment would be adequately protected. It dismissed the idea that genetic manipulation would have a negative impact on biodiversity, and in general terms supported the application of biotechnology to agriculture. It was in another government report, that the reasoning behind this approach was made clear. In a Bureau of Rural Resources (1991b: 62,64) document it was stated:

> Scientists cannot construct new forms of life. If they did create monsters, they would easily be identified and not released into the environment. ... even if an ecological disaster did occur, and that has not happened in the past from genetic modification, then scientific ingenuity can solve such a problem given funding for research and other activities.

For reasons discussed later, the state is very much behind the push towards biotechnological applications in agriculture. Its view of sustainability is one which endorses change along the present trajectory of productivity-driven outcomes.

The Agribusiness Sector

Agribusiness is increasing its influence in Australian agriculture. Agribusiness corporations are supplying increasing levels of inputs to farmers, and are taking increasing amounts of food and fibre for processing. In the view of a number of authors, and as has been explained in earlier chapters, the relationship between the corporate sector and the farm sector is one which may leave the latter in a position of economic vulnerability, and lead to increasing levels of environmental degradation. Reeve (1992: 218, 220) puts the point well:

> Where agriculture is structured such that the farm sector is a food and fibre transformer for the products of the input sector, individual farmers, no matter how concerned they might be about sustainability, have their choice restricted to what ever the input sector is able to produce profitably. Sustainability will require that the farm sector reduce its

dependence on a materials (and energy) intensive input sector ... The input sector has developed since World War II into an agrichemical technological monoculture. There are signs that this will soon be replaced by another technological monoculture based on biotechnology and genetic engineering.

The concern is that a 'corporate agenda' is emerging in which seed and chemical packages are developed and sold to farmers who, desirous of productivity increases, will uncritically accept the new products (Hindmarsh, 1994). If this input package advantages farmers, it is likely to be widely adopted by those wishing to remain in the industry. The movement to corporate-based agriculture is viewed as opposing the development of more ecologically sound forms of farming such as permaculture, and organic or biodynamic systems (see Hindmarsh, 1992; 1994).

On the output side, there are concerns that the 'global sourcing' strategies of firms in the food sector will reinforce the move to biotechnological applications in farming. Under contract to TNCs, many farmers will be required to grow the genetically modified plants and animals demanded by the food industry because of their perceived desirable traits such as higher levels of solids in tomatoes, increased sweetness in carrots, higher levels of amino acids in corn, and decreased levels of fatty acids in oilseeds (see Harlander *et al.*, 1991). Burch *et al.* (1992) argue that TNCs will largely decide the terms under which crops destined for the food processing industry are grown, and, since these firms have no regional loyalties, the environmental devastation which may result from the intensification of production, would simply result in the corporation leaving that area. Short term returns rather than the longer term well-being of land and water resources is seen to be the driving force for industry -- and this will compromise attempts by farmers to move to less energy intensive and less polluting forms of agriculture. In other words, the globalisation of the food industry and the 'biotech future' inherent in its contract production strategy is considered likely to threaten sustainability.

Farm Production and the Australian Economy

It is believed by government in Australia, that the most appropriate means of bringing down debt, and of creating a resurgence in export sales, is to add value to goods leaving Australian shores and to make our industries more internationally competitive. Together with workplace reforms, reductions in the social wage, and incentives for foreign capital investment, the restructuring of industry is considered an essential 'adjustment' to world market forces. In relation to rural industry, agricultural restructuring has occurred in a way which has left farmers increasingly exposed to the instability of international price regimes for agricultural goods, and has inevitably pushed them to increase their dependence upon agribusiness for ever-more productive inputs to farming, and, in the context of the dismantling of statutory marketing bodies, for the sale of farm produce.

It should be noted that this latter tendency is approved by the National Farmers' Federation (see NFF, 1993), and by the Federal Government (see Prime Minister's Council, 1991). It is asserted that Australia's 'natural' market is the Asia-Pacific region -- a region which will provide opportunities for producers as long as they link with agribusiness marketing firms and produce the sorts of products required by a burgeoning population (Dept of Foreign Affairs and Trade, 1994). The NFF has vigorously endorsed an OECD assessment which indicated that were biotechnologies not to be adopted in modern farming systems, agricultural productivity would begin to fall world-wide (see NFF, 1993: 84).

While it might once have been desirable for Australian farmers to produce as much food and fibre as possible, the realities of power relations on a global level are a constant reminder that those needing food and clothing are not necessarily the people who will receive it. Instead, increased production of rural commodities in the advanced economies leads -- in an era of stagnant demand -- to oversupply and 'dumping'. The prices being received for many of Australia's major export commodities are at an historic low.

The question must be asked in the context of the realities of world agricultural trade, whether it is economically sensible -- and in an era of economic rationality, socially desirable -- to genetically modify wheat plants to grow further inland (or on inferior soils), to produce transgenic sheep which are capable of growing significantly more wool, or altering sugar cane so that it can grow in cooler regions of Australia. These output and productivity advantages will mean little if the policies of competing nations result in continued subsidisation and the artificial lowering of the costs of production of farmers from competing nations. While biotechnologies -- when considered separately (divorced from the political economy of a global world order) -- appear to be a saviour for struggling farmers and a 'starving' world, the reality is that the conditions of world trade and the practices of transnational agribusiness appear certain to severely limit whatever benefits proponents of the new technologies predict.

Just as importantly, farmers under economic stress may adopt new biotechnologies which improve productivity. They will be capable of producing more on the same area of land, or of reducing land in agriculture. But the latter is unlikely. Increased productivity and output may provide an opportunity for farmers voluntarily to take land out of production. More likely, however, is an outcome in which farmers, eager to increase their level of income, utilise biotechnologies over the maximum possible area. Were this to occur, the much vaunted promise of environmental improvement through the removing from production of marginal and 'surplus' land would not eventuate. Sustainability would be less achievable in the context of the *forced* production which would occur in a world where productivity improvements went hand in hand with the expansion of farming into new (and generally more marginal) lands.

CONSUMER RESISTANCE TO GENETICALLY MODIFIED ORGANISMS

While the promise of a number of biotechnological applications is to clean up the environment, and, of others, to reduce the amount of land required for production (see House of Representatives Standing Committee, 1992), it is necessary to question the possibility for either outcome in Australia. While some biotechnologies have the potential to eliminate introduced pests like the fox (through biotechnologically induced sterility), to clean up oil spills, and to eliminate the use of herbicides and pesticides, there are suspicions that the introduction of genetically modified organisms (GMOs) in the environment will result in the increased applications of herbicides, the transfer of genes between species (including the imparting of resistance in undesirable bacteria and plants), the risk of escape of pathogenic organisms, and the disruption and potential damage to biotic communities (see Burch *et al.*, 1990; Hindmarsh, 1992). And, while increases in the efficiency of production of desirable plants and animals may in theory allow for reductions in land use, it is more likely that farmers will seek to achieve greater production from existing lands as a strategy to offset cost-price pressures through increased output (see Lawrence, 1987). Such an outcome would lead to increasing pressures being placed on Australia's fragile environment (see Lawrence, McKenzie and Vanclay, 1992).

The concerns regarding release of GMOs have been well documented elsewhere and will not be presented here (see Lawrence, 1987; Tait, 1990; Baumgardt and Martin, 1991; Busch *et al.*, 1991; Goodman and Redclift, 1991; Hindmarsh *et al.*, 1991; Hindmarsh, 1992, 1994). What is worth noting in relation to Australia is the nation's particular vulnerability to 'foreign' organisms including the potential extinction of indigenous species (see Hindmarsh, 1990), the incompatibility of GMO release with Australia's desire for biodiversity and sustainable development, and the trends in 'green consumerism' in food-importing nations.

In regard to Australia's ecological vulnerability, it is argued that parallel problems to the ones caused by the release of foreign species designed to improve the profit levels of farmers in the past, will occur again. When the cane toad was released to control the cane beetle, it was not envisaged that it would threaten the viability of many native species which prey on amphibians. As was suggested in Chapter 1, it is now spreading out of control in Queensland, the Northern Territory and in northern NSW. Insufficient research was undertaken to establish the likely impact of the toad on the Queensland ecosystem. It is argued that pressures for release of novel organisms will be great because of their profit-generating potential and that the scientists who traditionally advocate release are often those intimately tied to agribusiness through contractual or other arrangements (Hindmarsh *et al.*, 1991). In Australia there was the 'accidental' release of transgenic pigs when, without obtaining permission, a batch was sent for slaughter. While in this case there was virtually no potential for the escape of 'new' genes, the House of Representatives Standing Committee chose to discuss this release in terms of the need for tighter regulations, rather than to see it as an example of the likelihood of unintended consequences to occur despite the best intentions of scientists (see House of Representatives Standing Committee, 1992: 190-193). Some ecologists argue that scientists in Australia simply do not know enough about existing bacterial, plant and animal species to allow release into the environment of any transgenic organisms, particularly when there is some potential for the transfer of traits to Australian native species (see Hindmarsh *et al.*, 1991).

In relation to the issue of biodiversity, it seems likely that biotechnological applications will reinforce patterns of monovarietal production in Australia, which, while lifting productivity in the short term, might not provide long term economic or ecological benefits (see Burch *et al.*, 1990). The narrowing of the genetic base for agriculture is inconsistent with Australia's avowed desire to move to ecologically sustainable development. In its draft national strategy, the Ecologically Sustainable Development Steering Committee (1992) stressed the need for both nature conservation and environmental protection as part of a broader strategy to protect diversity. In this report and in the earlier document of the Working Group on Sustainable Agriculture (1991), the complicated issue of biotechnology's role in the promotion of biodiversity was not raised.

Finally, the likely problems for biotechnologically-oriented agricultural and food industries in a world of 'green consumerism' have not been addressed in any satisfactory manner. Overseas customers have been quick to reject chemically contaminated foodstuffs from Australia (see Lawrence, 1987), and it is quite likely that they will act to reject products which have been deemed to have been genetically modified in inappropriate ways. Some overseas nations have banned foods from Australia on what have been construed to be the flimsiest of grounds, leading experts in Australia to conclude that health was not the primary reason for concern. It is thought that the bans represent a form of trade barrier to protect local producers against lower priced imported foods. (A similar point has been made by Geisler and Lyson [1993] in relation to the EC's banning of US-produced beef.) Biotechnology may result in significant improvements in food output and efficiency in Australia, but may lead to the rejection of those foods by countries seeking ways of reducing food imports. Hoban (1989) has suggested that consumer opposition is likely to grow in instances where the public believes food has in some way been 'contaminated' by its manipulation with the new biotechnologies. He notes that 'public concern for technological risk is greatest when risks are seen as involuntary, exotic or unfair. These characteristics apply to biotechnology as seen by the public' (Hoban, 1989: 20).

If it is accepted that food 'quality' is socially constructed, and that consumers are beginning to reject the 'more quantitative logics pursued by agriculture and the corporate food system during the height of the Fordist period' (Marsden, 1992: 220), and if it is also accepted that consumers are becoming more suspicious of the ability of governments to ensure food safety (see Hoban *et al.*, 1992), it is not hard to envisage the development of global forms of consumer rejection of the new biotechnologies. The so-called 'greening of western society' (Harper, 1993) is likely to fuel opposition to genetically modified foods. In the USA, consumers are lobbying to have anti-biotechnology legislation enacted (see Geisler and Lyson, 1993) and there are concerns expressed by consumers in Britain and the EC (Tait, 1990; INRA, 1991). Significantly, for Australia, the Japanese are very concerned about issues of food nutrition and safety (Jussaume and Judson, 1992: 246). The Australian Confederation of Consumer Organisations (1990), in its submission to the House of Representatives Standing Committee on Industry, Science and Technology, argued that all food products derived from genetically engineered organisms must be labelled as such to distinguish them from 'natural products'. This suggestion was not taken up, but a modified proposal -- that 'all new foods, new strains of existing foods, or new food additives which are developed using genetic manipulation techniques should be submitted to the Release Authority ... as a precondition before release' (House of Representatives Standing Committee, 1992: xxviii) -- was. In following the US lead and not insisting that genetically engineered products be labelled, the Standing Committee has been accused of ignoring the interests of consumers and of producing a report which is 'a blueprint for fast tracking engineered products into the marketplace' (Phelps, 1992: 2). In fact,attempting to counter the view that genetically modified foods might contain greater levels of natural and novel toxins, the Committee argued 'unfortunately, not all 'pure and natural' products are safe...there may be considerable risk to human health from naturally occurring compounds in the diet' (House of Representatives Standing Committee, 1992: 197) -- hardly a convincing response to the concern raised.

At present, bovine somatotropin is banned for use in Australia. The reason given is not that it is considered dangerous to consumers, but that many of the nations importing dairy foods from Australia have not approved its use in their own countries (see *Australian Farm Journal,* November 1992: 30). It would not be too difficult to imagine a situation in which an importing country concerned about the presence of genetically modified substances in foods, or aware of the negative impact of a particular release in Australia, were to place a ban on food from Australia. Yet the strategy being adopted in Australian agricultural marketing is to promote Australia as having a low pollution agriculture and 'unsullied natural resources' (NFF, 1993: 64). Promoting Australia as the 'clean' food nation (Prime Minister's Science Council, 1991), the Australian government is seeking to have agriculture strategically placed to capture new market share in the unprocessed and processed foods sectors in the Asia-Pacific region (Prime Minister's Science Council, 1991). The inevitability of moving to biotechnology was emphasised in a report by the Bureau of Rural Resources (1991b: 61):

> It is essential to have public acceptance of recombinant DNA technology if we are to move to have commercially viable industries in agriculture and in biotechnology. It must be stressed that it is not just the biotechnology industry per se and its export potential that is at stake but the survival and competitiveness of our major industries in agriculture, both plant and animals that are also at stake. Major sections of the rest of the world are moving into using genetic modification to improve the efficiency of agriculture and we cannot afford to be left behind with outdated technology.

In this sense, biotechnology and its potential impacts are not in question: the problem, quite literally, is one of 'public relations' (ibid: 61). It is suggested that understanding biotechnology has required 'a large intellectual effort' by lay persons and that this has resulted in 'cognitive stress'. In such circumstances, 'fears and anxieties increase ... rather than decrease ... Emotion rather than objectivity ... prevail in some people' (ibid: 63). People, it seems, must *trust* and accept what the scientists are doing; concerns about food safety and health are obviously misplaced.

This simplistic trust in science is at the heart of the concerns raised by the environmental movement in Australia. Even *one* experiment which went wrong, or one release which had unintended outcomes, might damage irreparably Australia's international reputation as a reliable supplier of wholesome foods. Accidents aside, what biotechnology's proponents appear to ignore -- in circumstances of the 'greening' of policy and attitudes throughout the world -- is the distinct likelihood of consumer rejection of the very products which are being promoted in

Australia for their ability to improve farm productivity and increase output in the processed food industry.

CONCLUSION

It is possible to view many of the biotechnological developments occurring in Australia as conforming to, rather than challenging, the current non sustainable trajectory of Australian agriculture. This is not to deny that Australia must seek to achieve productivity increases if it wishes to continue to export primary products, nor is it to deny the potential for some biotechnologies to have major beneficial effects in plant and animal production. What is often overlooked by those who seek to evaluate technology on its intrinsic merits, or in terms of its potential economic contribution, is that technology is embedded within socio-political structures (see Buttel, 1993b). These structures determine the shape of technological development and the ways it is likely to impact upon society. For example, the new biologically engineered lupin plants may help farmers to improve soil fertility at the same time as they increase output. But they may lead to increased applications of herbicides and, because of the patents taken out on them, can only be obtained from the TNC which owns the patent. Growing lupins will tie the farmer to the corporation, and to the corporation's longer term economic strategy. Similarly, the promise of nitrogen fixation is that the amount of synthetic nitrogen in the soil would decrease. However, this would not occur if plant biotechnology resulted in the production of new crops capable of utilising more efficiently the synthetic fertilisers currently on the market. The outcome here would be increasing input costs for farmers, together with increased environmental problems (see Busch *et al.*, 1991).

Australia is linked firmly to the global economy, an economy dominated by the corporate sector. It is a sector which has little regional loyalty and has, at least in the past, looked to 'externalise' many of its production costs. The environment has suffered as a result. There remains considerable doubt about the possibility that biotechnologies will alter the course of production within the transnationalised world economy in a manner which will lead to significant environmental improvements.

FARMERS AND SCIENTISTS
WHAT WILL THE FUTURE BRING?

SCIENTISTS IN AUSTRALIAN RESEARCH INSTITUTIONS

The issues surrounding the development and application of new technologies in Australian agriculture are not unlike those in the USA and Europe. Debate centres upon the customers of the research, the effects of research, and -- especially in relation to the development of agro-biotechnologies -- ethical issues about genetic engineering. Australia has had a long history of public support for agricultural research and critics have claimed that there is likely to be a corruption of this research as the state seeks new (private industry) partners for experimentation and commercialisation. The shift from conventional methods of plant and animal breeding to the new biotechnological methods have, as in other nations, raised issues relating to animal welfare, the relationship of people to nature, the setting of research agendas, confidentiality, release, regulation, environmental and social impacts, and patents (see House of Representatives Standing Committee, 1992).

Very little social science research has been conducted into the attitudes of scientists in Australia. The best study to date has been that of Charlesworth *et al.*, (1989) who studied scientists at the internationally renowned Walter and Eliza Hall Institute of Medical Research in Melbourne. Their study was guided by anthropological concerns about the presence of a scientific 'subculture' and the rituals and myths which help sustain it. While virtually all the scientists were involved in medical research, rather than agricultural research, one of the study's findings is of particular interest: there was perceived to be very little concern among the scientists regarding the commercialisation of their work -- including the impact this might have on science.

AGRICULTURAL TECHNOLOGIES FOR THE FUTURE: THE HEALY STUDY

In 1988, a study was commenced by the Bureau of Rural Resources (see Healy, 1991) to identify the technologies which would help to maximise Australia's competitiveness in agriculture-based exports. In that study, an 'informed spread of opinion' (see Healy, 1991: 4) was sought from face-to-face interviews with 50 of Australia's leading research scientists. Those chosen represented a variety of disciplines, but all were either from the CSIRO or the university sector. Areas of research included: expert systems, veterinary therapeutics, genetic engineering, cell culture, fermentation and biomass research, textile manufacturing and climate modelling. The scientists were presented with a list of technologies which were being developed or employed in Australian and overseas laboratories. Two questions (with sub sections) were asked of the scientists -- to list the technologies which were being used or could be used in their area of research, and to assess the potential of the above technologies for use in Australia's agricultural industries. Eleven key technologies were identified. These were, in order of priority: genetic engineering, reproduction technologies (such as cloning), cell micropropagation, cell receptor manipulation, computers (microcomputers and expert systems), sensors and controlling equipment, mechatronics (that is, robotics), automation, advanced materials, protein engineering, and remote sensing (see Healy, 1991: 6).

Healy indicated the ways scientists considered the above techniques could be employed. In regard to genetic engineering, Healy summarised the views of scientists as follows:

- genetic manipulation technologies would assist Australia's rural industries to be internationally competitive;
- export markets are requiring chemical-free agricultural products; biotechnologies will help eliminate the use of agricultural chemicals in crop production; genetic engineering will, within two or three decades, produce a basis for sustainable agriculture;
- there would be a convergence of research in medicine and agriculture with human genes being inserted in animals to produce pharmaceuticals;
- there was a general perception that Australia's research base in genetic engineering was eroding as a result of pressures to move from basic to applied research;
- the major impediment to the development of genetic engineering was the conservative investment market, with *production* rather than R&D being the prime focus of private firms;
- overseas links were essential for the growth of Australian research into genetic engineering -- yet budgets were limiting the opportunities for international collaboration;
- Australia's overall capacity in genetic engineering was considered to be strong in comparison to other 'strategic' areas of technology, but it was unlikely that it would develop if left to current market forces (Healy, 1991).

Healy's report provided the basis of a Bureau of Rural Resources (1991) report in which a list of recommendations for government was compiled. This latter report is both consistent with, and underpins, much government policy relating to technological development and the future of agriculture in Australia (see Chapter 3).

THE SOCIAL ISSUES INVOLVED IN AGRO-BIOTECHNOLOGY: RESULTS OF A NATIONAL SURVEY

In 1991, funding was received from the Australian Research Council for research into the social aspects of agro-biotechnologies in Australia. A comprehensive study comprising four parts was developed. Semi-structured, face-to-face interviews with 50 biotechnologists were conducted during the early phase of the study. Those interviewed were selected across the broad span of private industry, university and public sector employment and across the many areas of biotechnology (plant and animal biotech, microbiology, biochemical engineering and so on). The aim was to obtain a variety of opinion about the issues of concern to scientists (see Lawrence, McKenzie, Vanclay, 1992). The second part was face-to-face interviews with farmers in four of Australia's rural industries (mixed farming in NSW, horticulture in NSW, dairying in Victoria, and sugar growing in Queensland) (Gray, Dunn and Lawrence, 1993). For this and the third component -- involving a questionnaire sent to representatives of farmer associations throughout Australia -- the aim was to discover the level of knowledge about and concerns regarding applications of biotechnology to agriculture. The fourth part of the study involved sending a questionnaire to biotechnologists who were involved in agro- biotechnological research in Australian laboratories (Lawrence and Norton, 1994; Vanclay and Lawrence, 1994b). This provided an opportunity to discover whether the concerns raised in the first three parts of the study were shared by the scientists. Some aspects of the national study will be presented in the remainder of this chapter.

OPERATIONALISING AND EVALUATING SCIENCE POLICY

Examining the Healy (1991) and Bureau of Rural Resources (1991) reports, and by taking into account the concern raised by Charlesworth *et al.* (1989), a series of six propositions for investigation can be developed:

1. genetic manipulation technologies will assist Australia's rural industries to be internationally competitive;
2. biotechnologies will reduce the need for heavy doses of agricultural chemicals as well as produce a basis for sustainable agriculture;
3. human genes will be inserted into animals to boost production;
4. Australia's research base in genetic engineering is eroding;
5. if left to existing market forces there will be little development of biotechnology in Australia;
6. there is little concern among scientists regarding the commercialisation of biotechnology and the impact this might have upon scientific practice.

These propositions -- or hypotheses -- were explicitly addressed in the national study. The intention was to determine how important scientists thought these issues would be. In a modified form of technology assessment (see Porter, 1995) or social impact assessment (see Burdge and Vanclay, 1995), the concerns likely to emerge from government implementation of an agro-biotechnological strategy were investigated. Since it is the future being dealt with -- and there is obviously uncertainty about what might constitute such a future -- the assessment of expert opinion is an important way of gaining an insight into the contours of change. Analysing the views of scientists is therefore valuable, but it is also complicated because scientists, like others in society, have vested interests. The extent to which Australia's agro-biotechnological scientists concurred with the above propositions, the extent of their support for the benefits of biotechnology, and the extent of their understanding of the social issues relating to biotechnological developments are important concerns.

A set of statements was developed which addressed each proposition. These were included in the questionnaire which was distributed to Australia's scientists involved in agriculture-related biotechnological research, development or administration. A sample size of 278 representing a response rate of 81 percent was achieved. By examining how scientists responded to the statements above, a conclusion can be made about each proposition.

1. Genetic manipulation technologies will assist Australia's rural industries to be internationally competitive.

Table 4.1: Genetic Manipulation and Australia's Rural Industries

Statement (row percentages)	Strongly Agree	Agree	Not Sure	Disagree	Strongly Disagree
genetic engineering will allow development of new products for export	44	41	9	5	1
genetic engineering will increase agricultural productivity	53	39	5	2	1
genetic engineering will decrease production costs in farming	31	36	24	8	1
if we don't move quickly in developing genetically- engineered products we will become less competitive in international markets	29	44	14	11	2

Scientists were very strongly supportive of the proposition that Australia's rural industries will be advantaged by the new technologies. About a quarter of the respondents were uncertain about the likelihood of production costs being reduced as a result of biotechnological applications.

2. Biotechnologies will reduce the need for heavy doses of agricultural chemicals as well as produce a basis for sustainable agriculture.

The majority of scientists appear to be convinced that genetic engineering and biotechnology will improve the environment and will lead to the reduced use of chemicals (see Table 4.2). They suggested that the conservation movement -- which, in Australia as elsewhere has been critical of the corporate agenda in agro-biotechnologies -- should support the new initiatives in biotechnology. Scientists apparently reconcile any concerns they have -- for example, that there will be 'unintended releases' (49% agreement), or that the transferring of genetic information to other organisms after field release is likely to occur (25% agreement) -- by believing that such outcomes will not have any detrimental ecological effects.

Table 4.2: Biotechnologies for a Sustainable Agriculture

Statement (row percentages)	Strongly Agree	Agree	Not Sure	Disagree	Strongly Disagree
genetic engineering will reduce the level of inputs such as pesticides and fertilisers	44	40	10	4	2
there should be more emphasis by researchers upon biotechnology products that enable farmers to use fewer chemical inputs	51	34	11	4	0
genetic engineering will increase the sustainability of agriculture	38	43	11	7	1
the conservation movement should support the development of agricultural biotechnologies	33	46	13	6	2
(damaging) secondary ecological effects ... will result from the release of GMOs	3	11	30	39	17
following the field release of GMOs genetic information is unlikely to be transferred to other organisms	13	36	26	20	5
it is certain that there will be unintended releases of GMOs as the biotechnology industry grows in Australia	10	39	18	28	5
public concern over the release of (GMOs) is out of proportion to the actual risks	23	49	14	11	3
the benefits of genetic engineering will far outweigh any possible risks	25	42	20	9	4
genetic engineering will improve the quality of the environment	33	40	20	5	2

3. Human genes will be inserted into animals to boost production.

Elsewhere in the study, 5 percent of scientists revealed that they thought it was unethical to genetically engineer animals, and only 2 percent of scientists considered it was unethical for plants and bacteria to be genetically engineered. There is very strong support amongst scientists for genetic manipulation, even involving human genes (see Table 4.3). Since the broader public is likely to regard genetic engineering involving human genes to be unethical (Hoban, 1989; Hoban *et al.*, 1992), how do scientists reconcile their ethical and professional social concerns? Some of the responses in the previous two tables help to explain this: scientists believe that the risks relating to biotechnological applications are not high, and they point to the environmental and other benefits flowing from current research.

Table 4.3: Human Genes for Animal Production

Statement (row percentage)	Strongly Agree	Agree	Not Sure	Disagree	Strongly Disagree
human genes should not be inserted into plants, animals or microbes even where positive benefits are the likely outcome	25	5	9	14	47

4. Australia's research base in genetic engineering is eroding.

Table 4.4: Erosion of Australia's Resource Base

Have you experienced any of the following? (row percentages)	yes	no	not sure
pressure to involve private organisations in your research work	52	43	5
funding cuts to your major research project	63	34	3
increasing administrative responsibilities	81	18	1
an improvement in the general conditions under which your work is conducted	37	58	5
a reduction in the level of information sharing between research scientists	58	38	4
increasing pressures on researchers to be more productive	90	8	2
increasing dangers in the laboratory because of overcrowding	43	52	5

There are clear indications that the structural changes which scientists are experiencing are perceived to be having negative effects. While over one third of scientists believed that changes have been beneficial, the majority believed that the conditions within the workplace have eroded. The increasing pressures on scientists to be more productive is not inconsistent with the general thrust in the public sector for efficiency gains. That over 40 percent of scientists considered that there are increasing dangers in the laboratory because of overcrowding is confirmation that public support for biotechnology is not occurring at the level which scientists believe it should be.

5. If left to existing market forces there will be little development of biotechnology in Australia.

Table 4.5: Markets and Biotechnological Development

Statement (row percentages)	Strongly Agree	Agree	Not Sure	Disagree	Strongly Disagree
Australia needs more 'scientific entrepreneurs' to help link researchers with commercial firms	29	42	12	13	4
developments in the commercialisation of biotechnology are being retarded by the lack of venture capital in Australia	45	42	10	3	0
(there needs to be) tax incentives for companies and individuals to invest in biotechnological research	53	26	14	6	1
(there needs to be) greater economic incentives for firms to become involved in funding or initiating biotechnological research	45	33	18	3	1

Other questions were also asked of scientists, including: 'Is the government doing enough to develop the agricultural biotechnology industry?', and 'Are commercial firms doing enough to the agricultural biotechnology industry ...?' In answer to the first question, some 11 percent of scientists said 'yes', another 58 percent said 'no' and a further 31 percent said 'don't know'. In regard to the latter, 9 percent said 'yes', 62 percent said 'no', and 29 percent said 'don't know'. There is quite a strong belief among scientists that both public and private investment is necessary for the continued development of biotechnology in Australia.

6. There is little concern among scientists regarding the commercialisation of biotechnology and the impact this might have upon scientific practice.

Scientists appeared to endorse the move to a more commercially-influenced biotechnology industry in Australia. They say this not from a belief that it will produce the most personally productive work environment (bringing out the best in scientists), nor that corporate funding provides the best opportunities for open communication and the exchange of knowledge between scientists, but, rather, on the grounds that -- in the context of cutbacks in

Table 4.6: Impacts of Commercialisation

Statement (row percentages)	Strongly Agree	Agree	Not Sure	Disagree	Strongly Disagree
linkages between public research institutions and private companies should be strengthened	37	52	6	4	1
the increased linkages between public agricultural researchers and private firms will enable more rapid transfer of new technology to farmers	21	52	16	11	0
a more commercial profit-driven work environment 'brings out the best' in research scientists	3	19	14	44	19
increased university-industries are essential in developing new technologies to meet foreign competition	43	41	6	9	1
the openness of communication between scientists often suffers when private industry funds research in university or government research labs	33	45	4	17	1
there is reason for concern about restrictions on researchers ... that often come with corporate funding of agricultural research	26	42	7	21	4
if linkages between agricultural researchers and private industry continue to increase, public research will have become too oriented to the needs of industry	13	33	13	36	5
basic or fundamental research will suffer if links between industry and the public agricultural sector become too strong	24	34	11	26	5
increased corporate sponsorship of public agricultural research is necessary because public research funds are no longer adequate	32	53	8	6	1

public research funding -- the perceived way that biotechnology will develop is through increased corporate sponsorship. Rather than being a 'don't care' attitude as Charlesworth *et al.*(1989) suggest, it is a pragmatic attitude which the scientists in this sample seem to have adopted. In other words, they do recognise some of the disadvantages of commercialisation (restrictions on researchers, reduced knowledge exchange, research biased toward industry) but are, on balance, prepared to accept that this is the price which must be paid for progress in the field. The commercial promise is for the transfer of new technology to farmers and the possibilities of challenging foreign competition. There is a certain altruistic slant to such beliefs -- that although their own scientific practice may suffer as a result of the commercial drive in biotechnology, the Australian farmers and the Australian economy will benefit. Of course, it might also be a reflection of the realities of the funding of science in the 1990s, where in the CSIRO for example, it is expected that at least 30 percent of research funds be obtained externally.

What is shown here is that Australian agro-biotechnologists are willing to be involved with private industry as a precondition for the development of their discipline and presumably the furthering of their careers. That some 70 percent of scientists consider that 'Australia needs more "scientific entrepreneurs" to help link researchers with commercial firms', attests to their genuine interest in seeking practical outcomes of research and to the desirability of ensuring the continued funding of their work in the face of government cutbacks. It is important to note that scientists in the sample believed that their own work would increase agricultural productivity (83%), improve the quality of the environment (60%), increase the sustainability of agriculture (68%), decrease production costs in farming (65%), increase farm output (71%), and assist farmers to remain in agriculture (51%). In considering such outcomes to be likely, the scientists appear to be recognising that the best way to survive and prosper -- and to achieve the outcomes they desire -- is to link with the private sector. They do this while anticipating that this is likely to have some negative impacts on scientific practice.

OTHER ISSUES OF CONCERN

Consistent with the latter suggestion is the concern of scientists for the regulation of the industry. If Charlesworth *et al.* (1989) were correct in their belief that scientists did not really care about the outcomes of commercialisation, it might be predicted that the scientists in this sample would be unconcerned about -- or opposed to -- the moves to increase regulation of the biotechnology industry. They would also show little concern for -- or be likely to endorse -- the granting of patents to firms or individuals developing new products.

Table 4.7: Regulation of Biotechnology

Statement (row percentages)	Strongly Agree	Agree	Not Sure	Disagree	Strongly Disagree
scientists should be required to put 'worst case' scenarios' to committees deciding on the funding of research into, or release of, GMOs	17	50	9	17	7
Australia needs a new body such as a GMO Release Authority to give approval for field trials and the release of products containing live GMOs	15	35	20	23	7
Genetic Manipulation Advisory Committee guidelines should be made mandatory for all genetic manipulation work	27	51	9	10	3
patents should be extended to cover complete organisms	9	27	29	23	12
patents should be granted for a DNA sequence	10	19	15	31	25
preventing the patenting of GMOs would deter the development of the biotechnology industry in Australia	22	44	11	15	8
products which contain, or have been made by, GMOs should be labelled as such when they are marketed	18	36	11	25	10

One of the major recommendations of the House of Representatives Standing Committee on Industry, Science and Technology (1992) was the creation of a GMO Release Authority to approve all future releases. This would be on top of the work of the Genetic Manipulation Advisory Committee which would be retained to grant approvals for laboratory-based research. The scientists appeared to endorse the extra tier of regulation. It will be of no surprise to learn that it is the basic/applied/developmental scientists rather than the scientist/administrators who primarily considered this new regulation to be of importance. Similarly, the spread of responses in relation to the patenting of a sequence of DNA, and the labelling of products, suggests that there is a degree of polarisation within the community of agrobiotechnologists. Similarly, researchers involved in basic research, and in particular those working at universities, were more likely than the other scientists to oppose patenting or to endorse tougher labelling laws. Just as with the views recorded regarding commercialisation, it would seem that while a sizeable proportion of scientists opposed or are not sure about the extension of patents, they saw such a development as necessary to the growth of the biotechnology industry in Australia.

It is important to note that the scientists were concerned about the socio-economic impacts of agro-biotechnologies. Some 86 percent of scientists agreed that scientists and research administrators need to spend more time talking to farmers about potential impacts of genetic engineering, and 56 percent believed that the social and economic impacts of genetic engineering in agriculture have been given too little attention. The need for more research into social and economic consequences of biotechnology was considered to be fairly or very important by 54 percent of scientists, and another 29 percent agreed that it was somewhat important.

WHAT DO THE SCIENTISTS SAY?

The following is a brief statement of the findings from the survey of scientists:

- the vast majority of agro-biotechnologists believed their work will have significant direct and indirect impacts upon agriculture and the food industry in Australia;
- the scientists were very supportive of the development and release of biotechnologies in Australia, and expected them to increase agricultural output and productivity, reduce the need for chemical applications, and increase the sustainability of agriculture;
- although some outcomes were considered likely to be negative, there was, according to the majority of scientists, no perceived threat to the environment from the release of GMOs;
- notwithstanding the above point, scientists considered that regulations need to be tightened to ensure biotechnological experimentation and application occurs in an environmentally beneficial manner;
- the scientists generally supported moves further to commercialise agro-biotechnology and do so primarily because of both the perceived benefits this will bring to agriculture and the deterioration that they have faced in state funding;
- the decline in state support has not, according to the scientists, been matched by an increased level of funding from private industry -- they considered that market forces alone cannot ensure the best conditions for the development of the biotechnology industry in Australia.

In their survey of agricultural scientists at US Land Grant universities, Buttel and Curry (1991) reported that there was quite strong support for the development of stronger links between private firms and universities. Their finding -- that the scientists endorse corporate funding because of the deficiency of public sector monies -- is reaffirmed in the Australian case. Buttel and Curry suggest that scientists' opinions have been shaped by the steady 20 year decline in the provision of funding in the USA. While the cutbacks have not occurred over such a long period in Australia, the same conclusion holds: the scientists have been quick to realise that alternative funding sources for their research are necessary. This is despite, in the Australian situation, biotechnology having been identified as one of the strategic technologies which should be given preferential funding treatment by government.

Just as with the Buttel and Curry study, scientists could argue in the majority for greater public-private collaboration, while -- also in the majority -- arguing that there will be negative outcomes from such affiliations. So, as in the US study, it can be concluded that although there is agreement by the scientists that public research needs to strengthen its relationship with commerce, there is also quite significant concern that problems will arise as a result of the growth of this relationship.

To the extent that the views of Australian scientists are in keeping with wider public opinion, more research will have to be undertaken. In the USA for example, Lacy *et al.* (1991) have reported that the public believes environmental protection must be foremost in the thinking of those legislating for biotechnology. The majority of US respondents identified four main problems relating to environmental release of GMOs: production of harmful bacteria (61%), creation of antibiotic resistant diseases (61%), development of herbicide-resistant weeds (56%), and the possibilities of problems in food supply (52%) (Lacy *et al.* 1991: 152). The majority nevertheless approved of releases of GMOs with the potential to clean up the environment or improve agricultural productivity. However, Hoban's research in North Carolina showed that a considerable proportion of people (38%) felt that the genetic manipulation of animals was morally wrong (see Hoban, 1990; Lacy *et al.* 1991). It might be predicted that a similar percentage would be found among the Australian public. Over 25 percent of submissions to the House of Representatives Standing Committee's Inquiry opposed genetic engineering on ethical or environmental grounds (see Hindmarsh, 1992). Further research may reveal that the views of scientists (only 5% of whom agree with the statement that it is unethical to genetically engineer animals) might well be understood as being out of line with that of the general public, and perhaps the international community of scientists. In Norway, for example, there is reported to be a good deal of concern among scientists about the ethical and environmental issues surrounding biotechnology (see Almås, 1992). It should be noted that in its report on genetic manipulation in Australia, the Parliamentary Standing Committee on Industry, Science and Technology tended to dismiss the concerns of the public and various consumer groups which submitted documents to the Committee. A very pro- biotechnology report was the outcome of two years' deliberations (Phelps, 1993).

The issue of food security was not looked at in any meaningful way by the Committee. It accepted that new products would be developed and that the proposed new Release Authority would be the best means of judging whether novel foods or food strains should be approved for general release. Overseas surveys suggest that the public is most concerned about the possible problems relating to the presence of 'novel' foods, which under some circumstances, might be construed as being contaminated by genetically- modified substances (see Hoban, 1989). There is the distinct likelihood that scientists -- in Australia and overseas -- are out of step with public opinion on this issue. In contrast to this, their endorsement of the need for better socio-economic impact assessment places them at the forefront of worldwide moves to appraise the likely effects on communities and individuals and to incorporate findings in those policies aimed at extending the influence of biotechnology (see Lacy and Busch, 1991).

Finally, there is the important issue of the interpretation of the meaning of the responses of the scientists in the Australian survey. As Busch *et al.* (1991) convincingly argue, science is not conducted in a vacuum but in response to the demands of clients, and such demands are expressed not necessarily through market mechanisms, but through the more sociologically-relevant concepts of negotiation, persuasion and coercion (1991: 49). Scientists are clearly aware of their own interests and might be expected to confirm the great advantages of continued experimentation and commercialisation of biotechnologies. As an articulate and powerful lobby group, scientists *would* be expected to endorse the current research focus in biotechnology and generally to downplay the concerns. On the other hand, they are the experts and their views might be seen to be those formed from engagement with the lived problems and philosophical preoccupations of those who are closest to the scientific workbench. Kenney (1986) was one of the first to suggest that any extension of industry-university links would be premised upon the deterioration in the public funding of biotechnological research, and it was Buttel (1989) and Busch *et al.* (1991) who suggested that the so-called 'useful' technologies and techniques would supplant the more basic research emphasis which had been part of the Land Grant focus prior to the 1990s.

Almås (1992) has indicated that Norwegian scientists tended to evoke the 'loss of international-competitiveness' justification in calling for increased government expenditure on biotechnology. It is feared in Norway as in Australia that the 'smaller' countries will fall behind the rest of the world in the development of new techniques and products unless the state provides increasing levels of support. But in Australia, unlike Norway, there is a belief among scientists that given the right infrastructural support, commercial firms will enter the industry for the benefit of biotechnology, agriculture and the Australian economy.

Have Australian scientists fallen for the ideology of economic rationalism (see Pusey, 1992) -- which would lead to an acceptance of the need to limit both those state expenditures on research which were not practically focussed, and to the desirability of incorporating the interests of commercial firms? Are the scientists ignoring public opinion and simply furthering their own interests by downplaying the likelihood of problems which might arise from the development of biotechnologies? Is the narrow training the scientists receive likely to explain their inability to anticipate some of the more controversial social and economic impacts of their work? These important questions can be answered by analysing the submissions and other documents put forward by firms and by biotechnology departments of public research institutions to the House of Representatives Standing Committee, and by incorporating qualitative research results into the present analysis.

Another step in the evaluation of the Australian data has been to establish the characteristics of the scientists who endorse or reject particular changes in the climate of research in Australian labs. What has been revealed is that while scientists as a group overwhelmingly endorsed the development of the new biotechnologies, the degree of support varies with the type of scientist. Significant results at the 0.01 level were recorded when public research scientists were compared with those working in the private sector; when scientists working in laboratories were compared with those who had become scientist/administrators; and when those who had never undertaken collaborative work with industry were compared with those who had. In all cases, those who had links with industry via collaborative ventures, private sector jobs, or via research administration, were very much more interested in the private commercialisation of biotechnologies in Australia. They also tended to be against increasing regulation and for a more market driven system of biotechnological experimentation.

THE VIEWS OF FARMERS AND SCIENTISTS COMPARED

To what extent might the views of the biotechnologists be shared by those Australian farmers who will, eventually, be using the products to improve their livelihood?

As part of the agro-biotechnology study, face to face semi structured interviews were conducted with some 245 individuals on 106 farms in four distinct regions: irrigated dairying (northern Victoria), sheep/wheat farming (Riverina region), citrus growing (Murrumbidgee Irrigation Area), and sugar cane production (Central Queensland). Results revealed an appalling lack of knowledge by the cross section of farmers of the experimental work being undertaken in Australian research laboratories. Very few farmers could provide any details of biotechnological research. And there was much confusion and misunderstanding. For example, embryo transplants were mentioned by several farmers: while this is an important new technology it is not biotechnology.

When asked the same series of questions as the scientists about the perceived virtues of the application of genetic engineering, the lack of farmer knowledge was further revealed. Between one third and one half of all farmers answered 'not sure' to the questions. The table showing responses of the farmers and scientists is provided below.

Table 4.8: Perceived Effects of the Application of Genetic Engineering to Agriculture -- Farmers and Scientists

Statement (row percentages)	Strongly Agree	Agree	Not Sure	Disagree	Strongly Disagree	Statistical Difference
increase agricultural productivity						
farmers	5	58	29	8	0	*
scientists	53	39	5	2	1	
improve the quality of the environment						
farmers	2	24	51	20	3	*
scientists	33	40	20	5	3	
increase the sustainability of agriculture						
farmers	3	41	41	13	2	*
scientists	38	43	11	7	1	
protect crops and stocks from pests						
farmers	4	55	33	7	1	*
scientists	53	43	3	2	1	
decrease production costs in farming						
farmers	3	30	40	25	2	*
scientists	31	36	24	8	1	
increase farm output						
farmers	3	58	33	6	0	*
scientists	38	45	12	4	1	
allow the development of new products for export						
farmers	4	55	35	6	0	*
scientists	44	41	9	5	1	
reduce the level of inputs such as pesticides and fertilisers						
farmers	4	53	35	8	0	*
scientists	44	40	10	4	2	
assist farmers to remain in agriculture						
farmers	4	44	33	19	0	
scientists	23	31	34	11	2	

* Denotes significant difference = 0.01

From Table 4.8, it can be seen that:

• the majority of farmers and scientists believe that genetic engineering will increase agricultural productivity, increase farm output, allow the development of new products for export and reduce the level of inputs such as pesticides and fertilisers;

• farmers, in contrast to the scientists, did not in the majority believe that genetic engineering would improve the quality of the environment, increase the sustainability of agriculture, decrease production costs in farming, or assist farmers to remain in agriculture.

Are the scientists -- with their intimate knowledge of advanced experimental work -- in a better place than the farmers to determine the likely impacts of the application of genetically engineered products to agriculture? Are the farmers being overcautious? Or are they simply not aware of the ways in which the new biotechnologies will affect their own farm production systems?

There are several important issues to be considered in this comparison. First, in terms of one of the concerns of this book, farmers do not believe, in the majority, that the new products will come to assist farmers in the ways science is promising. That roughly the same proportion agrees as disagrees that genetic engineering will improve the quality of the environment must be of concern to a federal government which has endorsed the continued development of biotechnology as part of a 'new' agriculture, and which has boasted of its 'green' orientation in terms of natural resource management. Will those farmers who do not believe that genetic engineering will be of benefit actively resist the new products? If such rejection is widespread, will this act to undermine the research being undertaken in Australia's research laboratories? With the majority of farmers remaining equivocal about, or disagree with, the view that genetic engineering will improve agricultural sustainability, there is likely to be a slow adoption rate, even of those biotechnologies which do show promise of improving the environment. One of the most important issues of the nineties will be the degree to which non sustainable production can be made more sustainable. Yet farmers do not appear to be linking genetic engineering with sustainability. Finally, if less than the majority perceive that genetic engineering will be a key to their remaining in agriculture, what incentives will the majority have to adopt the new technologies?

What we appear to have here is a classic case of the development of a technology without any involvement from the end users of that research. In past years (with different technologies) this has been a recipe for failure (see Part Two). It is sobering to consider that, in the answers farmers gave to other questions in the survey, some 40 percent considered that 'large farmers and agribusiness will gain the greatest advantage from genetic engineering', some 58 percent agreed that 'the social and economic impacts of genetic engineering in agriculture have been given too little attention'. The vast majority (78%) agreed that 'scientists and research administrators need to spend more time talking to farmers about the potential impacts of genetic engineering'.

In the following chapters, we will be considering the value of extension as a key to the promotion of a more sustainable agriculture. It is clear from the survey results reported here, that farmers are not aware of, and remain in some cases highly suspicious about, the very technologies which are being heralded as the 'future' for Australian agriculture. What role will extension have in informing the future farmers about the technologies they will need to remain productive and competitive while moving to a sustainable production base?

PART B

AGRICULTURAL EXTENSION

THE KEY TO SUSTAINABILITY?

ADOPTION OF ENVIRONMENTAL MANAGEMENT PRACTICES
FARMERS' ATTITUDES, KNOWLEDGE AND BEHAVIOUR

CHAPTER 5

INTRODUCTION

As was suggested in earlier chapters, land degradation is Australia's most serious environmental problem, and recognised as severe since the 1930s (Messer, 1987). Many techniques for preventing land degradation exist, some which have been around for 50 years or more, yet these have not been widely adopted by farmers. According to soil scientists, adoption of these practices would greatly reduce the long-term land degradation currently experienced on Australian farms. At first glance, the lack of adoption appears to be surprising, since many of these techniques would require little or no change to overall farm management, and many could be implemented without significant cost to the individual farmer (Pampel and Van Es, 1977; Chamala, Keith and Quinn, 1982; Donald, 1982). Some techniques -- such as the establishment of deep-rooted perennial pasture species, such as lucerne, which are recommended salinity mitigation strategies -- are considered to be profitable for farmers (Oram, 1987; Thorne, 1991). Why, then, do Australian farmers not adopt those soil conservation technologies which are readily available?

The lack of adoption of conservation farming practices by farmers indicates that land degradation is not primarily a technical problem. The issue is not the lack of techniques of soil conservation or of sound land management practices, but the social, structural, cultural, perceptual and financial situations and processes which act to prevent farmers from adopting those techniques. It is necessary to examine from the farmer's point of view, reasons for the non-adoption of practices that technical experts clearly believe would solve, or at least reduce, the soil degradation problem.

THE CALL FOR A CHANGE IN FARMERS' ATTITUDES

Politicians and conservationists often comment in off-the-record statements that farmers' attitudes to the environment are not conducive to effective land management. They consider that the solution to the environmental problems experienced on Australia's farms requires the changing of farmers' attitudes. Many urban people also consider that farmers are not stewards of the land, and that farmers have little intrinsic concern for the land. Of course, it is unlikely that public figures would wish to go on record stating this, even if this is their personal opinion. Nevertheless, former Minister for Primary Industries Kerin (1984) and former Prime Minister Hawke (1989: 44) have made remarks indicating that a change of attitude would be important in dealing with the land degradation problem.

The adoption of a land ethic is actively promoted by Dr Brian Roberts, a previous chair of the Soil Conservation Association of Australia, and a member of the Commonwealth Soil Conservation Advisory Committee (see Roberts, 1990); and it is also the platform of many (soil) conservation organisations. The Soil and Water Conservation Association of Australia considers that the problems of inadequate land management will remain 'until such time as the whole community accepts the need for stewardship and adopts a land conservation ethic' (Standing Committee on Environment, Recreation and the Arts (SCERA), 1989: 105). A key witness at the Inquiry into the Effectiveness of Land Degradation Policies and Programs, Dr Smiles, Chief of the CSIRO Division of Soils, also endorsed the notion that 'there needs to be a public reappraisal of attitudes to land management' (SCERA, 1989: 61). Furthermore, the National Soil Conservation Program (now the National Landcare Program) had five goals, the fifth being 'that the whole community adopt a land conservation ethic' (SCERA, 1989: 66).

These calls have a political element. By placing the failure of soil conservation adoption on farmers, governments can claim that the responsibility for the causes and solutions to the problem lies with farmers, not with government. Education campaigns to increase farmers' awareness of the problem are likely to be far less costly than other potential action. From a political perspective, the call for attitude enhancement is understandable. The land degradation issue is complex and costly, with actual payoff generally outside political time frames. In many cases, success would not be obvious -- and it is quite likely that small efforts by governments would have very little effect. But all this rests on the premises that farmers' attitudes are actually environmentally negative and that attitudes directly influence behaviour.

CONSERVATION AND AUSTRALIAN FARMERS

Although a fundamentally important concept in psychology, 'attitude' does not enjoy a uniformly accepted definition. As a general approximation, attitudes are some form of 'learned predisposition to respond in a consistently favourable or unfavourable manner with respect to a given object' (Fishbein and Ajzen, 1975: 6). Methodologically speaking, an attitude is an intervening hypothetical construct mediating the influence of an external stimulus on an individual's response to that stimulus (Figure 5.1).

FIGURE 5.1: SIMPLISTIC ATTITUDE MODEL

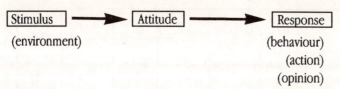

| Stimulus | ⟶ | Attitude | ⟶ | Response |

(environment)   (behaviour)
                                                     (action)
                                                     (opinion)

It is generally accepted that farmers will adopt soil conservation technology when they consider themselves to be at risk (that is, perceive land degradation on their land) (Rickson *et al.*, 1987). The attitude then mediates the relationship between the perception of the environment (stimulus) -- in this case the recognition that land degradation is occurring -- and the appropriate response which is the adoption of soil conservation technology. According to this model, farmers with the right attitude (those who are conservation minded) will adopt soil conservation technology when they perceive the need, while those with environmentally destructive attitudes, or less positive attitudes, will be content to allow land degradation to occur unabated.

Vanclay (1986, 1992a) tested this model by developing five attitude scales to measure the different aspects of farmers' attitudes to the environment: stewardship, conservation is economic, the importance of conservation, seriousness of off-site damage, and no erosion problem. Each scale consisted of several items scored on a five point Likert scale (1 = strongly disagree; 5 = strongly agree) with the total scale scores averaged to allow scoring on the original measurement. The scales were developed from a bank of attitude items completed by a sample of 92 Darling Downs farmers in a major study of farmers' responses to soil erosion.

Darling Downs farmers had high scores (on average agreed) for the scales: stewardship (mean=3.8), importance of conservation (3.9), and conservation is economic (4.0); with lower scores (on average were undecided) for the scales, no erosion problem (3.1), and seriousness of off-site damage (2.8). There was very little variance in the scores, indicating consensus among farmers on these issues (Table 5.1).

Stewardship refers to the notion that farmers are stewards of the land and that farming is a way of life that places implicit responsibility on farmers to look after the land for future generations. The stewardship concept recognises that farmers may have to make uneconomical decisions in order to protect the land. It embraces the notion that there is more to farming than economic management. Ninety-six percent of Darling Downs farmers had an attitude favourable to the notion of stewardship (had scores>3.0 on the stewardship scale).

Almost all the Darling Downs farmers believed in the importance of conservation. This was measured by a scale covering issues of the importance of conservation to farmers and to the community in general, especially as far as the future was concerned. All farmers also believed that soil conservation was economic. Given these attitudes of Darling Downs farmers, this should suggest that the adoption of soil conservation technology would not be a problem on the Darling Downs. Not only did these farmers have appropriate attitudes, they also believed soil

TABLE 5.1: ATTITUDE SCALES -- DESCRIPTIVE STATISTICS

	no of items	Cronbach alpha	min score	max score	mean score	std dev	% who agree
Stewardship	9	.74	2.1	4.9	3.8	.48	96
Importance of Conservation	8	.68	2.4	4.9	3.9	.48	94
Conservation is Economic	11	.73	3.2	5.0	4.0	0.41	100
No Erosion Problem	10	.63	2.2	4.2	3.1	0.45	60
Seriousness of Off-site Damage	5	.53	1.4	4.2	2.8	0.64	30

Potential range from 1.0 to 5.0; n=90.

conservation to be economic. There is no reason to believe that farmers on the Darling Downs should be any different, at least to any major degree, than farmers anywhere else in Australia. It is very likely that similar results would be obtained from any representative sample of Australian farmers in any geographical location. Although attitudes are learnt, and therefore changeable, they tend to be stable over time since they are the result of years of socialisation and of internalisation of experiences. It is unlikely that these attitudes would change from year-to-year or season-to-season. However, despite the attitudes remaining stable, other influences affecting resultant behaviour may change, so behaviour may change even though the underlying attitudes remain the same.

Unfortunately, the existence of these attitudes is not associated with the adoption of soil conservation technology or the absence of land degradation on the Darling Downs. Soil scientists argue that large proportions of Darling Downs (and other Australian) farms are not adequately protected against land degradation. According to the criteria of the Queensland Department of Primary Industries and the NSW Soil Conservation Service, Vanclay (1986) determined that 45 percent of Darling Downs farmers had not adequately protected their farms against soil erosion. Clearly, the fact that farmers have appropriate environmental attitudes does not guarantee that they will adopt the necessary practices. It also suggests that educational campaigns which aim, exclusively, at improving the attitudes of farmers are likely to fail. What then does explain the contradiction between farmers' attitudes and their lack of adoption of necessary practices?

THE CONTRADICTION BETWEEN ATTITUDE AND BEHAVIOUR

The first obvious explanation is that the measurement of farmers' attitudes is affected (biased) by the potentially enormous influence of social desirability in this sort of attitude measurement. Some might wish to claim that farmers are actually hostile to the environment, despite the results of these attitude scales. Farmers are astute enough to be aware of the politics of conservation. The most 'socially desirable' answer is obvious to anyone responding to the questionnaire: some will tell the researcher what they believe the researcher wants to hear. It would be difficult to rule out social desirability argument, except perhaps by repeating the research including some sort of social desirability measure. Alternatively, it could be assumed that social desirability affects farmers equally; that the mean scale score for each farmer is elevated, but that differences between farmers are still meaningful. If this were to be the case, those with higher conservation scores would be expected to have higher levels of adoption of technology and be more likely to protect their farm from land degradation. Vanclay (1986) undertook discriminant and regression analysis to identify the socioeconomic correlates of adoption of soil conservation technology, using 'protection' (a dichotomous measure indicating whether the farmer had adopted sufficient and appropriate soil conservation techniques to adequately protect the land against soil erosion) as the dependent variable. In that study, there was no indication that stewardship or conservationism (as measured by any of the five scales) was positively associated with protection. Furthermore, there was some evidence of a reverse relationship, that the non-protectors actually had stronger conservation attitudes. This finding supports the general conclusion that, even if the attitude scales are 'contaminated' by social desirability response bias, farmers' attitudes to conservation do not predispose them to adopt soil conservation technology.

The finding that attitudes are not generally predictive of behaviour is not unique to this study and is well recognised in psychology. It is only under certain conditions that attitudes are expected to have any strong effect on behaviour. Myers (1989: 558) lists these conditions as:

(i)when other influences likely to affect attitudes and actions have been minimised;

(ii)when the attitude is specifically relevant to the behaviour; and

(iii)in situations where individuals would be keenly aware of their attitudes.

In the situation of farmers responding to the environment and determining whether or not to do anything (Figure 5.2), the connection between the stimulus (the environment) and the response (adoption) is not only, if at all, affected by their attitudes. It is also affected by their perception of the environment (the perception screen) and by their personal and financial situation or context (the context/situation screen).

FIGURE 5.2: SOPHISTICATED ATTITUDE MODEL

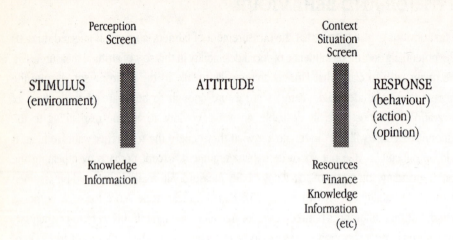

Farmers are unlikely to adopt soil conservation technology to the satisfaction of soil scientists if they have differing perceptions about the nature and extent of land degradation on their land. Furthermore, even where they do perceive land degradation, they are unlikely to adopt soil conservation technology if they lack appropriate information and/or have other demands on their capital and time. In the context of Myers' conditions:

(i) The situation of farmers' adoption of soil conservation technology is heavily affected by a wide range of other influences. The range of possible actions the farmer may undertake in response to the situation is considerable and there are many influences on farmers' attitudes, including processes that may lead to the denial of the problem (cognitive dissonance);

(ii) Attitudes to the environment (such as stewardship and conservationism) are very general attitudes consisting largely of 'motherhood' statements which also experience a high degree of social desirability. These attitudes do not determine specific behaviour. In the situation of land degradation, even where farmers recognise it occurring on their farms, there is a wide range of appropriate behaviours and there is much conflicting technical information.

(iii) Farmers are not generally aware of their attitudes to the environment. They think that surveys like this are a waste of time and do not conceive of or intellectualise their responses in the way that urban professional people might. Farmers are much more likely to respond according to their notions of good farm management.

Recognising the wider situation of farmers and the general nature of conservation attitudes, there are many reasons for why there might be strong attitudinal support for conservation, and why this might not necessarily lead to high levels of adoption.

On the Darling Downs, there is a further explanation for the contradiction. Darling Downs farmers not only had high scores on the 'stewardship', 'conservation is important', and 'conservation is economic' scales, they also believed that there was no (real) erosion problem and that the loss of soil from soil erosion is exaggerated by people who are not farmers. They also tended not to believe (were undecided) in the 'seriousness of off-site damage'. With their beliefs that soil conservation practices were economic and the small nature of erosion problems generally, farmers considered that most of the work required to be done to protect farms against erosion was already done (or soon would be) and that no major changes to agricultural management practices or technology were required. This suggests that the farmers may be less concerned about land degradation than soil scientists consider they should be and that they may not appreciate the full implications or seriousness of the erosion problem.

TABLE 5.2: FARMERS' CONCERN ABOUT EROSION (DARLING DOWNS)

	Darling Downs	Local Area	Own farm
not a problem	0	0	15
a small problem	1	17	37
a medium problem	11	37	37
a major problem	88	47	11
Total (n=90)	100	100	100

(modified from Rickson *et al.*, 1987)

TABLE 5.3: FARMERS' CONCERN ABOUT SALINITY NOW (VICTORIA)

	Central Highlands	Neighbourhood	Own farm
not a problem	3	12	28
a small problem	4	11	24
a medium problem	30	23	10
a major problem	45	24	5
don't know	2	0	0
Total (n=131)	100	100	100

(Vanclay and Cary, 1989)

**TABLE 5.4: FARMERS' CONCERN ABOUT SALINITY 20 YEARS IN THE FUTURE
(VICTORIA)**

	Central Highlands	Neighbourhood	Own farm
Not a problem	3	12	28
A small problem	4	11	24
a medium problem	14	35	24
a major problem	75	39	21
don't know	5	3	2
Total (n=130)	100	100	100

(Vanclay and Cary, 1989)

LAND DEGRADATION: A CONCERN TO FARMERS?

Farmers are concerned about land degradation as a general community problem but tend to
consider that it is not a problem that will affect them personally (see Tables 5.2, 5.3, and 5.4).
Farmers consistently understate and misperceive the extent to which their farms are affected by
land degradation (Chamala, Keith and Quinn, 1982; Rickson and Stabler, 1985; Cameron and
Elix, 1991). Research by Rickson *et al.* (1987) indicated that were farmers to appreciate the full
extent of land degradation that did occur on their farms, they would quite likely act to prevent
it. Rickson *et al.* found that farmers' estimates of anticipated yield losses for a nominated
hypothetical erosion rate of 5 mm per annum (the then accepted, estimated average erosion rate
for unprotected properties on the Darling Downs) exceeded the actual yield losses in field
experiments at a nearby site on the Darling Downs simulating that erosion rate. Discussions with
farmers revealed that theycould not accept that there was an erosion rate of 5 mm per annum
on their farms. The anticipated yield losses were high because farmers considered 5 mm per
annum erosion to be an enormous and greatly exaggerated erosion rate (Vanclay, 1986, 1992a).
Nevertheless, it does indicate that if farmers can be brought to accept that high rates of erosion
are actually occurring, they may be likely to adopt soil conservation technology. However, it is
also likely that their estimates of yield losses will be moderated as they come to accept higher
erosion rates as being normal.

THE RESPONSE OF FARMERS TO LAND DEGRADATION

Land degradation has pervasive and intensive forms (Barr and Cary, 1984). While farmers generally respond positively to the more obvious forms of erosion, extreme intensive forms of accelerated erosion may evoke a fatalistic acceptance response (Williams, 1979; Chamala, Rickson and Singh, 1984). The insidious nature of pervasive forms of land degradation, especially in their early stages, are such that the effects are slight, not obvious, and even if noticed are easily dismissed as being due to other factors. Roberts (1991) relates a story about an old South African farmer who, when asked whether he had seen any changes on his farm over his lifetime, replied, upon serious reflection, 'I think the rocks are growing'.

The principal forms of land degradation occurring on the Darling Downs are sheet and rill erosion, the subtle processes which together are responsible for eroding an estimated 5 mm of soil per annum (50 tonnes per hectare per annum) on inadequately protected cultivated land. Sheet erosion is not obvious at the point of erosion, while rill erosion is recognisable by the very small gullies (rills) that form as water runs across the paddock. Although in aggregate, these forms of land degradation erode an enormous amount of soil, at the individual level, on a day to day basis, the effects of this soil loss are not obvious. However, the ways to prevent soil erosion are well understood and soil erosion processes are relatively easy for farmers to understand.

Although soil conservation technology is costly and may require some change to farm management, there are clear benefits to the individual farmers who adopt it, probably within the farming lifetime of that farmer. Nevertheless, while there may be substantial, perhaps almost uniform, technical agreement that various forms of management practices (such as contour cultivation and stubble mulching) and structural practices (such as the use of contour banks, grassed waterways, and diversion banks) are practical, appropriate and required on most farms, technical disagreement exists over the appropriateness of so- called conservation cropping (at least when defined as zero or minimum tillage) (see Barr and Cary, 1992b). While farmers may, in principle, agree with extension officers about the use of some of the recommended practices, they tend to disagree about the extent of their use. For example, there is very little disagreement that steep slopes should not be cultivated and should be left as permanent pasture. Disagreement occurs in determining what constitutes a steep slope with, typically, extension officers recommending permanent pasture on slopes which farmers might normally cultivate (for example, slopes just over 8 percent).

Another more insidious problem, soil salting, is not only a slow process, but is also temporally and spatially distorted. According to the currently accepted model of dryland salinity, farmers in the discharge zones who experience salting are not necessarily the farmers whose farming practices were responsible for causing the problem, or those who must implement the longer-term solutions. The process of water infiltration into the watertable has occurred since the land was first cleared. Salinity control techniques which are implemented are unlikely to have an effect on watertable levels for a very long time. The model of the salting process is complex -- although not beyond farmers' understanding -- but is not necessarily generally accepted by them. Salinity control measures are costly, have almost no short-term or even medium-term effect on the severity of salting and may require major changes to farm management. There is also considerable disagreement about the technical and plausible solutions to the problem. This is recognised by the extension agencies in the development of what are referred to as 'best-bet' strategies. Consequently, there is little incentive for farmers to participate in soil salting control (Vanclay and Cary, 1989), and farmers' participation is likely to require a great deal of faith on the part of the farmers (Barr and Cary, 1992a). Importantly, there is some suggestion that farmers are being asked to grow trees where trees are unlikely to have grown before (see Cary and Barr 1992; Barr and Cary, 1992a).

KNOWLEDGE ABOUT LAND DEGRADATION

The extent of farmers' knowledge about soil salting was the focus of Vanclay and Cary's (1989) study of the Central Highlands of Victoria. Seventy-nine percent of farmers knew that dryland salting was a consequence of tree loss and/or watertable changes. Seventy- six percent knew that the solution to salinity required tree planting and/or the growing of deep rooted species. However, in an area where all farmers were in close proximity to discharge areas, only 57 percent were aware that salt-tolerant species were early indicators of soil salting. Clearly, of these three issues, farmers' knowledge of the early warning signs was the limiting factor in their overall picture of the salinity process.

The above figures relating to farmers' knowledge levels are overstated since very lax criteria were used. In terms of the early warning signs, any salt tolerant species was accepted. In reality, many salt-tolerant species, such as salt bush, appear only at the very late stages of salting, and even the recognised salt-indicator species such as barley grass and spiney rush occur at such a stage that it may be impossible to reverse the salting process.

For farmers to be environmentally conscious, it is important that they recognise the subtle changes in pasture composition and the lack of prolific growth among plants as being indicative of potential salting. When farmers recognise potential salting at this early stage they will begin to see that they themselves are personally at risk and will be more motivated to participate in salinity control measures, or in community programs aimed at controlling salinity.

The same argument holds true for soil erosion. If farmers become aware of the early warning signs, they will begin to recognise these signs on their own and other farmers' properties. The recognition of the farm to be at risk from land degradation is one of the factors that is predictive of soil conservation technology adoption (Vanclay, 1986). Furthermore, if farmers become aware of the early warning signs, they have an opportunity to respond to those visual cues while there is still time. The potential to dismiss the need for adoption because of a fatalism associated with dramatic intensive events is reduced. It is most desirable that farmers be made aware of the early warning signs.

The problem here is that the early warning signs are general -- rather than specific -- indicators of a 'problem'. In all situations of land degradation, the early warning signs could be attributed to other causes. For salinity, soil erosion, acidification and some other forms of land degradation, the early warning signs include poor seed germination rates, change in species composition in pasture, reduced proliferation and lack of vigour in plants. Farmers could easily and logically explain many of these changes as being due to the lack of fertiliser, too much fertiliser, the wrong sort of fertiliser, poor quality fertiliser, poor quality seed, the lack of rainfall, too much rainfall at the wrong time, too high temperatures, too low temperatures, pests, weeds, the influence of the neighbours' activities, residual influences from previous crops and sprays, and many other possible causes. Furthermore, for most of these early warning signs, it would also be impossible for an extension officer or other expert to determine precisely what was the real cause, without further testing.

For soil erosion by water, the warning signs could also include coloured runoff, turbid creeks and dams, build-up or loss of soil around fences, silted-up creeks and soil on the roadways. However, most farmers are so used to seeing these signs that they regard this as the usual situation.

The early warning signs for salinity include salt indicator species such as barley grass and spiney rush. However, these plant species are not restricted to salty environments and are frequently associated with general waterlogging, not necessarily being due to rising (salty) watertables. Nevertheless, the prolific establishment of these species is usually associated with high groundwater salinity (Jenkin and Morris, 1982), although farmers may not believe this to be the case.

Given that in most cases, farmers have not experienced reduced yields that are not seasonal fluctuations, farmers would be very reluctant to interpret early warning signs as indicators of land degradation, that is, as evidence that they would need to change their farm practices; rather, they would be far more likely to accept one of the many other possible explanations.

Since the visual cues to land degradation appear after significant degradation has already occurred and since these visual cues are easily dismissed, there is enormous potential for soil testing kits in promoting adoption of conservation farming techniques. Soil testing kits, when used on a regular basis, can identify soil salting, acidification and other forms of land degradation long before significant degradation happens and well before the visual cues become apparent. Since these kits give concrete indicators (that is, digital read-out) of rising salt levels or of increasing acidification, they provide indisputable evidence to the farmer that there is an increasing land degradation problem (see Powell and Pratley, 1991).

MEDIA IMAGES OF LAND DEGRADATION

Farmers have 'conservation-oriented' attitudes and are aware that land degradation is an important environmental issue, at least as a general issue. Yet they fail to perceive themselves to be at risk from land degradation. Rickson *et al.*, (1987) have demonstrated that farmers do accept that land degradation has serious economic implications and that significant yield losses may occur if they were to experience land degradation. The reason why farmers do not consider themselves to be at risk is because they do not know the early warning signs of land degradation and because of the presentation of land degradation in its most severe form in media images of land degradation. Any examination of land degradation in the media, be it the popular press, the conservation press, as well as much, if not all, of the extension literature, all rely on dramatic visual images of severe forms of land degradation (dry, salt encrusted bare patches, 3 metre deep gullies and so forth). The images are presented to visually shock the reader, and, potentially to shock the farmer or community into action to overcome the problem.

In a situation in which the most severe cases are presented as being representative of the general problem, farmers can be forgiven for not identifying with the problem. Very few farmers actually experience land degradation in the severe forms depicted in the media and extension literature. Consequently, while farmers' awareness and attitudes are being heightened by the images, the images themselves are telling farmers that because they do not have land degradation like those images, they must not have a problem. To this extent, the very people to whom the media are appealing are bound to reject the message which is presented. Vanclay (1992b) argues that the media and extension literature have been counter-productive to the identification of environmental problems by the farming community.

Since farmers are unlikely to adopt soil conservation technology when they do not believe themselves to be at risk (Pampel and Van Es, 1977; Bultena *et al.*, 1981; Chamala, Keith and Quinn, 1982; Rickson and Stabler, 1985), the promotion of dramatic images and the consequent ignorance of the early warning signs by farmers are major barriers to adoption of soil conservation techniques. It is obviously desirable that farmers recognise the early warning signs and that extension literature reduces the emphasis on dramatic images.

This may be difficult. State soil conservation departments employ publicity/publications officers who usually have an advertising, public relations or journalism background. The highlighting of the more dramatic images (an important technique in advertising) is at the expense of images that are less dramatic. The presentation of the less dramatic early warning signs may require a radical rethinking of how extension information is communicated to farmers.

FARMING SUBCULTURES

Society is not homogeneous. There are many groups within society and each group tends to develop a particular subculture, a set of behaviours and attitudes expected of people in that group. While still remaining part of the wider culture, each group develops a particular identity. The farming community is no different from any other group in this respect. Subcultures are not prescriptive and there can be diversity within a subculture. Furthermore, many people may belong to more than one subculture and may be placed in situations of having contradictory role expectations. Not all farmers will subscribe to all aspects of a farming subculture. Indeed, based upon differences in regions, climate, product type, history and so on, there is likely to be a large number of farming subcultures throughout Australia, and possibly in a given region. At present -- without the necessary sociological research -- we know very little about the specifics of Australian farming subcultures.

Because we are socialised into our culture and subcultures, in a continuous and subtle process called socialisation, we may not be aware that these subcultures actually exist and we may not be conscious of all of the aspects of them. However, this lack of recognition or cognition of subcultures does not prevent a particular way of thinking and set of values and attitudes from being an important part of our life or a significant factor in determining our behaviours and attitudes. Peer pressure is part of the enforcement of subcultural expectations: but peer pressure is intense and readily experienced by the individual. Peer pressure explains why individuals do things (and not do things) which might not be in accordance with more widely accepted behaviour. Socialisation into a subculture accounts for people's normal everyday behaviour, is not intense and is not necessarily experienced or perceived by each individual.

The obvious manifestation of what most people might recognise as a farming subculture is in farmers' dress: the 'uniform' is normally a combination of checked long sleeve shirts, moleskin trousers, elastic sided riding boots and Akubra hats. Driza-bones are an essential item when the rains arrive. A preference for country and western music and for conservative politics is also expected. Clearly, while this is an overgeneralisation, it does remind us that the farming subculture has certain definable 'features'.

'Agrarianism', one aspect of farming subcultures, has been a major theme within American rural sociological thought this century. Agrarianism is not a unidimensional phenomenon (Flinn and Johnson, 1974), and is generally conceived as having three major components: stewardship; farming as a way of life; and a unique form of (rural) political and social conservatism. Rural sociologists have tended to concentrate on the conservatism and the non-economic orientation to farming dimensions, often ignoring the stewardship aspect (see Flinn and Johnson, 1974; Buttel and Flinn, 1975,1977; Carlson and McLeod, 1978; Buttel *et al.*, 1981; Craig and Phillips, 1983; Singer and Freire-de- Sousa, 1983; Molnar and Wu, 1989). Australian farmers exhibit high levels of agrarianism (Craig and Phillips, 1983).

Subcultures work at two levels: at promoting certain attitudes, ideas and beliefs that members of a subculture are supposed to have; and at specifying certain behaviours and practices. This means that much of the behaviour of individuals may be in response to subcultural expectations (the sociological model), rather than as a result of the individual's own attitudinal response mechanisms (the psychological model). Part of the problem in relation to the adoption of new techniques or management practices is that these techniques and practices are not, on the whole, generally accepted within the various farming subcultures. Consequently, only the innovators within the community are likely to adopt them (see Rogers, 1983). Yet, once these techniques have gained wider acceptance within the various subcultures, the majority of farmers can be expected to adopt them.

Leaving aside the important task of deciding what are 'appropriate' and desirable techniques and management practices for any region, the aim of understanding the farming subculture in any region is to find a social mechanism for implementing change at the subcultural level. 'Using' sociology to discover how, and under what circumstances, decisions about the acceptance of environmentally beneficial practices occur, might appear utilitarian and a basis for social control. Similarly, 'using' the farming community's decision making processes to bring about change might be seen as manipulative, undemocratic and open to criticism as being a mechanism for imposing dominant ideology (see Vanclay, 1994c). These criticisms are not necessarily valid under circumstances where the extension officer is a genuine facilitator of farmer decision making rather than, as an agent of the state, someone who imposes solutions on the subcultural group. And, if the subcultural activities are known to be causing major problems about which the farmers may be unaware, the educational role of the extension agent is most important.

Some years ago there was a subcultural insistence that farms have perfectly straight furrows. In fact, rural show days often had competitions to determine who could produce the straightest furrows. This has now been replaced with an acceptance of contour cultivation. Contour cultivation is not universally adopted, of course, with some farmers finding the management of their farm too difficult with contour cultivation. Nevertheless, there is no longer a subcultural obstacle to the adoption of contour cultivation. Gradually, other aspects of conservation farming will need to become accepted parts of the farming subculture.

'Recreational ploughing' or 'recreational tillage' also needs to be understood in sociological terms. Farmers have a strong work ethic, yet farming is an activity that may mean at certain times of the year there is not a lot of work that needs immediate attention. Some farmers feel that unless they are doing something productive, like driving tractors, they are not working and many farmers are not used to the idea of leisure. With many Australian farmers overcultivating their land, we need to understand the extent to which some might use ploughing as a therapy to avoid some of the stresses of life. Ideally, the importance of the tractor in farming life needs to be de-emphasised and farmers need to be better trained to deal with the sometimes long periods of leisure time they are likely to enjoy.

SITUATIONAL CONSTRAINTS ON FARMERS' ADOPTION

Land degradation processes are complex, some control measures are costly and there is limited short-term return for investment in soil conservation technology. In fact, in situations of high interest rates, with future discounting entering into the calculations, it is likely that many soil conservation techniques and management practices are not economic (Quiggin, 1987). Except where land degradation reduces the capital value of the land or yields, land degradation is an externality to the economic situation of farmers. The off-site consequences of erosion and, in the case of soil salting, the temporal as well as spatial separation of consequences from management practices, make land degradation external to the immediate concerns of the farmer. Consequently, in situations of conflicting technical information, unpredictable markets and uncertain return for investment in soil conservation, it may be economically rational for farmers to avoid widespread adoption of soil conservation technology.

For reasons described in Chapters 1 and 2, farm incomes have diminished considerably over the past decade. Land values have also fallen, reducing farmers' equity in their properties and functioning to prevent further borrowing for capital improvement as well as preventing the transition of the smaller farmers out of agriculture. And, as has already been suggested, many Australian farmers are in a situation of 'agricultural involution' (Geertz, 1963) -- not being able to afford to undertake any capital improvement and not being able to change management strategies that involve any risk, or a perception of risk. No matter how environmentally aware these farmers may be, if they don't have the capital to outlay, or are prevented from borrowing further, they cannot undertake any adoption of soil conservation strategies involving additional spending. Their economic situation means that their primary concern must be their immediate economic survival. This economic barrier is a major constraint upon rational soil and water conservation strategies. What is also of concern is that adoption of conservation farming techniques has also been lower than desirable during times when commodity prices and farm incomes were high. When farmers' income is severely limited they have very little flexibility. At least when they have adequate incomes there is the possibility of adoption of new techniques and practices.

Having farmers adopt the recommended soil conservation technology and management techniques will often require their going against economic self-interest; of putting aside other priorities for capital; of rejecting some of their own ideas and knowledge about their local environment; and of accepting the models and knowledge of the extension agencies. As Barr and Cary (1992) suggest, much more than a leap of faith on the part of the farmer is often required.

Farmers tend to be older than the extension officers with whom they deal. Too often, extension officers and agencies fail to appreciate the experiences and knowledge of farmers. Farmers may have had a lifetime on their land. It is true that land degradation continues to exist on farms, but it continues to exist on many of the farms that may have complied with previous extension agency dictates about desirable land management practices. In many cases, advice given by extension agencies in the past has been wrong, or at least has not lived up to expectations, and may have caused more problems than it has provided solutions (see Frank and Chamala, 1992). Some farmers are tired of hearing from yet another extension officer that all they have to do to protect their land from land degradation is to adopt a particular practice or technique. Often, information provided by extension agencies has been ill-timed, making farmers consider extension to be irrelevant. Farmers also complain that they are treated as 'idiots' by extension agencies (Woodhill, 1991). The language used by the extension agencies and their staff is often patronising and prescriptive. We do not need to 'educate farmers' -- rather we need to learn from them, at least to understand their situation -- and to facilitate the discussion of their own problems in the context of a non threatening meeting with other stakeholders in the district. There is some evidence that the particular subculture of extension officers also tends to promote a patronising attitude. Extension officers generally perceive farmers' beliefs to be different from (inferior to) their own - although, as Earle, Brownlea and Rose (1981) have found, they tend to share the same beliefs as farmers.

Farmers are also placed in the situation of receiving contradictory advice. Soil conservation agencies are not the only agencies in the business of extension. In some States, the same agency that promotes soil conservation may have other extension officers whose job it is to promote commercial innovations. In other States, government agencies are structured so that commodity-based extension is the responsibility of one agency, while conservation extension is the responsibility of another. In both situations, there may be very little communication between (and within) agencies, and farmers are given different -- and often conflicting -- information. In addition to State government agencies, many other groups involved in extension. Various commodity bodies such as the Australian Meat and Livestock Corporation as well as agribusiness firms -- particularly agricultural chemical manufacturers and distributors -- also actively provide advice to farmers. In addition, farmers seek information from rural publications and from each other.

Even where farmers may accept the information presented to them, they are not always in a situation where they can comply. They have conflicting goals concerning the use of their time, the use of their capital, and the ideal ways to manage their farm. In times of unpredictable markets, farmers may wish to maintain flexibility. This limits the use of the deep-rooted perennial pasture species desirable for salinity control, because flexibility often rests upon a grazing strategy. Obviously, where achievement of sound land management requires considerable capital investment on behalf of the farmer, in terms of investment in new equipment, structural practices, seed and agricultural chemicals, the economic situation of the farmer is important. In situations where farmers have low equity levels, when interest rates are high, market prices for produce low and farmers have competing priorities for capital expenditure, investment in soil conservation is likely to be minimal.

The stage of life of the farm family may be important in determining goals for time and capital. There may be conflicting goals of improved housing or education of children. Many farms suffer from poor quality housing because farms are inherited, and farm housing tends to date from the time the land was first settled. Furthermore, owing to patterns of inheritance and the fact that farm families have tended to be relatively large, farms may have numerous shareholders, with the non-farming shareholders having different expectations and demands for the use of capital than the farming shareholders, usually preferring dividends to reinvestment of capital. The large size of farm families and the resulting inheritance 'battles' have produced considerable tension over landuse and property disbursement.

In other situations, the problem is exacerbated because the land degradation may be an off-site and non-point problem. That is, the farmers largely responsible for the problem may be different from the ones experiencing the negative effects of the problem. This is particularly the case with dryland salinity (see Introduction). Recharge areas may be a considerable distance from the discharge areas (usually the low lying areas) where the effects of salting are noticed.

Consequently, where the farmers experiencing soil salting are convinced that they need to do something, the accepted model of salinity requires them to convince other farmers in the recharge areas -- who may not be experiencing any ill effects from salting and are not likely to -- to participate in salinity control programs. Farmers who engage in such programs as the planting of trees (particularly on rocky hilltops) and the growing of deep-rooted pasture species on hill slopes, cannot restrict any benefit that adoption might have on watertable levels to themselves. Furthermore, because of the very slow rate of movement of subterranean water, it is likely that the farmers who suffer most will not benefit until a very long time has passed.

Although governments provide some financial incentives to encourage adoption of soil conservation measures, these seldom cover the full costs borne by farmers. All this suggests that farmers are unlikely to participate in adoption for conservation reasons alone. However, farmers tend not to act in an economically 'rational' way; they respond, instead, to farming culture and the notions of good farm management that exist within their community. In terms of farm management, farmers generally do what they regard is required, often consciously knowing that such an activity may not be economically rational. Such activities are justified as being part of the farming way of life (stewardship) and necessary in order to improve the farm for their children. This has meant that at times, farmers' expenditure patterns have been inappropriate -- something which has resulted in financial trouble with increasing interest rates and declining product prices and land values.

The constraints upon adoption, therefore, are not necessarily economic, but opinion- related. Farmers fail to adopt soil conservation technology because they are not satisfactorily convinced that it is necessary. In terms of salinity control measures, Vanclay and Cary (1989) found that many farmers failed to participate in adoption for very practical reasons. Based on the logic and premises of the farmer's explanation, the decision not to adopt appeared sensible. The task for extension agencies in Victoria was to change farmers' opinions of the particular deep-rooted species being recommended (phalaris and lucerne) -- something which would necessitate increasing the farmers' level of knowledge of these species.

THE VALUE OF LANDCARE

The causes of many of the problems associated with land degradation are social, not technical, in nature. In terms of the economic and social situation of farmers, the lack of adoption is understandable. Some extension agencies, and extension techniques, have alienated farmers and have failed to appreciate the extent of farmers' knowledge and experience in dealing with land management issues. The problem is also social in that many of the consequences of land degradation are off-site or outside the farming lifetime of the farmers. The solutions to land degradation therefore require community concern for the economic situation of farmers and community support for adoption of conservation farming strategies. Landcare, as a strategy for group extension, is likely to provide a suitable model for overcoming many of the problems that have been described.

In particular, Landcare is likely to empower farmers by making farmers themselves responsible for setting the agenda of the land management issue they address and the strategies they employ. It legitimatises their indigenous local knowledge (see Kloppenberg, 1991). Landcare will also potentially create a public acceptance of new ideas and land management strategies. Because farmers are meeting other farmers in a forum to specifically discuss land management strategies, new ideas are likely to gain legitimacy within the farming subculture much more readily than they would by diffuse innovation processes that occurred with individual extension strategies. As a local initiative, individual Landcare groups can respond to the particular needs of the members of that group (see Campbell and Siepen, 1994). Landcare is also likely to be a suitable organisation to assist farmers in dealing with the off-site consequences of land degradation.

However, in order to be effective, Landcare groups will need to be satisfactorily served by well-informed extension agencies in order to ensure that their information and other resource needs are met. State governments that believe Landcare will be as a strategy for reducing their commitment to extension ought to reconsider. The enthusiasm and energy of Landcare groups will quickly be lost if the are not properly serviced. And servicing Landcare is expected to require both new financial commitments and new approaches to community decision making. As Campbell and Siepen (1994: 296) have argued:

> While it is reasonable to expect good land management to prevent land degradation, it is simply unrealistic to expect farmers to pay for rehabilitating degraded land and water resources unless it will be profitable for them to do so, which is rarely the case. So more and better research into profitable and sustainable land management systems is essential, research which involves land users as key players from the start of the research and extension process. This may well require joint involvement in participatory training from researchers, farmers and extension staff.

Extension agencies and individual extension officers who see Landcare as simply a mechanism to be used by them to control or cajole farmers to do what the agency wants, rather than as a mechanism for empowering farmers, are likely to jeopardise the effectiveness of Landcare and contribute to the further alienation of farmers. The concept of 'ownership' that farmers attach to their Landcare group and the activities of their group, is likely to be very important in the success of that group and of those activities.

Landcare groups also need to ensure that they develop appropriate community organisational structures. Burnout of group leaders, loss of enthusiasm and eventual decline in the group will occur unless appropriate safeguards are implemented. Landcare is similar to any community organisation in most respects, and Landcare groups and the extension agencies sponsoring Landcare can learn a great deal from community organisational structures (see Chamala and Mortiss, 1990; Campbell and Siepen, 1994).

Extension agencies also need to be aware that while Landcare is about empowering farmers, only some farmers are actually empowered. Landcare becomes another organisation in which the politically and socially astute elite of the local community can dominant others. Far from Landcare empowering all farmers, it is quite likely that certain individuals will have their interests served by Landcare at the expense of other individuals (see Gray, 1992; Vanclay, 1993b, 1994c). This point was strongly articulated by Wilkinson and Barr (1993: 127-132) in their discussion of the 'lessons' from a study of involvement in catchment management of Victorian community members:

> one needs to be careful not to read too much into the description of some (catchment management) plans as 'community instigated'. The reality of community pressure is never as simple as these few words suggest. First, the community rarely acts as a single united entity ... there was ever only a minority of people in the community actively pushing for action. These people were unrepresentative of the wider community ... Second, the simple perception of community pressure for action often overlooks the crucial role played by government officers ... Even the most community-inspired plans required the efforts of departmental officers to guide the establishment and development of the groups ... Possible future problems (with the formulation of plans) raise the important issue ... of just who is representative.

Sociologist Ian Gray (1992) has recommended that sociologists begin to concentrate upon 'interests', especially the particular ideologies and organising activities of elites and others participating in group decision making, although Lockie (1994a, 1994b, 1994c, 1995) has suggested that the Landcare groups he studied fostered cooperation between members, thereby preventing the formation of any factional elites. More sociological research is being done (Lockie, forthcoming) and should help to clarify what is occurring -- in terms of the exercise of power -- at Landcare meetings.

Funding for Landcare needs to be carefully considered. Already there is the perception amongst some farmers that Landcare is just another way of securing funding (Woodhill, 1991). It is important not to let Landcare degenerate into just another social club, and it is likely that funding should reward positive action undertaken by each group.

There also needs to be some consideration given to the effectiveness of Landcare both in terms of implementation of conservation farming strategies (however this may be defined in each region) by members of Landcare groups and in terms of the coverage of Landcare. If large numbers of farmers are not being adequately serviced by Landcare, and continue to use environmentally unsound farming practices, consideration will need to be given to encourage their participation in Landcare, or to find other mechanisms which will encourage their adoption of conservation farming strategies. As Morrisey and Lawrence (1995) have warned, there is some evidence that farmers are adept at outsmarting other community members of Landcare groups when voting about the focus, tasks, and projects of the group is conducted. Setting a farmer oriented agenda may be perfectly sound and desirable, so long as environmental degradation is being addressed and so long as Landcare is not used as an instrument to prevent the 'greens' and other community groups with a growing interest in resource management, from implementing desirable change at the local level.

CONCLUSION

Land degradation has important, but often ignored, social dimensions. A disproportionate amount of research has been spent on physical research, with insufficient attention being placed on the social aspects of land degradation. There are known solutions to a large number of land degradation problems. While these solutions exist, many are not adopted by farmers for a wide variety of social, economic, cultural, perceptual and situational reasons.

Farmers do not have environmentally hostile attitudes. Rather, they endorse concepts of stewardship and conservation. It is highly unlikely that attempts to improve farmers' attitudes will be the key to the increased adoption of soil conservation and other environmentally sensible practices. Although adoption of soil conservation technology may not be economically rational for the individual in the short term, farmers do see conservation as having wider economic rewards and do appreciate that land degradation will significantly affect future yields. Farmers are also sufficiently concerned about the issue of land degradation to join local groups, discuss the issue and to lobby for funding. However, while most perceive some problems in their district, seemingly few consider that their own farms are at risk from land degradation. This is due to a misperception and underestimation of the land degradation processes. Farmers fail to recognise the early warning signs of land degradation because most media and extension literature usually present dramatic images of severe forms of land degradation. Although the protection of Australia's farmlands will, no doubt, be well served by a promotion of changes in farmers' attitudes, much more will be served by an increase in farmers' knowledge of land degradation processes and symptoms, and of the acceptance of conservation farming techniques. This, in turn, will be enhanced by sociological research which seeks both to understand the place of the environment within the farming subculture and to inform (that is, contribute to the development of) new extension practices and initiatives.

FARMER RATIONALITY AND THE SO-CALLED BARRIERS TO ADOPTION

INTRODUCTION

While in the past, it may have been of some concern that many of the production practices promoted by extension agencies were not being adopted by farmers (see Buttel *et al.*, 1990), the severity of contemporary environmental problems within agriculture provides an environmental imperative for farmers to embrace sustainable agricultural practices. In Australia, with rapidly degrading environments, the need for effective extension to promote the adoption of more appropriate environmental management practices is recognised as being great (Campbell and Siepen, 1994).

In traditional extension, the explanation of adoption behaviour was based on the social-psychological model of diffusion of innovations, as best represented by Rogers (1983). This model has become very limiting, contradictory, does not sufficiently explain farmer behaviour and has been substantially rejected (Buttel *et al.*, 1990). That there has not been an immediate 'replacement' with an agreed-upon model has left something of a theoretical vacuum in extension. The new models of group extension, such as Landcare, have been developed without a substantial theoretical basis and rest upon a certain amount of ideological faith about farmers' desires to join 'self-help' groups.

In Australia, extension agencies embody aspects of traditional extension thinking and, at the same time, a commitment to new methods of extension. Even though there is enthusiasm about these new models of extension, it is still adjudged that extension is not working and that farmers are reluctant to adopt the conservation technologies being promoted. Furthermore, extension agencies and agricultural research agencies are often unaware of the implications of these new 'bottom-up' (cooperative and group) approaches to problem solving.

This chapter proposes that the 'failure' of farmers to adopt technology, especially environmental management strategies, can be explained with reference to the rationality of farmers. It also argues that while traditional extension methods and philosophies may have been more or less successful in the promotion of commercial innovations, they are inconsistent with the promotion of environmental innovations. It is also argued that the barriers to adoption and the promotion of environmental management practices are problematic for modern extension approaches.

COMMERCIAL INNOVATION VERSUS ENVIRONMENTAL INNOVATION

Traditional extension is based on the model of innovation diffusion that dominated American rural sociology in the 1960s and 70s (Buttel *et al.*, 1990). The important feature of this model is that it is based on social-psychological notions of individual decision making. It does not see adoption as a simple, single act, but rather as a complex pattern of mental processes and activities occurring as a set of stages: awareness, information, evaluation, trial, and adoption. Adoption is theorised to occur as a sigmoid growth curve when graphed as cumulative percentage and which follows a pattern of normal distribution when graphed as frequency over time. This leads to classification categories such as innovator, early adopters, early majority, majority, late majority and laggards (see Rogers, 1983).

The classical model of adoption is predicated on commercial innovations that apply equally to all farmers for whom the technology is designed. Commercial innovation refers to those innovations developed primarily for economic reasons. With commercial innovation, non adoption affected none other than the non adopting farmer, and since adoption was in the farmer's self interest, it was assumed that widespread adoption would eventually occur.

With environmental innovations -- that is the use of techniques, methods and approaches to improve land management rather than to increase farm productivity -- the costs of adoption are borne by the individual farmer, while the benefits are usually social. Often the costs outweigh the benefits for an individual farmer, at least in commercial terms. Such adoption would not appear, in such circumstances, to be in the farmer's economic interest. Consequently, the result is large-scale non adoption. As will be argued later in the chapter, there are many other fundamental differences between environmental innovations and commercial innovations that make the adoption process of environmental management techniques much more complex, and their adoption much less likely.

Nevertheless, there are compelling social and environmental reasons why farmers' adoption of improved environmental management practices is socially desirable. Much of the impact from land degradation is in the form of 'off-site' damage -- a term referring to all the impacts that are of concern to people other than the commercial concerns of the individual farmer, including loss of the productive potential of the farm for future generations, impacts on downstream water users, impacts on neighbours, loss of wildlife habitat, loss of ecological diversity, water pollution, air pollution, exhaustion of non- renewable farm inputs (such as phosphates) and the destruction caused by their use.

A consequence of the existence of a difference between commercial and environmental innovations is that, while voluntary approaches were generally satisfactory for commercial innovations, different policy instruments including regulatory and subsidy approaches may be required for the promotion of environmental innovations. The problem, however, is that regulatory and subsidy-based approaches are the antithesis of 'bottom-up' approaches -- the very ones being endorsed by the state as a means of saving public money and encouraging group decision making at the local level. The question is, to what extent should the state intervene?

Significant off-site impact associated with land degradation and the uneconomic nature of many appropriate land management activities, especially on the large-scale, suggest that community support for land protection is desirable. A further reason to support community involvement is that, in many cases, fault cannot be placed with individual landholders but with government policies and social attitudes that encouraged the clearing of land in the first place. Extension agencies have also played a role in encouraging the adoption of what are now known to be environmentally unsustainable practices (Frank and Chamala, 1992). As was detailed in the Introduction, salinity is temporally and spatially distorted -- the watertable accessions that have caused dryland salting normally having occurred decades ago and possibly several kilometres from the discharge sites (Vanclay and Cary, 1989).

With environmental innovations, new technologies are not universally applicable. Rather than being concerned with adoption of the technology *per se*, a more appropriate measure to consider is that of 'protection' (Vanclay, 1986). Protection is a measure to determine whether a farmer has adopted or implemented a sufficient range of environmental management strategies appropriate to the environmental situation of that farm. Obviously there is no limit to what a farmer might do in terms of protecting the farm. However, for a particular production commodity in a particular region, a set of environmental management techniques can be devised which would be generally agreed upon as being the basis of what environmentally aware farmers should seek to achieve in order to manage their farm in a relatively sustainable fashion. In this type of analysis, farmers who happen to have the best tracts of land are usually required to do very little in order to qualify as 'protectors' (Vanclay, 1986), while those on poorer tracts may have to implement quite substantial changes to ensure environmental sustainability.

A further complication with environmental innovations is that they tend to be qualitatively different from commercial innovations. Commercial innovations tend to be what might be described as add-on technologies, which require little modification to farm procedures. Appropriate environmental management in agriculture requires major changes in land use and to farm management. It is well established that add-on technologies are far more likely to be adopted than practices that require major land use change, even where significant economic advantages can be demonstrated in the case of the latter (Donald, 1982).

It could be argued that commercial innovations were promoted by extension agencies using the traditional extension concepts focussing on the promotion of simple, single technologies. Effective environmental management, on the other hand, is more complex, requiring not only a change in management behaviour or the use of a particular technology, but, potentially, a different way of thinking: the adoption of systems thinking and whole farm planning. Röling (1993) argued that moving towards environmental management could be seen as a cumulative and incremental learning process: it was not about the 'adoption of innovations'. Australian extension agencies entrenched in traditional extension thinking have tended to perceive and promote environmental management practices as discrete practices or technologies (environmental innovations) in much they same way as they would perceive and promote commercial innovations. The only difference is that the goal has become environmental rather than commercial. Examples of the promotion of environmental management as a commodity or single innovation or technology abound, even though these practices are complex and often require a change in farm management: contour cultivation; so called 'sustainable crop rotations' to reduce artificial nitrogen use; establishment of deep rooted perennial pastures; improved management of stock rotations; stubble mulching; and zero tillage systems.

In addition, some conservation measures promoted by extension agencies possibly did not require major changes to farm management, and were also promoted as commodities to be introduced into the farm management plan. These included: contour banks and other structural works, grass filter strips, and strip cropping.

It is not necessarily the case that there will always be a conflict between environmental and commercial innovations. However, existing evidence of the widespread adoption of what might be described as environmentally sound practices, indicates that adoption of those practices occurs because of commercial reasons rather than because of the environmental benefits of those practices, especially among 'commercially oriented' as opposed to 'farming-as-a-way-of-life oriented' farmers (Buttel *et al.*, 1990). Thus, minimum tillage has been adopted because of labour and energy savings, and deep rooted perennial species have been adopted because of their cost effectiveness. Nevertheless, environmental benefits do accrue irrespective of the motivation for adoption (commercial or environmental). Commercially motivated adoption of environmental management practices does not, however, ensure that environmental benefits will be maximised.

THE RATIONALITY OF FARMERS

For turn-of-the-century sociologist Max Weber, the process of rationalisation represented the movement from a society based on substantive rationality to a society based on formal (capitalist) rationality (Beilharz, 1991). It was a process Weber was to lament -- but one he believed was inevitable. Weber considered formal rationality to be the explicit calculation of economic factors in monetary terms and the subordination of other goals or values in life. Substantive rationality is somewhat ambiguously defined by Weber, but in its simplest form is the opposite of formal rationality in that it is not constrained to purely formal or goal-oriented rational calculation (Weber, 1976 cited by Mooney, 1988). What is implied in the notion of substantive rationality is the legitimacy of value-oriented action.

Weber's notions of formal and substantive rationality have been applied to classify American farmers into two (Rogers, 1987; Salamon, 1985) and four (Mooney, 1988) ideal types. Salamon (1985) and Rogers (1987) classify 'commercially oriented' farmers as 'Yankee' farmers, while they classify 'farming-as-a-way-of-life oriented' farmers as 'Yeoman' farmers. Mooney (1988) adds C. Wright Mill's notion of craftship to the concept of substantive rationality to provide a more concrete notion of substantive rationality as applied to farmers. Placing the 'formal rationality -- substantive rationality' continuum on one axis, Mooney (1988: 68) adds a second axis of 'market situation' which reflects 'a continuum of positive and negative privilege with respect to the market in property and skills but also includes the level of market monopolisation of input and output factors'. This provides four sectors which he labels: 'Economists' Model Farmer' and 'Poor Farmer' at the formal rationality (capitalist) end, and 'Successful Family Farmer' and 'Marginal Family Farmer' at the substantive rationality (craftship) end. He also provides a description of each ideal type.

Jan Douwe van der Ploeg (1990, 1993) has also been classifying farmers into different groups based on his and Hofstee's (1946) concept of farming styles. The essential feature of the concept of farming styles is that different groups of farmers have different notions about the most appropriate way to farm in order to fulfil their objectives, which may include, but are not limited to, objectives relating to production levels, farming techniques, environmental management, animal welfare and so on. Somewhat similar to the concept of farming styles is the argument in Chapter 5 about the existence of (regional) farming subcultures into which farmers are socialised and which include norms about appropriate farm management (see Vanclay, 1992a).

Extension is based on the presupposition of economic calculation by farmers -- that is, formal rationality. Quite clearly, Salamon, Rogers, Mooney, van der Ploeg, Vanclay and others have identified considerable sections of the farming community that are not classified as adhering to formal rationality. That some farmers do not adopt some innovations which, according to formal rationality, are clearly economic, while other farmers adopt other practices which are clearly not economic, is further proof that much farmer decision making is not based upon formal rationality.

What follows is a discussion of the barriers to adoption of environmental innovations, and an argument that establishes how, from the farmers' point of view, such non adoption may well be rational. The importance of this approach is that it further legitimises the claim that more attention ought to be placed on farmers' concerns, and that farmers' opinions ought be considered more carefully in agricultural research and extension particularly in relation to environmental management and sustainable agriculture.

THE SO-CALLED 'BARRIERS TO ADOPTION'

As suggested earlier, in the classical adoption-diffusion model, adoption is regarded as being inevitable because the model assumes that the innovations are economically beneficial and that farmers are economically rational. In the case of commercial innovations, there should be no barriers to adoption. Here, lack of adoption tends to be explained solely by the lag time in the communication of the innovation from the extension agency to the individual farmer, in how long an individual farmer takes to try- out an innovation, and whether the farmer is psychologically and structurally an innovator or laggard in terms of the adoption curve. However, it is recognised that sometimes the opportunity to adopt new technologies might be limited by infrastructural constraints such access to inputs and to markets.

The notion of a 'barrier to adoption' is an attempt to adapt the classical model of adoption so that it might account for non adoption in circumstances where there might be reasons for such non adoption. In principle, this could apply to both environmental and commercial innovations in any expanded or enlightened model of extension and adoption behaviour that accepted the validity of substantive rationality. 'Barriers to adoption' recognises that some environmental management practices may not be in the best interests of individual farmers, even if their wide-scale adoption is socially desirable. A major aspect of the recognition of any barriers to adoption, is consideration of how farmers may be persuaded to change their behaviour, or how the barrier, or hurdle, might be overcome.

The problem with the 'barriers' approach is that it assumes there is a set position (or goal or objective) beyond that which currently exists, which is understood by one set of actors (the extension agents) but not by another (the farmers who are seen to be the barrier). It is, in this sense, part of an outmoded 'technology transfer' model. It sees farmers as needing external input to move them in a certain preordained direction, not as knowledge- rich producers with an ability to make decisions which are in their own interests.

In the new models of extension based on the Agricultural Knowledge and Information Systems (AKIS) concept of extension (see Röling, 1988; Röling, 1990; Röling and Engel, 1990), ideologies of 'farmer first', and 'bottom-up' approaches (see Chambers, 1983; Richards, 1985; Chambers *et al.*, 1989) mean that because farmers are responsible for setting the agenda and determining the priorities for extension activity, barriers to adoption do not logically exist, since there no longer is a normative reason (within the perspective) why adoption ought to occur. The moment that a normative argument for adoption is made, such as the need for adoption of environmental management practices, extension must be considered as a policy instrument (see van Woerkum and van Meegeren, 1990, and cf Röling, 1988). Thus, the concept of a barrier to adoption is inconsistent with an AKIS perspective.

Of course, having accepted that extension is a policy instrument and a legitimate tool of government for the modification of behaviour for socially desirable purposes, such as environment management, does not mean that AKIS-style methods of group extension (as embraced, for example, in Landcare) may not be the most appropriate or effective way to actually achieve that aim. Perhaps the most important difference is that the group facilitator must encourage (manipulate?), albeit subtly, the learning processes and knowledge environment of group members so that they, in the end, arrive at the socially desirable view (Vanclay, 1992a; cf Vanclay, 1994c).

In this method, it is unlikely that there will be substantial barriers to adoption, since once the farm study group has accepted the importance of a particular practice for commercial or environmental reasons and it has entered the subculture, or farming style, of that group, each individual farmer is likely to conform and adopt the practice. Similarly, until there is general recognition of the importance of a particular environmental problem and of the suitability of the management practice dealing with that problem, widespread adoption it is not likely to occur.

Many extension agencies have not appreciated the implications of these arguments about the barriers to adoption, and persist with notions about the need for persuasive extension, ignoring completely aspects relating to the rationality or otherwise of what is being promoted -- as perceived by farmers -- and the social context of adoption. The point made earlier can be reiterated: extension agencies promoting conservation practices tend to use similar concepts and thinking as is used with the extension of commercial innovations. To these agencies, even where an awareness of meaningful barriers to adoption exists, farmers who fail to adopt are often regarded as ignorant, short sighted, recalcitrant and/or laggards. Historically, and perhaps presently, the objective of much extension research has been to identify the perceived barriers and to establish strategies about how to improve the targeting of the message so as eliminate the barriers, with little consideration that farmers may be carefully choosing not to adopt, or that their reluctance to adopt may have, in their minds, a perfectly 'rational' basis.

A Classification of the Legitimate Reasons for Non Adoption

Many different reasons are given by farmers why they have not adopted a particular technology or management practice. Often non adoption is for very pragmatic reasons, where the technology being promoted is simply not suited to the new environment or social context (see Röling, 1988; Frank and Chamala, 1992; Frank, 1995a, 1995b). While many of the reasons relate to the specifics of particular commodities, environments and the technology or management practice being promoted, it is nevertheless possible to identify a number of key considerations (Vanclay, 1992d,1992e). Some of these points are recognised within the traditional extension model (see Rogers, 1983) while others have been made by some of the critics of traditional extension (for example, Buttel *et al.*, 1990).

1. Complexity. In general terms, the more complex the innovation, the greater the resistance to adoption. Complexity makes the innovation more difficult to understand, and generally requires greater management skills. This increases the risk associated with the innovation. Many environmental management practices are complex and require a detailed understanding of physical processes. In some cases, such as with salinity, farmers may know what is being stated about the process and what is being promoted to address the problem, but they may not believe or agree with the scientific explanation for salinity (Vanclay and Cary, 1989; Barr and Cary, 1992; Cary and Barr, 1992; Vanclay, 1992a; Vanclay, 1992b). Farmers are acting quite rationally by preferring to adopt less complex innovations over more complex ones or by not adopting complex practices at all.

2. Divisibility. Divisibility allows for partial adoption. Farmers can adopt that part of an innovation that they like or that is consistent with other farming objectives. Obviously, therefore, the more an innovation is divisible, the more likely it is to be adopted. Under the traditional model of adoption of commercial innovations, partial adoption will inevitably lead to complete adoption. Partial adoption is viewed as a form of trial adoption. Where innovations are not divisible, they are not likely to be adopted, especially if they have other detracting attributes. In this case, farmers must be totally committed to the new innovation before adoption. Such a commitment is unlikely for a range of reasons, and consequently farmers are acting rationally when they do not adopt technologies that are not divisible. Because they are about total farm management, environmental innovations tend not to be divisible and are, as a consequence, less likely to be adopted.

3. Congruence -- Incompatibility with Farm and Personal Objectives. Farmers are more likely to adopt innovations which are compatible with other farm and personal objectives. Where innovations are complex and indivisible, they are also likely to represent major changes in the management of the farm and therefore not be compatible with other operations on the farm. Farmers' personal needs for the use of capital and income -- such as the education of children, expenditure on household goods, as well as farm requirements such as the purchase of new machinery -- may mean that capital expenditure is not consistent with farm and personal goals at that point in time. The desire to maintain flexibility because of uncertainty in the market place also means that innovations that are not consistent with this goal are also likely to be resisted. Because of the fundamental changes to agricultural practices associated with most new environmental strategies, most environmental innovations are not compatible with current farm management practices. Non adoption under these circumstances is, again, rational from the farmer's point of view.

4. Loss of Flexibility. Many new environmental management practices reduce farmers' flexibility. Farmers like flexibility because it means that they can change commodities in response to prices and climatic conditions. Perennial pastures lock farmers into grazing. Zero-tillage systems with chemical control of weeds restrict the range of crops that can be grown and the rotations of those crops. Farmers are quite likely to resist the adoption of new technology that restricts their flexibility. With fluctuating market prices, farmers are acting rationally by wanting to maintain flexibility.

5. Economics. Under the classical model of adoption of commercial innovations, the more likely an innovation will provide concrete economic benefits, the greater the likely rate of adoption. While there are many factors that affect farmers' decisions to adopt, and given that farmers do not necessarily act in an economically rational way (Vanclay, 1992a), everything else being equal, it would be reasonable to expect that the more economically beneficial an innovation, the greater the rate of adoption. The ratio between short term and long term benefits will also affect the decision to adopt, with the adoption of practices having a higher ratio of short term benefits taking precedence over practices having only long term benefits. Because environmental innovations rarely provide direct economic benefit to the individual farmer, especially when future discounting techniques are applied (Quiggin, 1987), there would be very little adoption of environmental innovations if farmers were to base their adoption decision solely on economic criteria. Fortunately, farmers employ a range of criteria in their decision making processes. Nevertheless, it is a truism that the more expensive environmental management practices are (in terms of immediate financial and intellectual capital outlay and the labour required, and in terms of the benefit/cost ratio over time), the less likely adoption will be. If farmers were being strictly rational, little adoption of environmental innovations would occur. They ought not be criticised for not adopting when the economic situation does not warrant it.

6. Implementation Cost -- Capital Outlay. In addition to the economics of the innovation (its perceived capacity to increase profits), it is necessary also to consider the capital required to adopt the new technology. Much commercial innovation, and some environmental innovation, requires considerable capital outlay in the form of new machinery, seeds, agri-chemicals, and earthworks. Often, adoption of new techniques may require the farmer to forego income until the new system is established. In this situation, the farmer must have the resources, not only to adopt the new technology, but also to survive the period until the new innovation produces income. In the current period of farm financial crisis, many farmers have negative net incomes, and with declining farm land values and equity levels, many farmers have no borrowing power. In other words, farmers just do not have the capital resources available to them to adopt any new technology that requires a capital outlay. In addition to the lack of capital to outlay, the farm financial crisis means that most farmers are unwilling to take any risk because failure might have disastrous consequences. Risk taking behaviour is more likely when the farmer can afford the consequences of failure (but see Cancian, 1979). For the more marginal producers -- even in cases where there may be clear economic reasons for adoption -- marginal farmers may be unwilling to adopt new technology. They are structurally unable to deal with the consequences of potential failure and they normally lack the capital required to invest in any change.

7. Implementation Cost -- Intellectual Outlay. In addition to the capital costs associated with adoption of new technology, there are also intellectual costs. Farmers may have to learn new ways of doing things. Many of the new recommended farming strategies require much greater knowledge about cropping systems, and about the chemicals that are used in modern agriculture. This classification is similar to 'complexity' but relates to the knowledge base of the individual farmer rather than to an objective measure of complexity. Farmers would not be unique in attempting to minimise the amount of knowledge needed in order to conduct their operations. Many farmers have not had a good formal education, many are in their 50s and 60s, and many have not had the motivation, or financial wherewithal, to engage in further education. In such circumstances, the intellectual task of mastering a new technology may not be viewed by the farmer as worthwhile (or even possible).

8. Risk and Uncertainty. Risk is usually associated with commercial innovation because it refers to farmers' concerns that the capital and other resources invested in adopting the technology will not result in any benefits. However, the concept also refers to environmental innovations, in that farmers need to be sure that the conservation technology will actually provide the anticipated environmental benefits and outcomes. There is an element of risk. Farmers could expend resources adopting a new technology, buying new machinery, and altering the management of the farm in order to farm more sustainably, but with the new technology actually failing to solve the environmental problems it was intended to solve. In this sense, the risk is always greater for environmental innovations than for commercial innovation. With commercial innovations, the only risk is capital outlay and perhaps a yield difference for one season. With environmental innovations, the risk includes not only the capital resources expended -- which are often considerable when production strategies are required to be altered -- and the production for that season, but the chance of continued environmental degradation and the production of future seasons if the degradation is not stopped. While farmers do not necessarily make conscious and sophisticated analyses of the degrees of risk in adopting technology (the information required to do this is seldom available), they are aware of the implications of particular choices.

9. Conflicting Information. No new technology, especially that designed for conservation purposes, has unequivocal support in relation to its applicability and effectiveness. Farmers receive information from numerous -- and often contradictory -- sources (Vanclay, 1992a). In a situation where there is already some uncertainty, conflicting information further suggests that non adoption is an appropriate management strategy. That many farmers interpret the drive toward 'sustainability' as one directed by governments and promoted by 'green' movements is another reason that they may be suspicious about, and reluctant to adopt, conservation practices. Some feel that 'city' ideas are being forced upon them -- something which, unfortunately, can act to undermine the status and legitimacy of sustainability (Morrisey and Lawrence, 1995).

10. Environmental Perception. The media, especially the rural press, are an important source of information for farmers (Woods *et al.*, 1993). Conflicting information within the external sources of information is one reason for non adoption, but another reason for non adoption is when images presented by the media conflict with the farmer's own experience and knowledge. Considerable research has established that farmers are likely to adopt environmental management techniques when, among other things, they consider themselves to be personally at risk from environmental degradation (Vanclay, 1986; Rickson *et al.*, 1987). However, as suggested in Chapter 5, much of the extension literature, conservation literature, and general media reports, depict land degradation in its most dramatic forms -- something which militates against the acceptance by farmers that their own properties might be in need of land and water conservation measures. They will often claim that their own farms look nothing like what is portrayed in the media (which is likely, indeed, to be true) and also tend to deny that their farms may need conservation works -- even when it is accepted that serious environmental problems may be occurring in the locality (Vanclay and Cary, 1989; Vanclay, 1992a; Vanclay, 1992b). Where farmers actually do experience land degradation in its most severe forms, farmers may feel powerless to address the problem, and adopt a fatalistic attitude rather than to undertake any reclamation action or to change, in any fundamental way, their management practices (Williams, 1979; Chamala *et al*., 1984).

11. *Physical Infrastructure.* Economists and physical scientists readily accept that the lack of appropriate infrastructure in the region is a barrier to adoption. Many types of commodities are tied to particular marketing infrastructures that may not exist in certain areas. Consequently, adoption is not likely unless the appropriate infrastructure exists. Suppliers (and supplies) of inputs, the existence of equipment (which could be seen as a capital cost), the available of contractors or a (skilled) labour force if necessary, access to markets, and a mechanism or delivery to markets, are all components of the necessary physical infrastructure. The availability of consultants and/or extension personnel skilled in the productivity enterprise being considered, as well as the available of other sources of information, could also be regarded as physical infrastructure.

12. *Social Infrastructure.* In the same way that we can conceive of a physical infrastructure, we can also consider a social infrastructure. Farmers frequently suggest that other farmers are an important source of information about farming. Where centralised marketing arrangements have existed -- such as was the case in past decades, in Australia -- many farmers have not regarded themselves to be in direct competition with their neighbours, making sharing of ideas, knowledge, and sometimes equipment, commonplace. Except for a small number of maverick innovators, most farmers would not want to be the only one to undertake a new practice, or grow a new crop. Consequently, adoption must normally wait until there is sufficient interest in the innovation to promote wide-scale adoption. An 'agreeable' social infrastructure is necessary for widespread adoption.

13. *Farming Subcultures and Styles of Farming.* The notion of a social infrastructure is helpful in viewing farming as a social and cultural activity. Yet, it still maintains a physical conceptualisation of the 'barriers to adoption'. To fully appreciate the notion of farming and farm and environmental management as a cultural practice is to accept the legitimacy of farming subcultures and farming styles. Sociologically, it is known that the influence of the farming peer group is of great importance (Vanclay, 1992a), and the concept of opinion leaders has been fundamental to the establishment of trial sites in extension practice. Conforming to subcultural norms is a fundamental aspect of social behaviour in cohesive groups which are different from (although forming part of) wider society. Thus, it is possible to talk of an academic subculture, a 'deviant' subculture, an 'inmate' subculture (see Waters and Crook, 1993) or one of the farming subcultures (farming styles) in a particular region. As suggested in the preceding chapter, farming subcultures endorse acceptable views about the agricultural practices of that group. Part of the reason why land degradation occurs is because farming subcultures have not, up until this time, imposed significant sanctions against inappropriate environmental management. Within farming subcultures, in Australia at least, there is a notion of individualism -- that is, that individual farmers have the right to do what they like with their farms. This notion of independence also means that farmers do not critically comment on the farming practices of other farmers directly to those farmers, even when they do not agree with the way those farmers are running their farms. (This is not to deny, of course, the extent of discussion -- in other social settings -- about the practices of farmers.) The subculture -- based on the perpetuation of a particular set of values -- tends to ostracise those whose views, opinions, values and attitudes do not accord with those within the subculture. This social control mechanism both justifies continuing practices and excludes those who are unwilling to conform to those practices. The subculture is not always prescriptive -- change is possible and not all individuals adhere to the subculture -- but the subculture is, nevertheless, a powerful force in resisting change.

An important feature of farming subcultures (or farming styles) is that if specific environmental management practices are not part of the subculture, adoption in that group is unlikely to occur -- irrespective of the benefits which may be predicted. Conversely, when environmental practices and environmental thinking enter the subculture, mass adoption has a greater likelihood of occurring, irrespective of any perceived disadvantages. The important thing in the promotion of environmental management is the acceptance of the practices and thinking within the subculture or farming style.

Evaluation

The above factors help to explain why farmers' non adoption of commercial and especially environmental innovations is understandable, logical, and quite likely rational (certainly within the concept of substantive rationality). As such, farmer interest in innovative environmental management practices is unlikely whether traditional extension techniques or the 'new' extension approaches are used.

Furthermore, farmers' adherence to what might be considered non-rational aspects of farming subcultures or farming styles, such as having an anti-change sentiment, or a distrust of outside 'urban' experts, must be considered both as an understandable response in situations where past advice has been found wanting, and as a legitimate and acceptable aspect of decision-making. Scientists -- as with every other group in society -- are enmeshed within social power relations which help to promote particular solutions to particular problems in ways which support their own interests. It might be entirely appropriate for farmers to reject advice they perceive to be in the interests of some other group, rather than their own. Scientists, like all other groups in socety, engage in legitimate behaviour that would not necessarily be interpreted strictly as rational. Behaviour that is consistent with social and cultural expectations, but is nonetheless not rational, should be considered legitimate human behaviour. When research scientists or extension officers patronisingly criticise farmers' behaviour as being not rational, they are not making an informed evaluation about farmers' behaviour, they are passing a normative or value judgement about farmers. Non adoption should be seen as both rational, and legitimate, from the perspective of the farmer.

The acceptance by extension practitioners of the factors discussed above is growing, particularly in terms of the physical and technical difficulties, however there still remains a refusal to accept the cultural and social bases of farm management. The fundamental point that farming must be seen as a cultural practice continues to be ignored (see Guerin and Guerin, 1994).

CONCLUSION

When examining adoption of innovations from the perspective of the farmer, the non adoption of much new technology, especially many of the environmental innovations, has a rational basis. In addition to technical reasons for non adoption, the reasons given by farmers for not adopting can be classified into several broad headings which provide rational reasons -- in the eyes of farmers -- for non adoption. Other aspects of farmer resistance to change which form part of farming subcultures and farming styles must be considered to be legitimate aspects of social organisation and interaction, not as deficiencies in the behaviour or attitudes of those farmers.

Given this perspective, and the fundamental nature of the differences between commercial and environmental innovations, the promotion of environmental management in agriculture by agricultural extension agencies will be problematic. This is especially so given the severity of environmental degradation in Australia and the apparent necessity for action by extension agencies.

Nevertheless, in past decades, Australian extension agencies have been using traditional models and concepts of extension which are based on an inappropriate model of adoption and which fail to deal satisfactorily with environmental issues. Although some extension agencies and universities have attempted to change the basis of extension knowledge (through the development, for example, of new theories about group facilitation) and extension practice (as with Landcare and other group extension approaches), the notion still persists that recalcitrant farmers have not been capable of recognising what is in their own best interests. Patronising attitudes displayed by agricultural research groups, and occasionally by extension officers, are the result of a failure to appreciate the issues at the farm level.

Given the environmental necessity of overcoming degradation in Australian farming systems, agricultural extension should be considered as a relevant policy instrument. What should be understood is that the greatest potential for change in environmental management appears to be change of the farming subculture or style of farming, and that group extension and similar approaches which promote shared learning are likely to be most appropriate.

Many of the criticisms by farmers of environmental management practices relate to the perceived inappropriateness of those practices. This clearly suggests that agricultural research is out of touch with farmers, and that extension agencies which naively promote the products of agricultural research are failing -- in the context of the community concerns for the impacts of environmental degradation -- properly to understand and serve the interests of farmers and the community as a whole.

Further social research into understanding farming subcultures and styles of farming, and into developing mechanisms that will facilitate adoption, especially of environmentally sustainable techniques and strategies, through these farming subcultures and styles, needs to be undertaken. New extension models which incorporate farmer concerns need to be developed (see Clark and Coffey, 1993). We may even see, as agricultural science and extension are reconstructed, the 'laggards' of the past becoming the innovators of the future (see Flora, 1992), at least in terms of environmental management. The task is not necessarily to speed up the transfer of knowledge that is already known (that which may contain the biases of traditional science), it is to overcome the partial ideological and compartmentalised nature of existing thinking in agricultural science (see Kloppenburg, 1992) and to move to more holistic ways of understanding the farmer in the context of the wider social world (see Dunn, 1991).

This task will not be easy. Consideration also needs to be given to the wider structural issues affecting farmers, and of which farmers themselves may not be aware (Lawrence, 1987; Buttel *et al.*, 1990; Lawrence and Vanclay, 1992; Lawrence and Vanclay, 1994). Finally, extension practices which seek to achieve involvement of farmers but do not address these structural issues nor deal adequately with group processes (see Chamala and Mortiss, 1990), farmer subculture (Vanclay, 1992a), the influence of rural elites (Gray, 1991a; Gray, 1992) and the power of agrarian ideology (Gray, 1991b) are unlikely to provide anything but partial solutions to complex eco-social problems.

AGRICULTURAL EXTENSION FAILURES AND VIRTUES

INTRODUCTION: THE CRISIS OF EXTENSION

As a consequence of their own financial constraints and altered priorities State governments in Australia are reducing extension services, segmenting their client base, and privatising their operations. Despite rhetoric about 'community development', 'group facilitation', and 'farmer directed extension', many modern extension programs such as group extension are being adopted by governments not because of their superior effectiveness, but rather as a means of reducing the costs of providing those services (Lawrence *et al.*, 1992; Vanclay, 1993b,1994b,c). Older forms of publicly-funded agricultural extension have been severely criticised in recent times (Buttel *et al.*, 1990; Kloppenburg, 1991; Vanclay and Lawrence, 1994a) and support of such extension is waning, both in terms of the withdrawal of state support and in terms of the lack of advocates. Within extension agencies (which might be expected to champion the need for enhanced extension services) there appears to be a grudging acceptance of the new economic order and what this means for extension. These agencies have been preoccupied with rationalisation and restructuring, cost recovery and user-pays, and appear to have fully accepted the economic rationalist rhetoric promulgated by government. While, in Australia, there has been a growing commitment to newer, group extension practices, and to so-called 'bottom-up' models of extension, this has occurred largely because of the disarray in traditional extension and not because of any evaluation of the effectiveness of the new models to deliver more desirable outcomes. And where these new models are adopted, not only is their use inconsistent with the objectives of State agenda, but their effectiveness is being compromised because of the political and economic environment in which they are being utilised.

Nevertheless, at the same time as there has been a growing realisation that traditional extension methods have not been sufficiently effective in promoting adoption of new management practices and technologies (particularly those relating to environmental concerns), there has been -- as a direct outcome of the mounting severity of environmental problems -- an increasing need for extension. Thus, in Australia and the USA, and to a lesser extent Europe, agricultural extension is in a period of crisis. The crisis has taken a number of forms: a financial crisis relating to the continued reduction in government funding and support; an effectiveness crisis based on the recognition that traditional extension programs appear to be less than successful in promoting desirable environmental management practices; a legitimation crisis concerning the questioning by farmers of the relevance of the services provided to the farm sector; and a theoretical or paradigmatic crisis where the rejection of traditional models of extension has left a theoretical void (Vanclay, 1993b).

THE FAILURE OF TRADITIONAL EXTENSION

Traditional extension methods have only had limited success in promoting the widespread adoption of new management practices and technology. The characteristics of technologies that were readily adopted have been widely studied and identified. In general, technologies that were: add-on; commensurate with other farm activities; clearly profitable; did not require a substantial capital or intellectual outlay; involved little risk; did not require a major change to farm management; were simple; could be adopted in parts; were widely and uniformly supported by extension agencies, other farmers and farm literature; and did not reduce farm flexibility, were more likely to be adopted than those which did not exhibit these features (see Chapter 6 and Buttel *et al.*, 1990; Vanclay, 1992a,b,d,e). Many production-oriented practices clearly fitted the description of innovations likely to be adopted. Conservation practices, however, tend to be very different and are less likely to be adopted.

Traditionally, extension has been a 'one-to-one' activity, with individual extension officers attempting to change the behaviour of individual farmers. Recognition of the existence of farming subcultures and viewing farming as a cultural activity provides sociological substance to farmers' reluctance to change. Normally only maverick, entrepreneurial or innovative farmers were prepared to take a chance with new technology (Vanclay, 1992a). Although real differences between extension officers and farmers may be slight (Earle *et al.*, 1981), real and imagined differences were exacerbated within the subcultures of both groups, and consequent stereotyping produced perceptions and attitudes not conducive to trust and respect -- requisite bases of effective extension. Among some extension service providers, a condescending attitude towards farmers has been identified which accords little respect for the knowledge and experience farmers possess. Farmers may also not understand the role of extension and of agricultural research, and may view extension advice as either impractical or irrelevant to the immediate needs of the farm. In a social environment bordering at times on mutual distrust, there can be little productive interchange of ideas.

With many extension officers receiving, at best, a smattering of social science training, few have been aware of the important social factors affecting adoption and farm life: for example, the social constraints under which farmers operate, the importance of group processes in endorsing change in agriculture, the role of women in farm decision making, and life cycle and inheritance factors which influence decisions to adopt new technologies and practices. Typically, there is only a partial understanding of farmer decision-making processes. There is also a tendency, on the part of extension officers, uncritically to accept the products of science as the salvation for commercial farming. In other words, in a postmodern world which has come to reject Big Science, extension personnel might be accused of having a dated faith in the ability of science to produce results of benefit to society and the individual farmer. Extension officers have also tended to assume that farmer decision making, their own, and that of scientists, is based on a logical calculation of risks, costs and benefits. Not only is there no provision within this view that there might be various weightings put to different components in the equation (decision-making process) by different groups, but there is a general refusal to accept that farmer decision making -- and their own -- may be based on more nebulous processes (such as what is considered to be socially and culturally acceptable by members of their social group). Farmer decision making appears to be based largely on what farmers believe to be 'good farm management'. And this, in turn, is part of a locally sanctioned approach to farming which tends to endorse particular approaches and actions over others. Within such a framework, farmers adopt a farming style which is normally in accord with local norms which both proscribe and prescribe acceptable practices.

There is also a personal, psychological, dimension to farmer resistance. Farmers are likely to be, on average, much older than the extension officers with whom they deal. They may have had many extension officers telling them many things over many years. In virtually all cases, the practice being promoted was one 'sold' to the farmer as the key to profitability and management effectiveness. In some cases, the promised benefits did not eventuate. Farmers are, and may be justified in being, a little sceptical of the packages, products and knowledge which extension officers promote. In the last chapter, a range of reasons was provided detailing why it was rational for farmers not to adopt new technology.

When Australian farmers have been surveyed about agricultural extension, it has been revealed that one of the most important concerns is the lack of practicality of the advice being provided (Vanclay and Lockie, 1993; Vanclay and Glyde, 1994). Another is the declining funding of extension services. It is important to note that although farmers may be quite critical of extension services, they are still strongly in favour of keeping them.

THE IMPORTANCE OF AN ENVIRONMENTAL IMPERATIVE

In traditional extension with respect to commercial innovations, non adoption is inconsequential -- perhaps it might mean that non adopting individual farmers would be financially disadvantaged. Since adoption was regarded as an individual decision, the consequences of non-adoption were largely individual. At the aggregate level, governments have historically been keen to promote new practices because of the national benefits to be gained from enhanced production, but there was no overwhelming motivation for concern about non adoption. In more prosperous times, there has been no need for accountability of extension agencies or extension methods. Adoption of new technology did occur, and the extension agencies were given the credit, whether they deserved it or not.

Environmental concerns add a new dimension to the issue of effectiveness in the delivery of extension services. The effects of non-adoption of environmental practices are borne not only by an individual farmer but more so by other people: other farmers, downstream users; people who share the catchment; and future generations. Since agricultural land is, ultimately, a non-replenishable resource -- one that is being continually diminished by urban expansion -- the nation may be viewed as suffering as the resource base declines through environmental degradation and through loss of agricultural land to non-farm use. Thus, the community has a vested interest in ensuring the widespread adoption of environmental management practices and the effective and efficient delivery of extension services.

As described earlier, salinity is a major problem affecting land users and downstream water users. Increasing soil acidity reduces the productive potential of the land. Erosion leads to a loss of the productive resource and to downstream (and downwind) siltation problems. Nutrient decline and declining soil structure lead to irreversible damage to the resource. Erosion and the leaching of excessively applied fertilisers and pesticides lead to water quality problems, particularly eutrophication of waterways and the increased occurrence of toxic blue-green algae blooms. Overgrazing and the activities of introduced species such as rabbits, goats, and donkeys lead to accelerated erosion. Activities of other feral animals, particularly cats, have a major effect on wildlife reserves.

All these causes of environmental degradation have long term effects for the whole community. Consequently, while extension agencies could reasonably ignore the fact that some farmers did not adopt production-related innovations, environmental issues pose a new problem. Non-adopting farmers are not so much threatening their own livelihood, but are affecting the livelihood of future generations of Australians. Thus, governments, agricultural extension agencies and the whole community have an increased responsibility to ensure that widespread adoption of beneficial environmental management practices occurs.

THE APPROPRIATE ENVIRONMENTAL POLICY INSTRUMENT

The existence of an environmental imperative does not necessarily lead to the acceptance of an argument that the public must subsidise with cash 'handouts' on-farm environmental improvements, but it does provide strong support for concern about non adoption and for concern about the effectiveness of extension. The Working Group on Sustainable Agriculture (1991) canvassed the idea of subsidising inputs to agriculture which were environmentally beneficial (such as lime to combat acidity). Three problems were recognised. First, if the problem is on-site and has no external effects, subsidisation will benefit only the individual (there is no public gain). Second, even where there are offsite 'externalities', it may be impossible to use subsidies in a way which targets particular unsound management practices.

Third, once subsidies are capitalised into land values they lose their effectiveness in catalysing change (Working Group on Sustainable Agriculture, 1991: 77). Another concern has been raised by Rose (1992). If production subsidies are employed, they will have the effect of increasing the intensity of production -- of land and of applications of synthetic fertilisers, pesticides and herbicides. In so doing they contribute to the environmental degradation which they were expected to help overcome.

This aside, it has been convincingly demonstrated, at least on one occasion, that the economic losses associated with soil degradation are unacceptably high and that programs to address them are not only needed but are cost effective. Avery (1992) has reported that Victoria experiences productivity losses of about $48 million from soil structural decline which affects about 14.5 million hectares of that State. It was further calculated that about $12.5 million in productivity could be retained by the implementation of an appropriate crop management program. Called SoilCare, the program was expected to cost some $260,000 over the two years of its operation -- a benefit to cost ratio of some 50:1. Importantly, the program combines both group processes and one-to-one extension services -- something which it is hoped will lead to the incorporation into the program of those who might otherwise not participate.

The Working Party on Sustainable Agriculture (1991), after looking (albeit briefly) at the expenditure of public dollars on subsidies and other forms of assistance, endorsed Landcare activities as the most effective. Community group activities which were based on 'awareness programs' and other forms of group information exchange were the preferred strategy for public investment. Advantages of the group approach were viewed as: the farmer peer group can support and encourage change; groups have a wide skill base necessary for discussion of complex issues such as sustainable agriculture; extension agents' resources are used more efficiently and effectively; community attitudes are incorporated into decisions (Working Party on Sustainable Agriculture, 1991: 88). The role of extension (in its broadest form) was seen as crucial in the Landcare approach to environmental improvement in agriculture -- although its pro-agribusiness recommendation that there should be an 'integration' of private and public sector extension services was made without grounds (and without, one might expect, a great deal of thought). Reeve and Black (1993) reported, from a national survey of farmers, that there was majority support for increased education to alert farmers of the damage being done by existing agricultural practices. Farmers in the sample also endorsed government provision of financial incentives which might assist farmers to move quickly to those practices -- such as stubble retention, deep ripping and new rotations -- which have been shown to be environmentally beneficial.

STRUCTURAL ADJUSTMENT

Structural adjustment in Australian agriculture, promoted by governments wanting to assist efficient farmers to remain in agriculture and to induce those deemed unviable to leave, is one of the major platforms of agricultural reform in Australia (see National Farmers' Federation, 1993). But there have been questions raised about the ultimate outcomes of the scheme --

particularly its overall effectiveness in improving the benefits which farmers and the nation gain from ever-larger farms (Lawrence, 1994). The argument that Australian farmers must obey international price signals -- largely independent of any other considerations -- is essentialist and apolitical. By placing the emphasis on the economics of production, rather than, say, the ability of the farmer to produce in a manner which improves sustainability, the scheme endorses production for unstable, increasingly competitive, markets. It thereby reinforces the tendency for farmers to use inputs for productivity and efficiency gains. These products -- from synthetic fertilisers to agri-chemicals -- and the land management techniques necessary to produce the large volumes of output required for economically viable operation, are the ones which have contributed to the degradation of the environment. At a time when resources are being depleted and the world marketplace is glutted with products, it must be questioned whether state assistance for adjustment is preferable to state assistance for the promotion of sustainable options.

Australian governments and farmers appear to believe that the economic logic of their arguments at GATT (where the Cairns group of free traders was largely responsible for having agricultural protection discussed and new 'free trade' policies implemented) -- will lead, in some inevitable fashion, to increases in returns to Australia's relatively unprotected farmers.

This position is politically naive. In Britain and France, for example, any dismantling of protection for agriculture is sure to be matched by 'replacement' heritage or other schemes which, in paying farmers to keep their hedgerows, or maintain walkways for the public, or restore farm buildings, will effectively be farm subsidisation by another name. The point is, the 'rural' in those nations is a place for consumption as much as production (Marsden *et al.*, 1993). Tourists, people pursuing active outdoor recreation, those wanting to purchase regional produce on weekend drives, retirees, and the new 'gentry' who restore fifteenth century cottages in rural locations, have ensured that their 'meanings' for rural have had prominence in countryside planning. Through heritage and other schemes European society is therefore paying its farmers to create what it wants: picture-card rural scenes which are quintessentially English (or Dutch, French, or German). But they also continue to produce foods, and that production must be seen to be subsidised. Its subsidisation will continue to prevent Australian farmers from gaining market position. It makes good sense in the eyes of the Europeans to help to preserve rural villages, peasant farming, small scale agriculture and other features of regional culture.

In Australia, the Rural Adjustment Scheme is a particular policy instrument designed to produce a particular outcome: a more efficient and competitive agricultural sector. It takes no account of the needs of rural communities and, to date at least, has had little interest in the environmental sustainability of the properties with which it deals.

The marketplace has penalised young farmers with large debts, or those who expanded before interest rates peaked, and/or who paid artificially high prices for land. The very farmers who were likely to have been more productive and who responded to the market's (and government's) call for a more efficient agriculture, have suffered as interest rates have risen and as commodity prices have continued to fall relative to input costs. The Rural Adjustment Scheme has tended to perpetuate what the market has 'determined' -- endorsing the very market signals which have contributed year after year to the further marginalisation of a section of producers, and the subsequent need to increase farm size of some by removing others (see Lawrence, 1987; 1994).

Another governmental strategy that appears to have had a detrimental impact on farmers has been the dismantling of state monopoly commodity marketing boards. One of the alleged purposes of this action was to allow differentiation of grades of produce and to allow high quality producers to gain full advantage of their better product. Premiums for quality produce were paid by the marketing boards, but it was considered that there would be more differentiation under a deregulated privatised system. Under a new system, it was argued that farmers would be more attuned to the market and would respond in a more appropriate way to market demands. Economic rationalist discourses which pervaded public service decision-making in the 1980s and 1990s justified free enterprise solutions rather than those (Keynesian-style) interventions which had characterised agricultural policy throughout the period from the First World War to the mid 1970s (Lawrence, 1987; 1995).

Economic rationalism ignores farmers' interests in having their (largely homogenous) products sold internationally via farmer-organised monopolies. Far from being cheaper for farmers, the percentage payment to the marketing agent is often greater than that charged via state marketing. In addition, there is no guarantee that a private commodity agent will handle all the bulk produce harvested by the farmer. Farmers now have to make a variety of decisions based on when to sell their products. This has lead many into the unfamiliar world of future trading. All in all, it means that farmers must invest considerably more time in the marketing of the product. In some cases, farmers are ill- equipped for the social and technical skills they need to undertake this analysis.

The economic crisis in agriculture has meant that farmers' disposable incomes have been reduced to a minimum. Many have faced an uncertain future. Employing what amount to little more than 'survival strategies' to minimise input costs and to see them through the crisis has meant that adoption of environmental management practices has been a low priority. Furthermore, when their overall concentration is upon ensuring their survival, new management practices and new ideas take second place.

The economic constraints of farming must be blamed for hampering what might have been much greater activity on the part of farmers to improve the agricultural environment. Farmer surveys consistently reveal that farmers are environmentally aware and concerned, and that they have a stewardship ethic (Vanclay, 1986,1992a). Nevertheless, it has also been found that a reliance on voluntary action in this situation does not lead, unequivocally, to increased adoption of environmental management practices. If the environmental imperative is to be taken seriously, extension agencies need to take deliberate and considered action.

It is somewhat revealing to consider the findings of the national study of farmers undertaken by Reeve and Black (1993). It would appear that a significant minority of farmers are not so enamoured of current practices as to dismiss the moves toward a low input, organic, agriculture for Australia.

> If organic or low-input farming systems were available with the same management complexity, risk profile, profitability, marketing arrangements, information availability and local back-up as for chemical-based systems, it is likely that 20 to 30 per cent of Australia's farmers would make the transition to organic or low-input systems. This ... highlights the importance of continuing research both on the biophysical aspects of agricultural sustainability and on the social and economic structures which would facilitate the adoption of organic or low-input practices (Reeve and Black, 1993: 132).

TRADITIONAL EXTENSION AND ITS DEFICIENCIES

There are numerous criticisms of traditional extension and the use of the adoption diffusion model dating back to the early 1970s. It has, for example, been criticised for being a scientific research based, largely top-down, process about the transfer of information and ideas - one which accords with a social-psychological model of individual decision making (Buttel *et al.*, 1990; Vanclay and Lawrence, 1994a). As such, it has been accused of being reductionist, unable to provide a basis for the incorporation of a large number of farmers, and as being simply a vehicle for the imposition of technical solutions for what are complex (and often largely 'people-based') problems. Nevertheless, institutional inertia and other reasons have meant that Australian extension agencies have been required to work within the constraints and limitations of the traditional model. Some agencies have attempted to incorporate new models of extension -- even though these models have not been perfected and bring with them their own problems. Because of the commitment of extension agencies to traditional thinking, it is worth recounting the fundamental criticisms of traditional extension. Five important criticisms of traditional extension are predominant and have relevance in the promotion of environmental innovations.

First, extension -- based on the linear model of knowledge utilisation -- has accepted, uncritically, the products of agricultural science research as being improvements (Fliegel and van Es, 1983) and has taken 'a promotional posture toward technological change' (Buttel *et al.*, 1990: 46-7). Technology has been viewed as an 'autonomous force' (Buttel, 1994). Extension has identified its task as 'selling' technology to farmers without considering its appropriateness (usefulness and impacts). Kloppenburg (1991) argues that extension (and rural sociology) has become the handmaiden of the scientific-industrial agribusiness complex. It has tended to accept that all farming problems can be overcome by the continued application of conventional science. Even when it is perceived that science has caused the problems, the solutions have been framed within the existing paradigm -- more 'science' must be harnessed in the discovery of those solutions. From this perspective, extension agents are seen literally as 'agents of the state' in the promotion of practices which the state endorses and which, ultimately, conform to the economic desires of an agribusiness sector which sells technical packages/products to the farming industry.

Secondly, this uncritical acceptance by extension has resulted in considerable social (Röling *et al.*, 1976; Goss, 1979; Lowe *et al.*, 1990) and ecological (Stockdale, 1977; Clark and Lowe, 1992) impacts as a result of the technological change fostered by extension. The adoption/diffusion model itself ignores many of the important social issues such as the unequal distribution of impacts and benefits of the technology (Röling *et al.*, 1976; Goss, 1979). The service provided by the extension agencies reaches, differentially, the better educated and more economically powerful farmers.

Thirdly, the adoption/diffusion model only applies to production innovations and not to the adoption of conservation technology. Despite establishing that the correlates of adoption for environmental innovation are different from those for commercial innovation (Pampel and van Es, 1977; Taylor and Miller, 1978) extension has not, until recently, examined in any self-critical manner, its previous overwhelming commitment to the adoption/diffusion model. One aspect of this issue is that extension based on the linear model is seen as the promotion of discrete technologies (those having the characteristics of a commodity, see Röling, 1992a) whereas environmental management is not only about individual technologies but about different ways of thinking and about the management of whole systems (Dunn, 1991). A further serious implication of the failure to perceive of the difference between commercial and environmental innovations is suggested by Buttel *et al.*, (1990) who claim that by this approach, rural sociology (as a discipline) supports, in a narrow way, voluntarist (non-regulatory) approaches to resource management. It tends to overlook or reject alternative positions, such as regulatory approaches, because the model assumes that adoption of the desired technology or behaviour will always eventually occur.

Fourthly, farmers' 'indigenous technical knowledge' (local knowledge -- about such things as weather cycles, ploughing times, vegetation growth or livestock management -- which farmers accumulate as part of the practice of farming, but which might not have any official status outside farming circles), has been marginalised, trivialised, subordinated and ignored by the 'techno-strategic discourse' that has dominated agriculture (Kloppenburg, 1991). Traditional extension tended to assume that the majority of farmers had little to contribute to the discussion about what was needed in agricultural technical development. Given the hegemony of technocratic discourse within advanced capitalism, those adopting were seen as 'innovators' and held in high regard, while those not adopting (and/or rejecting) new technologies were labelled as 'laggards' and viewed disparagingly. In this way the knowledge and skills of the latter group were marginalised and discredited, virtually eliminating any challenge, from 'below', of 'scientific' agriculture. Agricultural extension is seen in these terms as espousing, uncritically, pro-corporate ideology and the expansion of transnational agribusiness (see Lawrence, 1987).

Finally, the social, political and cultural context of agriculture and of adoption behaviour has been ignored. Adoption is seen as an individual decision based on formal rationality, while the structure of agriculture itself is taken to be independent of any social or political context (Long and van der Ploeg, 1989; Vanclay, 1992a).

In addition to these general criticisms it is apparent that the classical adoption/diffusion model has other faults. Adoption does not always occur according to the predicted distribution. In practice, the shape of the cumulative adoption curve, or the frequency/time curve, varies considerably (Buttel *et al.*, 1990). Adoption does not necessarily follow the suggested stages from awareness through knowledge, trial and adoption. With environmental innovations, it is not always possible to trial the new technologies since the new technologies tend to be indivisible and therefore cannot be adopted in 'part'. Farmers are understandably cautious about committing themselves to complete adoption of management practices that they have not trialed. The classical model assumes that awareness and knowledge will always filter through to all sections of the farming community -- something shown to be not necessarily the case. Even with a concerted awareness-raising campaign, knowledge of an innovation does not permeate to all groups. Farmers utilise a range of information sources and different farmers have different information sources. Furthermore, as we pointed out in Chapter 5, awareness and knowledge do not always lead to adoption. In some cases, particularly with environmental innovations, awareness and knowledge may be held by farmers, but because of other factors affecting the decision making process, adoption does not occur. (In the traditional model of extension these are known -- as suggested above -- as the barriers to adoption.) Sometimes the knowledge basis necessary for adoption is held by farmers but rejected by them -- often for good reason -- because the knowledge basis defies the farmers' notion of common sense and historical experience (see Barr and Cary, 1992).

Campbell and Junor (1992) have pointed to several other concerns with traditional extension: there has been confusion about the meaning of extension, leading to a lack of direction in the provision of services, and a loss of professionalism; and that one of the main deficiencies has been the failure to engage farmers in the early stages of research and development.

THE RECONSTRUCTION OF AGRICULTURAL SCIENCE AND SUSTAINABLE AGRICULTURE

Kloppenburg (1991) endorses the 'farmer first' approach (see Chambers, 1983; Richards, 1985; Chambers *et al.*, 1989) on the grounds that the present scientific 'way of knowing' is inappropriate as a model for future sustainable development and for the extension of democratic principles. It is only in relatively recent times (coinciding with economic crises in agriculture, environmental pollution, agribusiness domination, corrupted markets and concerns about food quality and the impacts of new technologies) that criticism of scientific agriculture is emerging as a strong force in capitalist nations such as the United States and Australia (see Buttel and Newby, 1980; Lawrence, 1987). Kloppenburg argues that by 'reconstructing' agriculture, new insights and perspectives will supposedly develop. Local knowledge can be rediscovered and incorporated into an understanding of sustainable options; feminist approaches can alert us to issues of 'diversity, affection, responsibility, [and] accountability' (Kloppenburg, 1991: 539) and systems thinking can remove current barriers between farmers and agricultural scientists. Unorthodox, alternative approaches are likely to emanate, Kloppenburg argues, from the rediscovery of local knowledge and from the continued critical examination of the impacts of orthodox science. For Kloppenburg, then, the 'crisis' of extension cannot be viewed in isolation from the more general crisis of agriculture -- one brought about by adherence to a narrow set of technocratic methods, products and ideas.

Clearly, Kloppenburg and others (for example, Chambers, 1983; Richards, 1985 Chambers *et al*., 1989) place faith in farmers' ability to develop their own sustainable, affordable and economically productive ideas and techniques which will challenge (and displace) the existing science of agriculture. The assumption is that farmers' knowledge can produce sustainable outcomes in the context of economically productive farming systems. This is to ignore the facts that farmers' knowledge has been utilised in the development of existing practices and knowledge; that farmers have come to rely heavily on existing practices and knowledge and generally endorse scientific applications in agriculture; and that scientific agriculture may be just as capable -- if not more capable -- as indigenous knowledge of finding sustainable solutions (see Molnar *et al*., 1992).

Molnar *et al*.'s (1992) major criticism of Kloppenburg is that he distorts the importance of local knowledge and neglects the limitations, especially the potential short-sightedness and sectionality associated with it. They also claim that farmers are involved in the research process, but that access to involvement tends to be class-related. Greater contribution of farmers to the research process may not, in such circumstances, redress the class imbalance (see Gray, 1992).

Kloppenburg reiterates that extension knowledge is a particular form of knowledge, which, as an uncritical form of pro-agribusiness ideology, is in urgent need of revamping. The challenge would appear to be to alter the mode and context of extension -- from an elitist 'trickle-down' approach to the facilitation of group interaction and problem solving at the local level (see Flora, 1992; Lawrence *et al*., 1992; Röling, 1992b; Vanclay, 1992a). In this way the rejection of farmers' attitudes and farming styles as 'irrational' is less likely to occur. This is likely to facilitate the extension of environmentally sound practices, and have the potential to result in the subsequent improvement in land and water management.

BENEFITS OF TRADITIONAL EXTENSION

Despite these and other criticisms, what should not be overlooked is that some aspects of traditional extension may be quite useful in dealing with environmental issues. Furthermore, the environmental imperative -- to solve the problems of the agricultural environment as a prerequisite to long term agricultural sustainability -- gives a renewed call to extension agencies to evaluate which aspects of their work might assist in the promotion of better environmental practices. It should also be remembered that an essential feature of traditional extension has been that governments have (in general terms) provided it as free service to all farmers. Although it may have been deficient in not having serviced the needs of all farmers, the possibility, at least, existed.

There is one particular feature of traditional extension that allows us to consider it differently from the user pays approaches which have evolved in recent times. There was a social equity principle which provided an undergirding to the provision of state services. All farmers, in this view, were entitled to extension services not matter how poor, distant, old, or (in terms of farm size) small.

Social equity has been, and should continue to be, an important consideration in the provision of extension services. Political and social considerations were often responsible for establishing minimum and maximum farm size, for limiting and promoting farm expansion (by direct regulation, interest rate policies, and other policies that affect land prices), and, via subsidisation and price manipulation, for encouraging the growth of certain types of agricultural production over others.

Today, the farmers being structurally adjusted out of agriculture because of their marginal status are in many cases not marginal because of their own inability to farm, but because of policies which have helped to determine the size of their farm, the products that they grow, the prices that are achieved, the manner in which their produce is marketed and, in a more general sense, their competitiveness in the marketplace.

Given this perspective, and the social role played by agriculture, equity considerations become increasingly important. However, equity considerations achieve their greatest importance in terms of environmental issues. Environmental issues in agriculture, particularly land degradation, suggest there is an obligation on the part of the state to intervene. While the extension agencies were forgiven for any lack of concern about non- adoption of commercial innovations (the non adopters were assumed to be harming no one but themselves) environmental problems create a situation where extension agencies are obliged, in the interests of the wider public, to intervene. There is an environmental imperative on the part of the state to ensure that natural resources are managed in a sustainable manner. Farmers not serviced by extension agencies may wittingly or unwittingly create new, or exacerbate old, environmental problems. Save the introduction of increasingly severe legislatively-based regulation and controls, extension provides one of very few ways the state can monitor, advise and 'cajole' farmers into adopting practices which are considered to be desirable for long term sustainability. (Another is to provide economic or other incentives for farmers to adopt new approaches to farming -- something which does not accord with the anti-interventionist stance of the Federal Government, Opposition and those in Treasury and the Industries Commission, and which, as previously detailed, may bring its own set of problems.)

CHANGES TAKING PLACE TO EXTENSION

Earlier in this chapter, agricultural extension was identified as being in a period of crisis, which could be identified as having the following forms:

- a financial crisis where governments are reducing funding to extension agencies;
- an effectiveness crisis in that extension does not appear to be successful in promoting adoption particularly of environmental innovations;
- a legitimation crisis in that there is a (false) perception that because farmers are critical of extension, farmers believe that extension agencies are therefore not useful; and
- a theoretical or paradigmatic crisis in that the rejection of traditional models of extension and of adoption behaviour has left a theoretical void as there are not sufficiently well developed theories that are widely accepted to take their place.

This crisis of agricultural extension is manifested not only in reduced extension services to farmers, but also in the reduced funding to government-sponsored extension research, in the closure or reduction in the size of university departments of extension, and in the change of name of these departments as they try to gain a new identity. For example, what was the Department of Extension Science at Wageningen Agricultural University in The Netherlands has recently changed its name to the Department of Communication and Innovation Studies. Some of the US Land Grant Universities have had their Land Grant status altered; others have reduced their extension interest. The crisis is further manifested in the confusion that is occurring in Australian extension agencies about the objectives of extension, and how to achieve those objectives.

Extension agencies have developed a range of responses to the economic and environmental crises in agriculture, generally involving the following strategies: to segment their client base and deal only with so-called top-end farmers; to adopt group extension processes partly embracing a bottom-up approach; and to adopt a private sector philosophy and move towards user pays services. In response to farmers' criticisms that extension was not practical, to increase the perceived legitimacy by farmers of extension services, and to give credibility to the new strategies being implemented, extension agencies have utilised farmer participation in the extension and agricultural research process. These strategies also have their problems. Before traditional extension methods, theory, and structures are abandoned or subverted -- fuelled by the desire to bring about changes in farming in the quickest and most effective way -- it is necessary to reconsider what problems might be envisaged as arising from the new approaches.

Problems With The Segmentation Approach

One strategy being employed by extension agencies suffering from reduced funding is to segment their client base. Extension agencies are aware of their limited success in promoting the adoption of new technology. They believe that so-called top-end farmers are better farmers, and that these farmers are the farmers who tend to adopt new technology. They consider that they achieve maximum benefit from their scarce financial resources by concentrating on those farmers whom they believe will adopt new ideas.

Segmentation is not a strategy of targeting. Targeting accepts that there are different client groups that have different interests, and that extension needs to address each group individually. Segmentation is based, instead, on the principle that only top-end farmers need be considered. Extension agencies feel that they are further justified in this approach by the structural aspects of current production: that is, some 80 percent of the output is produced by the top 20 percent of farmers using 80 percent of the land. Why, the argument would go, should we bother with the rest?

While it is generally accepted that top-end farmers are more likely to be adopters (at least adopters of commercial innovations), this may be because extension services have not adequately addressed the needs of the non-adopters. Under traditional models of extension, extension agencies often only dealt with top-end farmers for a wide variety of self-satisfying reasons (see Röling, 1988). Such a strategy was legitimised by the belief that new ideas would eventually trickle-down or diffuse to all sections of the farming community, 'even while you sleep' (Röling, 1988). While such a view may have been naive and self-serving, at least there was still the assumption that eventually all farmers would benefit. Under the segmentation approach, there is no longer such a belief -- extension specifically addresses itself solely to top-end farmers. Traditional extension has been criticised for being patronising and dismissive of average farmers, but such an attitude was only implicit in the extension process as manifested by individuals. With market segmentation this position is explicit -- farmers who are not regarded as top end, do not deserve attention.

The strategy of segmentation is arguably acceptable when concern is about the promotion of commercial innovations, although it is not clear why the general public should pay for extension which will increase the economic efficiency of the already wealthy top-end farmers. Yet, when concern is about environmental management practices, adoption needs to be universal. Because it will not necessarily be obvious to farmers that they have environmental problems, and because the solutions may not be known to farmers, traditional extension is required to reach all farmers.

Although there is no empirical research to substantiate this point -- and there are alternative explanations -- extension officers anecdotally report that poorer, more marginal (so-called 'bottom-end') farmers tend to be worse environmental managers than top-end farmers. The marginal or sub-commercial (lifestyle) farmers who have non-commercial reasons for remaining in agriculture are also unlikely to adopt environmental management practices unless they are certain of their importance (Rickson *et al.*, 1987; Vanclay, 1992a). Without extension, many farmers may fail to appreciate the extent, nature and solutions of environmental problems. Bottom-end farmers tend to have the worst land, land that is most prone to erosion, and land that may well be in the recharge zones responsible for causing salinity. Because of the generalised nature of environmental problems, particularly salinity, a concern (even for top-end farmers) requires a concern about the activities of all farmers in a catchment.

Problems With The User Pays Approach

Another method adopted by extension agencies is to embrace a user-pays approach to the provision of services. Importantly, user-pays approaches are not 'extension' in any traditional sense, since it is about providing a commercial service, not about expanding the knowledge base of people. Such strategies lead inevitably to a conflict of interest between the provision of commercial services for income generation for the agency, and the social objective of encouraging adoption of environmentally sound management practices.

A user-pays approach will implicitly become a segmentation strategy since extension agencies adopting this strategy are more likely to align with top-end farmers who are more likely to make use of their services. This will occur for a variety of reasons. First, farmers will only make use of services that they feel are necessary. The issue of concern is that with many environmental problems, farmers are unlikely to recognise the severity of what is occurring. Furthermore, farmers who are suffering from declining incomes see this situation as a temporary, not a permanent situation. Australian farmers are used to income drops for short periods, due to fluctuating prices, climatic events such as floods and droughts, or plagues of pest species such as rabbits and locusts. In times of low income, Australian farmers adopt survival modes, usually involving reduced inputs. Thus Australian farmers are likely to forego the use of consultants, or the advice of extension agencies if they have to pay for it, in order to reduce their capital expenditure. So, while farmers generally are in favour of maintaining extension services, they may not have the economic ability to utilise those services (Vanclay, 1992a; Cary and Barr, 1992; Barr and Cary, 1992). 'User pays' extension may mean that a great majority of Australian farmers will not have access to the services offered. Farmers, in these circumstances, will not be receiving information which the state believes will enhance agricultural sustainability.

Second, in being charged for information, farmers might be expected to change their attitude towards it. It is quite likely that farmers will cease to share information and ideas for which they have, individually, had to pay. Where such information relates to issues of national significance, such as environmental issues, the much slower diffusion of the ideas would hamper effective environmental management.

Finally, with user pays approaches, extension agents lose contact with farmers. This occurs even when the user pays charges are only levied against the production side of extension. Such loss of contact reduces the agency's ability to involve the farmer in environmental matters, as well as 'removing' individual extension officers from farmers and their problems. This contributes to a loss of learning on behalf on the extension officers as much if not more than it does to farmers (Röling, 1988).

There is an ethical dimension to the issue of user pays charges for environmental management. Many environmental problems are generalised, not localised in their benefits. We have already argued at length that with problems such as salinity, the farmers responsible for causing the problems (creating the accessions to the watertable) are often not those experiencing the problems (experiencing the discharge). In a privatised system of paying for environmental innovations, farmers are unlikely (voluntarily) to pay for advice about management practices from which, individually, they are unlikely to gain benefit. When it is also realised that problems such as salinity may have been caused not by the current management actions of individual farmers, but by the history of landuse -- including governmental policy decisions requiring the clearing of land -- farmers are unlikely to accept that they should shoulder the blame and the costs both of extension advice and of restorative action. Many other environmental problems occurring over large areas -- such as weeds, pests and erosion -- are of a similar 'group' nature. Group approaches would seem, in these circumstances, to be highly desirable.

Full recovery user pays approaches are likely to be appropriate in situations where an extension agency provides an individual service to an individual farmer for a largely commercial reason (even if there are environmental benefits), such as with advice about crop rotation schedules, disease diagnoses, advice about yield improvement, soil testing, or advice about fertiliser requirements. In fact, for some activities, especially soil testing and other forms of testing undertaken on a regular basis, it may be asked why an extension agency is providing these services at all. Partial cost recovery (for example subsidised services) may be appropriate where the agency provides an individual service to an individual farmer, but where there are wider social and environmental benefits and where the cost of the service might be prohibitively high if a full commercial rate was charged, such as the development of farm plans, advice and implementation of structural works such as contour banks, grassed waterways and flumes. Some activities where there is little individual benefit and great public benefit probably should be provided free to farmers, with farmers contributing their time and machinery. This would apply to common access areas, creeks, road reserves and other public land, as well as to awareness raising activities.

Many private consultants earn a good living by providing technical advice and testing equipment. However, it should be realised that not all farmers who need advice of the sort mentioned will be able to pay for that advice. The state is making a conscious decision to 'abandon' to the marketplace those farmers who are economically marginal. Research needs to be undertaken to ascertain the impacts and consequences of the move to 'user pays' in agriculture.

Problems With The Group Extension Approach

Another strategy being adopted by extension agencies is to endorse group and interactive approaches instead of individual extension. Some of the new processes have great promise for encouraging farmer involvement and the sharing of knowledge at the local level (see, for example, Campbell and Siepen, 1994). A critical sociological approach warns us not to overlook the ideological element of the change in focus towards group approaches and sustainability (see Buttel, 1994 in relation to the latter). It may be, for example, that the current rhetoric about a commitment to self-actualisation, farmer empowerment, and of farmers setting agendas and finding solutions to their own problems, masks an intention on the part of the state to reduce its funding and overall commitment to agriculture.

If the motivation for extension agencies to adopt group approaches is based on a commitment to financial constraint, rather than to a more sustainable agriculture, group extension approaches will certainly fail to reach their potential. If resources are insufficient to allow an adequate response to the needs of farmers, they will fail to be an effective means of agricultural extension. In Australia, group extension approaches have actually increased the need for individual extension (Department of Primary Industries and Energy, 1992), because of their effectiveness in motivating change among farmers.

The major problem with a number of group extension approaches is that they rely upon farmer awareness of their own problems. Farmers may not, however, be necessarily aware of the environmental problems which they face either individually or as part of a catchment. Farmers themselves may not be aware of the extent of the environmental problems affecting their land, since many of these processes are invisible and insidious, and farmers may not have any knowledge about how to deal with these problems. As was suggested in earlier chapters, surveys of farmers frequently reveal that although they believe certain environmental problems to be serious, they often feel that the problem is not one they experience on their own properties (Rickson *et al.*, 1987; Vanclay, 1992a). This has to be demonstrated to them, if they are to accept that they do, in fact, 'own' the problem with others in the district.

To the extent that group extension is promoted by governments as a cost saving approach to environmental management, further problems might be expected to develop. An earlier point is of importance here: group extension may increase the demands for individual extension. Failure to respond to those needs will result in lost enthusiasm and to the potential undermining of farmers' commitment to group extension.

There is also some confusion about what constitutes 'bottom-up' extension. To some, bottom-up extension is any process that involves consideration of farmer concerns. To others, farmer involvement is something of a pretence since the agency is still firmly in control of the agenda. Complete bottom-up extension is a process that empowers and facilitates farmers to use their own skills to determine what problems affect them. They are encouraged to set their own agendas. They are encouraged to find solutions to the problems which they, themselves, have identified. In this process, the role of extension agents is not so much the extension of knowledge but of group facilitation.

As part of the philosophy of bottom-up extension, farmers must be free to make mistakes. They may, for example, falsely diagnose their problems or come up with what the experts may consider to be inappropriate solutions. In this system, reliance on farmers' local knowledge to solve problems that are new to their experience, such as many environmental problems, is unlikely to be successful. The insidious nature of such problems means that farmers may still not recognise them -- even after extensive damage might have occurred. While it is possible that many traditional problems may be solved with new extension methods, new problems, particularly environmental problems, may be best dealt with through a combination of new and traditional extension. The cost implications of this may not appeal to state governments which are in the process of dismantling the older forms of extension.

As suggested earlier, a further problem with group extension, particularly the complete concept of group-based extension, is that the groups themselves potentially become manipulated by vested interests with the groups (Röling, 1990; Gray, 1992; Vanclay, 1992a; Leeuwis, 1993a,b; Lockie, 1994a, 1994c, 1995; Morrisey and Lawrence, 1995). Quite likely, the more wealthy, more articulate farmers will come to dominate the groups -- and therefore the new extension process. These are the very same farmers who have been the main clients of (have come to dominate) traditional extension.

It may be possible that the use of group extension and other techniques as part of an educational program of top-down extension would be an effective method. The use of facilitators to encourage solutions to come from within the groups to give the appearance of bottom-up approaches, and thus for farmers to have a greater commitment to the solutions may also be effective. This is somewhere between the completely top-down extension approach, and the completely committed bottom-up approach, and is somewhat akin to the Dutch notion of extension -- voorlichting -- holding the light in front of the farmer so that they may find the path for themselves (Röling, 1988). It is also based, unfortunately, on the view that farmers should be 'manipulated' -- albeit subtly.

Problems with Farmer Participation

In principle, participation by farmers in agricultural research and extension is highly desirable. There is enormous potential for the effectiveness and efficiency of research and extension to be enhanced through the involvement of farmers. Many stages of research and extension -- including: problem identification; the undertaking of research; the dissemination of results; the evaluation of the effectiveness of research; and the setting of research priorities -- would all benefit from the involvement of farmers, and this would ultimately lead to more useful products of research and enhanced adoption rates.

These benefits of participation are largely recognised and accepted by the extension and R&D agencies. The Boards of the R&D agencies have farmer representatives, and require research that is funded to exhibit evidence of farmer participation. But, there is real danger that the participation that does occur is token or symbolic, rather than genuine. Furthermore, there are reasons why having farmer representatives does not demonstrate participation.

In the first place, the diversity within agriculture has already been argued. The small number of farmers who are appointed to the various committees or to be involved in research could not possibly hope to represent the diversity that exists within agriculture. The representatives tend to be appointed from the ranks of top end farmers. In that sense, they do not share the same structural experiences or (sub-)cultural identities as other farmers. Many top end farmers have non-farming identities as well, in business or the professions. They may be appointed to boards because of their demonstrated skills in their non-farming activities, with their being a farmer an added bonus to provide legitimacy and credibility. Either deliberately or accidentally, these token farmers will not represent the interests of all farmers, they will only represent the views of the farmers who share their farming style -- that is, other top end farmers.

Even if the representatives were altruistic, fully intending to attempt to represent the diversity of farmers' interests, they could not do so because of their marginalised status on the committees. The farmer representatives constitute only a small percentage on the committees, and are therefore not a significant voting power. In any case, the nature and operation of committees is such that if the representatives were novices, they would be subsumed by the formal procedure and find that they have little ability to influence proceedings. Where the representatives are not novices, they are at risk of becoming bureaucratised, such that they have fully accepted the hegemonic agenda and no longer share a value system or ideology with other farmers.

A final problem, both contributing to the marginalised status of genuine and altruistic farmer representatives, and to their inability to influence proceedings, is that the nature of the subcultural location of farmers is at odds with the subcultural location of the other members of these boards and committees. In terms of the other members, the farmer representatives may not be able to explain themselves sufficiently clearly. Because of the different subcultural locations there is not a shared language, ideology or value system, and there may be differing cognitive processes. Representatives may not have thought about the issues the way farmers see them or, not having thought about an issue, they may not be able to conceptualise a problem in the way the experienced and practically- oriented farmer might. If they have not personally experienced a problem, or discussed such a problem with other farmers, they may not be able to pass on that view to policy makers.

All of these points are not to be interpreted as criticisms of individual representatives. They are explanations of processes that occur, and provide the sociological reason why simply having a small number of representatives does not change anything -- why having representatives is not true participation (see Roberts, 1995).

CONCLUSION

Traditional extension, especially as it has been practiced by extension agencies in the past, has exhibited many faults. However, it must be accepted that traditional extension was not mal-intentioned but rather socially naive. It has, at various times, been ignorant of the environmental consequences of the practices it promoted. There is no justifiable reason why public funding should continue to support an extension service which fails adequately to address the needs of the majority of farmers, and which is linked in an uncritical and promotional way to the wider profit-making motives of transnational agribusiness. To the extent, however, that there is an environmental crisis in agriculture, there would appear to be a need for the state to assist in the solution to that crisis. There is, in other words, an environmental imperative for decisive action which, in the context of the preferred method of bringing about change in agriculture, provides extension with a new *raison d'etre*. Extension practice has been unsatisfactory because of problems in the way the extension process occurred, including its assumptions and the training of its practitioners. The fundamental basis of traditional extension -- that it was a free service provided to all farmers (and which most continue to desire today) -- has been conveniently overlooked.

The environmental crisis gives renewed importance to extension and for it to be made more relevant to the needs of farmers; it also requires more resources, not less. Extension agencies are beginning to appreciate that the failure of extension has had more to do with the inadequacies of the extension theory and practice, than with the inadequacies of farmers. Yet, to abandon all traditional methods of extension would appear to be short sighted in terms of the new environmental agenda in Australian and world agriculture.

New group processes are indeed exciting and they promise to reinvigorate the discipline of extension. They could, if appropriately resourced, provide farmers with the sorts of services they will need in a complex social, political and economic environment. These new approaches have been viewed by many as a means of usurping the discredited methods which have arisen from an out of touch, authoritarian and state-driven extension service -- one based on an outdated paradigm. What we have argued here, though, is that there remains some virtue in combining the best of traditional extension with what are quite obviously superior group-based approaches derived, largely, from sociology, social psychology and organisational theory. It would be tragic for Australian farmers and for the environment, if the replacement of an older paradigm with the new became little more than a vehicle for the state to abrogate its responsibility of assisting farmers in their efforts to perform the very difficult task of enhancing their efficiency and productivity while improving the sustainability of their farmlands.

TOWARDS A SOCIOLOGY OF CONTEMPORARY AGRICULTURAL EXTENSION

INTRODUCTION

Previous chapters have described and theorised the environmental and social consequences of agriculture, and we have mounted an argument for the existence of an environmental imperative within Australian agriculture for a greater commitment to a socially and environmentally sustainable agriculture. Ultimately, it will be agricultural extension (perhaps in a quite different form) which will be responsible for promoting sustainable agriculture. Extension has been considered throughout this book, but has not been explicitly theorised. This chapter seeks to examine and evaluate different perspectives of agricultural extension. It also considers other relevant rural sociological perspectives important to any understanding of contemporary Australian farming and the agricultural environment.

THE CHANGING NATURE OF AGRICULTURAL EXTENSION SCIENCE

Agricultural extension science has undergone considerable change over the past decade or so, with substantial rethinking about the relationship between extension agencies and farmers (Röling, 1988; Leeuwis, 1993b). The early concern for extension was: 'how do we get farmers to adopt new technology?', with extension science focussing on the theories and techniques of the diffusion of innovations and on adoption behaviour (see Rogers, 1962; Rogers and Shoemaker, 1971; Rogers, 1983).

The failures of extension (such as the slow rates of adoption of new technologies, and social inequalities as a result of differential adoption rates) that occurred under this model led to the questions: 'why don't farmers do as they are told?' and 'why don't farmers adopt the new technologies?'. The perceived solutions to these problems were the better targeting of extension efforts to the specific audience and the fine-tuning of the message by way of market research and greater interaction with clients (Kotler, 1975; van den Ban and Hawkins, 1988) (and see also Röling, 1988; Röling and Engel, 1990, 1991; Leeuwis, 1993b; Vanclay and Lawrence, 1994a). The orientation remained one of 'top- down' technology transfer from scientific research to farmer via the extension agency, with agricultural extension being defined, rather naively, as help for farmers (van den Ban and Hawkins, 1988). This is still largely the position of the extension agencies in Australia and most other countries.

As we saw in previous chapters, a more reasoned and less partisan analysis of the barriers to adoption inevitably leads to a discussion about farmer rationality and reveals that, given the constraints under which farmers operate, non-adoption may be logical from the farmers' point of view. In other words, non-adoption may have been due to the opportunities or otherwise for change which were experienced by rural people -- not to individual resistance to change. When the structural opportunities existed for adoption, adoption occurred at great pace, far more rapidly than might have been predicted (Röling, 1988).

The other important point is that when adoption did occur, it was because of its appropriateness to those adopting the innovations, or because it was adapted to be appropriate and to fit in with the local style of farming and local farming subculture. Adaption -- rather than any unreflective adoption -- was what was occurring in the process of the transfer of technology, but the extension agencies failed to appreciate this, and extension science has only recently begun to address this aspect of the process.

More recently, in Europe, extension scientists have questioned the applicability of the messages that have been promoted by extension agencies and have started to consider the many factors that contribute to the appropriateness of those messages. Extension is no longer conceived as a matter of interactions between agencies and clients as in the past, it is now seen to involve many participants and to require a very broad understanding of the various systems in which farmers operate. Extension science in its European mould developed into a complex discipline focusing on both the context in which communication takes place, and the content of what is being communicated (Röling, 1988; Leeuwis, 1993b). Far from being concerned about the transfer of technology, extension science (if not extension practice) is now concerned with rural people's 'sense making activities' -- how people make sense of the activities in which they are engaged (Röling, 1992b).

THEORETICAL PERSPECTIVES
IN AGRICULTURAL EXTENSION SCIENCE

Extension science can be conceived as having a number of theoretical positions. It is difficult to determine the number because the positions are not mutually exclusive and exist at different levels of analysis. Some are not central to extension practice but relate to very specific issues, others are borrowed from other disciplines and are useful in understanding aspects of extension. Nevertheless, agricultural extension science can be considered as consisting of three major or core theoretical positions: Transfer of Technology (ToT), Agricultural Knowledge and Information Systems (AKIS), and Policy Instrument (PI) approaches -- and several important, although peripheral, positions that are borrowed from other disciplines, of which the following are noteworthy: farming systems research, indigenous technical knowledge approaches, farming styles, and the actor perspective.

The transfer of technology (ToT) model is premised on diffusion of innovations and the linear transfer of technology, and is common to traditional extension thinking. Few extension theorists would currently accept or subscribe to this position, although it would be widely held amongst extension practitioners in extension agencies, and by many of the various Research and Development Corporations. This does not mean that extension theorists believe that the adoption of new innovations does not occur, or that extension agencies ought not be involved in attempts to transfer technology, but rather that the theoretical position that has developed surrounding the transfer of technology is not very useful in understanding all aspects of the process. Diffusion of knowledge and adoption of innovations still takes place, but for different reasons than those posited under the technology transfer model.

The Policy Instrument (PI) perspective (in agricultural extension) sees agricultural extension activities as one of many policy instruments of government, which together, when carefully coordinated, can be used to achieve a particular policy objective. Although a component of the disciplines of policy science and communication science, the PI approach has been adapted and expounded explicitly for extension science by Cees van Woerkum. However, the Dutch do not distinguish between the various forms of extension, accepting promotions, communications, public relations, and information provision activities as extension (voorlichting) (Vanclay, 1994a), and thus van Woerkum does not exclusively refer to agricultural extension. Unfortunately, most references applying the PI approach to extension are in Dutch, and those works in English (eg van Woerkum, 1989, 1991, 1992; van Woerkum and van Meegeren, 1990, 1991) are not particularly good articulations of the position (Vanclay, 1994a).

The Agricultural Knowledge and Information Systems (AKIS) perspective was developed by Niels Röling (eg Röling, 1985, 1988, 1992a; Engel, 1990; Röling and Engel, 1990) and considers that farmers operate in complex social and physical systems involving many actors. Consequently, any understanding of those systems requires a consideration of the interactions between the actors and agencies in those systems. This position concentrates on the knowledge and information operating within the systems, and particularly on the linkages between components of the systems.

There is a difference in how these latter two positions conceive of the role of extension agencies. In the AKIS perspective, extension has 'a facilitating function in processes of joint social learning, and thereby in the development of higher quality collective agency' (Leeuwis, 1993b: 56), while in the PI perspective, extension is conceptualised as a legitimate persuasive and coercive tool of government which needs to be carefully coordinated with other policy instruments, policies and communication (or extension) strategies to achieve an effective result.

This functionalist view of extension is based on the notion that what is defined as desirable by the state will (or should) automatically accord with what is desirable for the farmer. It ignores the likelihood of conflict over resource use, and is little more than an ideological justification for state intervention.

The AKIS perspective is implicitly multi-directional with respect to knowledge and information transfer, and is about promoting learning on all sides. The PI approach is top- down, with market research being used by the extension agency only to better target the message. The PI approach is more sophisticated than traditional extension, but is not fundamentally different in philosophy or ideology, whereas the philosophical or ideological base of the AKIS perspective is different from traditional extension.

The AKIS perspective -- based on extension experiences in non-western countries -- accepts that the client groups may often have considerable knowledge and experience, and may in fact have the answers to their own problems if the appropriate context for discussion of these problems occurs. The task of extension agencies then, is to facilitate discussion of these issues. The position recognises that there will be multiple actors in any situation. Extension agency client interaction should not be seen outside the complex social setting of which it is part. Because of the recognition of multiple actors, there is no inherent validity of any one point of view; knowledge must be negotiated -- something which is operationalised by Checkland's (1981) soft systems methodology (see below). It is also accepted that different actors have different levels of power, and in order to create an effective arena for negotiation, farmers must be provided 'countervailing power' (Röling, 1988).

At the extreme, there are problems with both perspectives. The persuasive communication strategy of the PI approach rests on acceptance of the legitimacy of the government view of the world, and on a denial that the knowledge farmers generate should be part of a process of negotiated change (see van Woerkum, 1992). The position tends to exaggerate the effectiveness of extension in changing behaviour, is excessively mechanistic and simplistic in its understanding of the knowledge creation and transfer process.

Also at the extreme, AKIS approaches are internally inconsistent for extension: if farmers have so much knowledge already, why is it that they need help? From a critical perspective, AKIS approaches are naive, not because they fail to appreciate that different actors have different levels of power in the negotiating process and that agenda setting is related to the relative strengths of different actors (they do recognise this point), but because they consider that such imbalances can be corrected by countervailing power. 'Countervailing power' is a concept which is not satisfactorily defined, nor is the implementation of such a concept adequately described. Groups and group processes are likely to continue to manifest traditional power relationships (Gray, 1992; Vanclay, 1992a). Furthermore, because of the concentration on knowledge and information, and even with the emphasis on the linkages between components of the system, the position tends to ignore the socio-economic (structural) environment in which farmers operate. It should be noted that such an extreme view is not Röling's (current) position. Niels

Röling (Röling and Jiggins, 1994; pers com) accepts that extension takes place within a policy context, but argues that too much attention is paid to the policy context and not enough to the knowledge and information systems that operate. His support for focussing on the AKIS does not mean that the policy context, and the structural situation, are not also important. However, other advocates of the AKIS perspective appear to ignore structural issues completely.

The major difference between the two perspectives is in terms of coercion versus learning facilitation. If a mutually exclusive dichotomy is erected, then at any time extension is used for planned intervention or for persuasive communication -- such as when extension agencies promote the adoption of environmentally sound management practices -- then, implicitly, a PI position is necessarily being taken, because of the element of intended coercion, no matter how altruistic the intention may be, and no matter what the expressed philosophy of the agency (Vanclay, 1994c). However, this may sit uncomfortably with extension agencies, because some other aspects of the PI position are unappealing, and there is much merit in aspects of the AKIS perspective. AKIS and PI perspectives are therefore best conceived as being polar opposite, ideal types at each end of a continuum, rather than as mutually exclusive dichotomous categories, and it is better not to endorse completely one perspective.

Since agricultural extension agencies are in the business of changing behaviour, definitions that see extension simply as 'help' for farmers (see van den Ban and Hawkins, 1988) are either inappropriate or deliberately misleading about the functional or instrumental value of extension. Leeuwis (1993: 59) considers that definitions which ignore the political context of the adoption process 'have been quite helpful in mystifying this clearly instrumental aspect' of extension. Extension will always be coercive when it is a state-directed activity. It is better to appreciate this point and negotiate about the content of the message, than to naively assume that extension will not, or should not, be coercive. Even voluntary associations and non-government organisations which are engaged in extension might at times stand accused of having hidden agendas: the interests of these organisations may conflict in major ways with what is desired by the client group. At the very least, there is a tendency for associations and organisations to survive even after the need for their activity has ceased. Yet in a true bottom-up AKIS approach, the organisation should cease to be needed, once group dynamics take over. Those in the group are serving their own needs and will have broken any 'dependency' relationship with the agency.

As has been argued throughout this book, the environmental crisis within agriculture creates an urgent need for change -- one providing extension agencies with a new mandate for action to attempt to alter farmers' environmental management strategies. Furthermore, the nature of environmental problems -- and the previous outcomes of state involvement in agriculture -- means that governments have an obligation to assist farmers with environmental management. Some environmental problems have not been previously experienced by farmers. They may be unfamiliar with the signs and symptoms of these problems. Their experiences in farming may not be sufficient to allow them properly to address those problems. It is therefore appropriate that scientific research agencies consider the causes and potential solutions to these problems and seek to promote the use of new management practices among farmers.

There is a responsibility to assist in the change of farmers' behaviour. Yet behavioural change is a difficult task, and is likely to require a blend of approaches, a mixture of policy instruments -- potentially including persuasive communication, media campaigns, subsidies (of a sort), incentives and cross-compliance mechanisms, as well as direct regulation. The achievement of this task will require careful coordination of instruments, as well as coordination with other policy objectives of governments. There is reason not to dismiss the potential inherent in the PI perspective.

Facilitating farmers to develop an increased awareness about environmental management and success in changing their behaviour will be more likely to occur if they are personally committed to such change and feel that they have 'ownership' of the problem and the solution. An understanding of the knowledge and information systems in which farmers operate, and an appreciation of the difficulties in which farmers operate may well result in the development of farmer-friendly strategies which produce greater compliance than by the use of other, more coercive, methods. In other words, AKIS approaches and related methodologies must become part of any mix of policy instruments adopted by government and extension agencies in the promotion of effective environmental management.

This position is a little different to the usual AKIS position which would not have such a specific agenda in relation to the role of facilitation. In AKIS approaches, the usual procedure or view is to facilitate a discussion which leads to a situation of a desirable outcome under circumstances where the outcome is not preconceived. Such a position is premised on the notion that farmers have worthwhile knowledge and potential solutions to contribute to the debate. This is a desirable, and an ethically and ideologically appealing position. However, it is not a position that is totally applicable in the case of environmental management in Australia.

The environmental problems facing Australian farmers are problems that are largely outside farmers' experience and, in many cases, farmers deny the existence of these problems. Consequently, farmers have no specific knowledge that relates to these problems and have, in aggregate terms, no specific solutions to these problems. Agricultural scientists have undertaken research and developed new management practices which can reduce land degradation and which in their opinion, and the opinion of the state, should be adopted by farmers. With this view, the role of extension agencies concerned with environmental management is to promote the use of these practices. By utilising group facilitation approaches, and by subtle manipulation of the issues that are discussed and the information that is provided to the group, group facilitators can 'engineer' a discussion in such a way that farmers arrive at the desired outcome. Such a procedure, because it involves farmers, and the solutions are perceived as deriving from farmers (although the discussion has been staged to force the identification of the solution), is likely to have most success in voluntary compliance.

Here exists a contradiction for extension and extension theorists. The environmental degradation problems of today result, in part, from the activities of extension in the past in the form of the uncritical acceptance of, and promotion of the adoption of what are now considered to be unsustainable, environmentally degrading, production oriented practices. This situation occurred because of scientific ignorance about the potential environmental effects of the products of science, and because extension then held to a top-down model of technology transfer, which did not see farmers contributing to research and innovation, and which perceived farmers as non-evaluating acceptors (adopters) of what was promoted. Given this view of extension and of agricultural science, what certainty is there that what is currently being promoted is not also environmentally and/or socially undesirable? Will analysts in the future question the applicability of the 'solutions' being promoted today?

There is no answer to this, but by involving many stakeholders including farmers, environmentalists, industry representatives, concerned citizens, and well as scientists and social scientists in the total process -- especially in the establishment of research priorities, the funding of research, the monitoring of research, the fine-tuning of products and of extension processes -- there is greater likelihood that mutually acceptable outcomes will be found.

The philosophical issue at stake is whether group extension is simply the means to an already-determined state-oriented end (to improve sustainability), or is based upon a genuine desire to have farmers themselves determine the nature and extent of the problems they face as well as to assist them to come to appropriate solutions. In the latter case, farmers may not be able, or wish, to discuss environmental issues. In adopting new, more participatory and apparently more effective techniques for changing farming practices (Douglas, 1992), is the state not simply harnessing different approaches to achieve the same end as that which was apparent in the traditional extension model -- that which the state has predetermined is best for the farmers?

While rural sociologists must remain sceptical, extension practitioners like Douglas (1992) suggest the answer would be a definite 'no'. Douglas argues that in the new forms of extension, closer involvement with client groups is multifaceted and that a concern for the environment has been paramount. In all States, new developments in extension have included -- alongside traditional agronomic and animal husbandry extension -- producer demonstration sites, Local Best Practice group meetings, neighbourhood farm trial groups, computer decision aids, knowledge and information systems, self-help property planning, whole farm planning, and integrated catchment management. Success of these approaches is premised upon the wider use of community participation methods and the expected advantages to producers of group adult learning and self-help strategies for property planning (see Campbell, 1992a; Chamala and Mortiss, 1990; Douglas, 1992; Frank and Chamala, 1992; Martin, Tarr and Lockie, 1992; Stone, 1992).

In Queensland, for example, there has been a move for extension to embrace extra-agricultural (broader rural community) concerns. A study commissioned by the Department of Primary Industries (see Jensen, 1993) indicated that given the inevitability of changes to extension philosophy, the changing characteristics of farmers, and the declining relative standing of agriculture as an economic (and social) activity, extension should broaden its focus. It was argued that the welfare of the farming sector and that of rural communities was 'closely related', that no one department was responsible for rural community development, that the concerns for agriculture in the 1990s were social (for example, educational and managerial) rather than technical (Jensen, 1993: 19). While rural sociologists have been making these claims for decades, rural sociology (as a discipline) was again overlooked as the basis for the training of the 'new' extension officer. However, at least their future education is to be of a social science nature (population analysis, impact analysis, community economic analysis were some of the new skills specifically mentioned). Extension agents would be involved in regional development activities using new group processes which involved community participation and decision making. The potential here for moving from agricultural sustainability to rural community sustainability is obvious.

INDIGENOUS TECHNICAL KNOWLEDGE

This position recognises that local inhabitants -- in the context of this discussion, farmers -- have knowledge, insights and adaptive skills which are based on personal experience, and on knowledge accumulated in the culture. Such knowledge and experience is variously called 'indigenous technical knowledge', 'indigenous knowledge', or 'local knowledge' (see Chambers, 1983,1993; Richards, 1985; Chambers, Pacey and Thrupp, 1989; Thrupp, 1989; Warren, Brokensha and Slikkerveer, 1991).

The position developed as a recognition of the failure of the Green Revolution to be useful to farmers in all agricultural ecosystems, and in an attempt to deal with the social inequalities induced by the Green Revolution (Reijntjes, Haverkort and Waters-Bayer, 1992). The Green Revolution worked reasonably well for wealthier farmers in regions with well-developed infrastructure, which were suitable for irrigation, and which were fairly homogeneous (such as parts of Asia), but did not work for small farmers in rainfed areas especially in Africa (Lipton and Longhurst, 1989; Brouwers, 1993). The Green Revolution was premised on the need to give new (western) technical solutions to rural people who were seen as ignorant, and whose farming methods were seen as being excessively simple, lacking in any inherent value, and having low productivity. However, as more research is being undertaken, it is increasingly acknowledged that indigenous peoples in many parts of the world are very skilful in choosing optimum crops, locations for cropping, and crop rotations, and have a vast store of knowledge relevant to their local situation (Brouwers, 1993). This knowledge may not necessarily be in the form of western concepts of knowledge, but is tied up with various aspects of the local culture (Thrupp, 1989).

There are fundamental differences between the orientation of agriculture in western and non-western countries. It is not true to suggest that all farmers in industrial nations are in the business of industrial agriculture, but industrial agriculture can be characterised as one with a market-induced obsession with efficiency, productivity and output as the main measures of farm and farmer performance. In some countries, notably The Netherlands, many farmers are concerned with maximising gross sales rather than maximising net profits (Leeuwis, 1993b). Farmers in industrial nations have a range of concerns including personal lifestyle (working hard, but not too hard), manner of farming, passing the farm onto their children in a better condition than they received it, which all form part of a farming subculture, or what van der Ploeg calls 'styles of farming'.

Indigenous agriculture is not simply concerned with yield, but with achieving an optimal solution to a range of concerns relating to things that are of importance in the context of agriculture within those cultures, societies and ecosystems. Brouwers (1993; based largely on Dommen, 1988) describes them as follows:

- an ability to work with the environment rather than attempting to override it;
- a deliberate utilisation of diversity of micro-environments;
- the purposeful selection throughout the production period of crops planted and cultivation practices used and the integration of livestock into the system as a means of maintaining soil fertility;
- the deliberate staggering of outputs in space and time; and
- the use of crop combinations which give a higher return per person per hour during the major labour bottleneck period and which give a more dependable result in variable rainfall.

Thus 'traditional' farming systems are complex, strategically integrate different resources and farming techniques, and, most importantly, act to maintain stability and productivity while conserving the natural resource base (Reijntjes *et al.*, 1992, cited by Brouwers, 1993). Such farming systems demand as much skill from the farmers as industrial agricultural systems such as glasshouse horticulture (Brouwers, 1993).

Integration or articulation of indigenous knowledge and scientific knowledge is desirable in order to modify technology to make it more useful to farmers, and to utilise farmers' knowledge, experience and experimental capacity in the design of the technology. Such a process which combines farmers with commercial and scientific organisations is called Participative Technology Development (Chambers and Jiggins, 1986; Haverkort, van der Kamp and Waters-Bayer, 1991; Jiggins and de Zeeuw, 1992).

There are a number of problems with the concept of indigenous technical knowledge and the usefulness of such a concept. A major problem is that of the potential marginalisation of the local knowledge as it is 'incorporated' by extension agencies. Because such knowledge does not consist of discrete packets of information but is integrated into complex cultural systems of language, behaviour, rituals, ceremonies and myths (Brokensha, Warren and Werner, 1980), there is a problem that attempts at scientification (for example, extracting and abstracting the knowledge) will ignore the social milieu from which the knowledge was drawn. As a corollary, there is a danger that this process will not pay sufficient regard to the extremely complex subtleties and nuances of such cultural practices (knowledge) (Thrupp, 1989; Brouwers, 1993). This has also led to an ethical and legal concern about the ownership rights relating to such knowledge. Who 'owns' it and who, if anyone, should be compensated if it is used to produce outcomes which have commercial benefits?

The major criticisms of the concept of Indigenous Technical Knowledge which arise outside the perspective relate not so much to the fairly obvious consideration that rural people have knowledge that should not be ignored, but to the implications of their possession of such knowledge. If it is accepted that rural people have local knowledge, how does this change extension or development practice?

First, the position tends to romanticise and glamorise non-western cultures which leads, in its most uncomplicated form, to a view that local people posses all the requisite knowledge and do not need help. Such a position fails to appreciate the difficulties that these people experience. Difficulties might include population growth (which often has less to do with population pressure *per se*, but to the structural conditions under which resources are distributed), changing social relations, and changing agricultural practices resulting from past development or political interventions. The problem is that so-called traditional societies no longer really exist. As a result of interaction with western nations, through colonialisation (the activities of slave traders, missionaries, and political and military concerns), as well as the well-intentioned and not-so-well intentioned extension efforts of development agencies (see Jiggins, 1995), the cultures and physical environments of these peoples have been significantly altered. It can legitimately be asked what constitutes 'indigenous' knowledge under these circumstances and to what extent should it be given priority in extension?

It needs to be accepted, as Brouwers (1993) suggests, that such knowledge, to the extent that it does exist, is not uniformly distributed in the community, and that such knowledge is not internally consistent. It has been suggested, in this context, that 'experiences of agro-ecological (mis)fortunes are not always shared within the community' (Brouwers, 1993: 6).

Proponents of the position appear to combine the ideas from an outdated functionalist-based environmental determinism (see Harris, 1968, 1975, 1977). Such a position sees culture as being determined by the environment in which it exists, and that all aspects of the culture have some functional or rational quality. Today, very few anthropologists and sociologists would be impressed with this position. The school of cultural anthropology (see Keesing, 1976) views culture as being largely independent of such a direct relationship between cultural practices and the environment, and would not accept the immediate or obvious functionality (or disfunctionality) of cultural practices. It would tend to provide an approach which accepts that cultures manifest many behaviours and practices that may be completely independent of any direct relationship with the environment. Such a position does not mean that some cultural practices do not have a 'functional' quality in environmental terms, that cultural practices do not contribute to social stability or have other cultural and social value -- or that cultures must adapt to the environment in which they exist -- but it does accord greater freedom to cultures to develop a more diverse range of practices. Consequently, many cultural practices may have little at all to do with some improperly assumed environmental 'functionality'.

As the basis for the development of satisfactory solutions to environmental and other problems, it is important for extension agencies to work with the knowledge and intelligence possessed by farmers. Attempts to force them to change against their will have been an abject failure. It is also true that extension agencies will learn something from farmers. It is a moot point however whether farmers -- who may not have experienced the 'new' environmental problems -- have any 'privileged' knowledge of, or experience in dealing with, those problems. Farmers will, though, have a lot to offer in terms of the fine-tuning of practices and in the of implementation of practices which may help reduce environmental degradation.

There are many examples of development assistance to non-western societies where the extension agency and the local culture were very removed from each other, and where the applicability of the message or the technology has been questioned (see Jiggins, 1995). In those circumstances, any consideration of local culture greatly assists in improving the extension message, or in adapting the technology to suit local conditions. Methodologically crude but cost-saving techniques such as Rapid Rural Appraisal (RRA) or Participatory Rural Appraisal (PRA) can be used to gain an impression of the local culture. They have been employed by extension agencies in Australia because of frustrations with structured questionnaires and surveys, dissatisfaction with the ways data are collected and analysed, and results disseminated, and the inability of data gathering approaches to empower, in any way, those who provided the information -- the farmers and members of rural communities (see Dunn, 1994).

The growing distrust of the empirical tools of a positivist sociology aside, in western countries such as Australia, extension agencies are not so removed from farmers. Extension officers may often have a farming background themselves. And they do, for the most part, relate well to the farmers with whom they deal. Where the extension message is, for the most part, accessible to farmers, and the techniques being advocated are not fundamentally removed from farmers' experience, the likelihood of rejection is minimised. In Australia, there is a great deal of farmer support for extension agencies. Despite specific criticisms made by farmers and extension scientists about Australian agricultural extension agencies, it must be accepted that extension agencies do provide a useful service to farmers. In such cases, the use of techniques such as RRA and PRA, may only have a minor or marginal role in providing additional helpful information. This does not mean that extension agencies cannot be improved, or that there are not significant differences between farmers and extension agencies, or that there are no problems with extension practices. It does mean that concepts, theories and methodologies which may be useful in understanding development in non-western countries maybe of less relevance in western countries.

One approach which recognises the validity of indigenous technical knowledge and attempts to harness this knowledge to develop and test new agricultural technologies with client groups is 'farming systems research'. Advocates of this approach accept that farmers operate in a complex physical environment involving many different physical systems. Under this philosophy, extension -- if it is to be effective and to deliver innovations that are likely to be useful to target groups -- must respond to the various physical systems of agricultural production. The position tends to be locally based and agro-biologically dominated. Much useful research that adapts innovations to local conditions has been undertaken (see Jiggins, 1982; Shaner, Philipp and Schmehl, 1982; Jones and Wallace, 1986). The position is an improvement on the technology transfer model, in that there is a bi-directional flow of information, but does not question the fundamental concept of extension. Nor does it appreciate the power imbalances that exist between different parties, and the socio-economic constraints under which farmers operate.

SOFT SYSTEMS THINKING

Within extension science, there is considerable support for soft systems thinking. A system can be defined as an 'arrangement of parts (elements, components, subsystems) which interact to achieve some common purpose' (see Hurtubise, 1984; Röling, 1988: 186-188). Systems approaches to problem solving involve taking a broad view, including all parts of the problem, and concentrating on interactions between different parts of the problem (Checkland, 1981). 'Hard' and 'soft' refers to how the functions and organisation of the system are perceived. Hard systems are conceived as having unproblematic and transparent functions, causes and purposes, while soft system approaches recognise that systems are social constructions with normative boundaries. Soft system theorists do not attribute purpose to entities but only to the individuals who make up these entities. The actors participating in these systems have different viewpoints and the task of the system is negotiation of the different viewpoints.

Soft systems also differ from hard systems in that in hard systems thinking, social systems (organisations) are assumed to be goal seeking, thus organisations should be rationally managed to achieve that objective (Checkland, 1985). By contrast, soft systems theorists consider that 'human activity systems' must be considered as complex entities in which people have different 'worldviews' (Checkland and Davies, 1986). There will be, as a consequence, different interpretations of the problems that exist, the goals that ought to be achieved, and the boundaries of the system itself (Leeuwis, 1993b). In response to the complexity of these systems, soft systems theorists have developed soft systems methodologies (Checkland, 1981; Engel *et al.*, 1992) in order to reach consensus between stakeholders in a system.

Checkland's soft system methodology was developed in a commercial business environment to assist in the development of organisational policy. Such a setting is far more simple than the environment of real world issues. Corporate executives who must determine corporate policy may have different opinions, but are largely from one 'subculture'.

Soft system methodologies are useful under certain circumstances, but the assumptions governing their use are likely to make the concept of minimal use as an extension strategy, despite the enthusiasm they receive from some extension scientists.

The primary assumptions required for soft systems methodologies to work effectively are:

- there must be a certain commonality or homogeneity among participants, at least a high level of mutual understanding, if not a common subcultural and class location;
- participants must have equal access to information about the issue and equal resources to research the issue further should they so wish;
- participants must be willing to negotiate and must contribute in a positive manner to the debate. This means that they must bear no animosity towards other participants;
- participants must be committed to the process and willing to negotiate their position; they must not have immutable intransigent positions (this does not mean that they necessarily must not be more committed to certain positions than others);
- participants do not need to have the same level of power in society or the organisation, but they must act in the negotiation process as if they did have equal power;
- the process should be conducted in a pleasant environment free of time constraints and other pressures.

These requirements are very stringent and not at all like real world situations. With any major issue to be debated, the participants are likely to have very different backgrounds which will make it difficult to understand each other's worldview. In the context of an important issue, it is likely that participants will have developed strong feelings about the matter, may already have intransigent positions, and may well have developed hostility towards people holding different opinions. It is unlikely that a situation can be created in which power does not affect the debate. Participants are not likely to have equal power at negotiating, access to information or resources to access information. Key stakeholders may have been deliberately (or accidentally) excluded from the debate. However, power relationships are not only overt, they are also embodied in social roles, and consequently are part of social exchange. Social concepts such as charisma and prestige will obviously affect the negotiations, but so will issues such as experience, ability to articulate one's thoughts (both in terms of cognitive abstraction and elocution), social skills, and issues relating to ingrained attitudes. In all likelihood, people belonging to many different socially groups would be disadvantaged in these situations, including but not exclusively and not necessarily in all cases, women, older people, young people, migrants, indigenous people, non-professional people, people who are labelled as 'deviant', and so on. Attempts at 'countervailing power' (Röling, 1988) and other such naive suggestions to overcome this problem, while laudable, are unlikely to resolve the power imbalance because of the extent to which it is ingrained in our social roles and interpersonal behaviour. Thus, it is very unlikely that a shared learning experience will take place in an open and harmonious atmosphere, and that a mutually agreeable, more or less rational, outcome can be achieved in most cases.

Another problem is that negotiated outcomes are often not satisfactory to any of the participants, certainly to participants who held particular positions prior to negotiation, and especially when the negotiated position involved the diluting of a proposal -- as is usually the case. Where radical action is required, the negotiating process may well mean that the solution, even if acceptable to the people involved, actually fails to deal with the problem.

Jackson (1985, 1991), Ulrich (1988) and Leeuwis (1993b) have all criticised soft systems approaches for failing to acknowledge that power structures affect the debate and that stakeholders do not have equal say in the discussion, nor equal access to resources. Jackson (1985: 144) suggests that the application of soft systems methodologies can easily lead to a reinforcement of the status quo:

> Soft systems thinking cannot pose a real threat to the social structures which support the Weltanschauung [worldview] with which it works. It can tinker at the ideological level but it is likely simply to ensure the continued survival by adaptation, of existing social elites (Thomas and Lockett, 1979; Jackson, 1982). This is not at all what the designers of the soft systems methodologies intended. Nevertheless, there is some evidence that it is what is achieved by these approaches. Churchman, Ackoff and Checkland are baffled that their methodologies when applied to the real world tend to lead to conservative or, at best, reformist recommendations for change. Examples of such bafflements can be found in Churchman, 1971: 228; Ackoff, 1979; and Checkland, 1981: 15. (Jackson, 1985: 144 quoted by Leeuwis, 1993b: 41).

Because of the difficulty of satisfying the conditions under which soft systems methodologies could work effectively, there must be some doubt about their efficacy in helping to solve many problems, such as the environmental problems of Australian agriculture. A worst case scenario would consist of a situation where the people with the most power manipulated the process to achieve their own personal objectives, while deceiving the other participants into believing that they did participate in a shared learning experience and negotiated outcome. The process could also be used to suppress dissension, or to divert responsibility for decisions, such as in the case of decisions that might, otherwise, be deemed by others as inappropriate or self-serving.

The environmental imperative of having farmers adopt more sustainable practices may mean that negotiated outcomes that are compromises of original proposals may not be satisfactory for the environment. What the farmers may have decided is 'good' for them may not be what is good for the environment. Facilitation should involve farmers in the discussion of strategies to improve farming practices. Such involvement does not necessarily mean that a complicated framework such as a soft systems methodology is required, nor does it mean token representation by a small number of farmers. There is reason to believe that participatory approaches are the way forward. At this time, however, the soft system adherents have failed -- in the context of environmental change within agriculture -- to demonstrate the superiority of the method over other participative mechanisms.

As a consequence of the problems with soft systems thinking, a third type of system thinking -- critical systems thinking (as opposed to soft or hard systems) -- has been advanced, based largely on the ideas of Jurgen Habermas (see Jackson, 1985, 1991; Lyytinen and Klein, 1985; Ulrich, 1988; Fuenmayor and López-Garay, 1991). Habermas (1981) posits an 'ideal speech situation' of undistorted communication in which the participants are able and willing to respect and have empathy for each other's positions, and a willingness to scrutinise their own and others' logical premises. If such a situation could exist, conflicts of interest would be resolved simply by the force of rational argument, and the outcome would be based on rational logic and not on negotiated compromise, or strategic action. Habermas does not believe that the ideal speech situation is achievable, but he considers that the desirability, if not potentiality of the concept of this ideal type of ideal speech underpins all human communication. Habermas uses the concept as an ideal type to develop an alternative, more realistic, concept of systematically distorted communication, which is then used as the basis of a critical analysis of society.

It appears likely that the critical systems theorists have not fully understood Habermas. They appear to be advocating the establishment of these ideal speech situations as an actual communication tool (rather than as an ideal type). They argue that decisions or outcomes arrived at through this communicative rationality procedure are not necessarily objectively correct in any epistemological sense, but the process is the most desirable form of conflict resolution. They believe that since such decisions are based on a shared consensus of what is true, communicative rationality has a normative validity rather than an empirical validity (Ulrich, 1988).

There are a number of problems with this approach. Most importantly, it not likely that Habermas' 'ideal speech situation' can actually be created, implemented and maintained. The position requires a sanguine view of human social interaction as it assumes that individuals will not take a self-interested position and that communicative rationality will not deteriorate into strategic rationality (cognitive instrumental rationality). This is slightly surprising because the logical (enlightened self-interested) position for individuals would be one based upon strategic rationality, not of communicative rationality. Habermas does not propose any solution to the contradiction of assuming that individuals are rational individual actors operating only on at the level of communicative rationality and not on the basis of strategic rationality. His approach assumes that conflicts of interest are irrational, and therefore will not occur in an ideal speech situation, and that rationality is purely cognitive. In other words, he does not accept the sociological or cultural basis of knowledge and the primacy of culture in determining behaviour. The sociological and anthropological position would recognise that all behaviour, knowledge and rationality itself is determined by the cultural and subcultural positions of individuals.

GIDDENS, LEEUWIS AND STRUCTURATION THEORY

Giddens' (1984) theory of structuration attempts to bridge the schisms of macro and micro, actor and structure, and structuralist and interpretivist frameworks. Giddens argues the social sciences ought to focus analysis on social practices rather than on individual experience or on social structure. Giddens does not accept that social structure exists as an empirical or objective entity, but rather that social systems, as reproduced by social practices, exhibit structural properties. Structure therefore, according to Giddens, is manifested in social systems in the form of the 'reproduced relations between actors or collectivities, organised as regular social practices' (Giddens, 1984: 25). Social practices are recursive, that is, they are continually recreated by social actors, and thus structure exists as recursively organised sets of 'rules and resources, or sets of transformation relations, organised as properties of social systems' (Giddens, 1984: 25; adapted from Leeuwis, 1993a: 293).

Leeuwis (1993a) has adapted Giddens' theory to make it more consistent with a constructivist position. He argues that Giddens' framework is more useful than Habermas' position, because it accepts that communication is implicit in every social interaction, and because 'the production of meaning (and therefore the production of information) is inherently connected with the operation of power and normative sanctions' (Leeuwis, 1993a: 296). Unlike the actor perspective, it also provides an explanation about why structures exist, and how actors are involved in reproducing those structures.

Leeuwis (1993a) also argues that extension scientists should base any new approaches on Giddens rather than Habermas. He argues that his adaptation of Giddens' theory is useful to the AKIS perspective in order to broaden its scope in dealing with communication and information in a more integral way. The theory is also useful to the Policy Instrument perspective to encourage the transcending of 'the rather narrow focus on the individual, the mechanistic conceptualisation of communication and the deterministic implications of outdated social psychology models' (Leeuwis, 1993a: 300). Finally, Leeuwis (1993a: 300-301) argues that Giddens provides advice for extension agencies:

> Professional communicators [should] aim at capitalizing on what Giddens calls the 'double hermeneutic' of the social sciences. Thus, we should not look at extension as having a 'neutral' facilitating function for developing higher quality collective agency (as is the case in the AKIS perspective), or as an attempt to persuade individuals to change and/or adopt particular behaviours on the basis of rational argumentation (as implicit to the PI perspective). Given the close interconnections between social structure, knowledge and power, it is better to look at extension activities as active and inherently political communicative interventions by which professional communicators aim at the production and/or reproduction of particular structural properties in society.

ACTOR PERSPECTIVE

The actor perspective as developed in rural sociology by Norman Long (1968, 1977, 1984, 1989, 1990; Long and Long, 1992; Long and van der Ploeg, 1988, 1989) is an extension of symbolic interactionalism (Long, 1990). It seeks to explain 'differential adaptations or responses to the same or similar [structural] circumstances' (Long, 1989: 222). It argues that cultural variations and organisational differences are the result of the different ways actors respond to problematic situations and interactions with other actors. Such actors, in a rural context, are not only farmers and their families, but all people and institutions whose interests intersect within the rural domain. The position accepts that actors are 'knowing, active subjects' who problematise situations, process information and develop strategies to deal with other actors, whether they are individuals or institutions, and regardless of their level of power (Long, 1989: 222). The position considers structure to be important, but not to be deterministic (see Long, 1988).

Long utilises Giddens' (1979, 1984, 1987) concept of 'agency' which attributes individual actors with:

> the capacity to process social experience and to devise ways of coping with life ... Within the limits of existing information, uncertainty and other constraints (eg physical, normative and politico-economic), social actors are 'knowledgable' and 'capable'. They attempt to solve problems, learn how to intervene in the flow of social events around them, and monitor continuously their own actions, observing how others react to their behaviour and taking note of various contingent circumstances (Giddens, 1984: 1-16; cited by Long, 1989: 223).

The important feature of the concept of agency is that it does not refer to actors' intentions, but refers to the inherent 'capability of the individual to "make a difference" to a pre-existing state of affairs or course of events. This implies that all actors (agents) exercise some kind of "power", even those who are in highly subordinated positions' (Giddens, 1984: 14, cited by Long, 1989: 223). All people, including those who are subordinated, are viewed as being able to influence those who subordinate them, and thus are involved in the construction of their own social worlds.

Social structures are seen as having both constraining and enabling potential for social behaviour. Again, following Giddens, structure cannot be comprehended without accounting for agency:

> In following the routines of my day-to-day life I help reproduce social institutions that I played no part in bringing into being. They are more than merely the environment of my action since ... they enter constitutively into what it is I do as an agent. Similarly, my actions constitute and reconstitute the institutional conditions of actions of others, just as their actions do mine. ... My activities are thus embedded within, and are constitutive elements of, structured properties of institutions stretching well beyond myself in time and space (Giddens, 1987: 11; cited by Long, 1989: 223-224).

The actor perspective as developed by Norman Long assumes that actors are capable of formulating decisions and acting on these decisions, and of innovating and experimenting with new forms of behaviour. All this can occur even in situations where the social space of actors is severely restricted. The fundamental notion of the actor perspective is that individuals can always make choices, however limited, between different courses of action, as well as having some process to judge or evaluate the appropriateness of their actions.

Hindess (1986) argues that the reaching of decisions requires the use of 'discursive means'. Types of discourse vary and form part of the available stock of knowledge and resources available to all actors. Thus actors have a choice of discourses, as well as 'a repertoire of different life styles, cultural forms and rationalities' which can be utilised 'in their search for order and meaning' (Long, 1989: 224).

> [Because] the strategies and cultural constructions employed by individuals ... [are selected] from a stock of available discourses (verbal and non-verbal) that are to some degree shared with other individuals, contemporaries and even predecessors ... the individual is ... transmuted metaphorically into the social actor, thus signifying that 'actor' (like the person in a play) is a social construction rather than simply a synonym for the individual person or human being (Long, 1989: 225).

Long (1989: 225) argues that the principal elements of the concept of agency, knowledgeability and capability, 'must be culturally translated if they are to be fully meaningful. ... Cultural expressions of agency vary and reflect different philosophies regarding the capacity of the individual to influence actions and outcomes' (see also Strathern, 1985).

The term 'actor' and the concept of 'agency' can be applied to various institutions, such as government departments, corporations, and specific social groups, providing that they 'have means of reaching and formulating decisions and of acting on at least some of them' (Hindess, 1986: 115; cited by Long, 1989: 225). These concepts should not be applied to social collectivities or agglomerates which because of size or internal heterogeneity are structurally incapable of formulating or implementing decisions.

Long (1989) anticipates the two criticisms levelled at the actor perspective: first, that it might be construed to be based on methodological individualism; and second, that it may overlook the influence of the macro structural setting. Long argues forcefully that an actor-oriented analysis is not based on methodological individualism. He points out that individuals make decisions contingent upon the social conduct of others, and their behaviour is also affected by more diffuse external institutions, structures and cultural factors that transcend the immediate social setting experienced by the actor in question. Such influences on the actor are not only the results of direct interactions, or through the activities of entities like the mass media, but are based on the collective cultural history, such as implied by Bourdieu's (1981) notion of 'habitus' or 'embodied history' (Long, 1989, 1990). (Bourdieu is discussed later in this chapter.)

In response to the criticism that the actor perspective concentrates on the detail of social life at the expense of structural analysis, the argument is more complex. Long (1989) first utilises Collins' (1981) argument that sociology should concentrate on the analysis of micro situations lest it place itself at risk of reifying macro structure. However, Long rejects this view by applying Giddens' (1981) concept of 'emergent structures' (emergent forms). The argument is that there are certain macro structures which cannot be fully explicable or describable in terms of micro events. Ultimately, Long (1989, 1990; Long and Long, 1992) adopts a position he calls interface studies, which means that both macro and micro sociological analyses need to be undertaken, with attention given to how the two levels of analysis can be integrated. The interface is a methodological device for analysing critical points of discontinuity, accommodation and negotiation processes and emergent social forms. While Long accepts the macro influences, the actor perspective concentrates on actors (including institutions), on how these actors respond to macro processes, and on the contextualising aspects of discourse and authority structures.

One theoretical assumption of the actor perspective which is appealing is that actors are viewed as having the capacity to make a difference and to exercise choice -- no matter how limited the range of choices available. In contrast, critical sociology, with its focus on the limits placed on action by macro structure, views action as contingent, limited and usually incapable of removing inequalities without profound change to the structures of oppression. If the former is optimistic, the latter, in contrast, might be viewed as pessimistic. The actor perspective focuses at the practical level on what can be done to make a difference -- on intervention practices rather than on intervention models and theoretical positions (see Long and van der Ploeg, 1989).

An important criticism of the actor perspective is that it exaggerates the rationality of individuals. A cultural relativist notion of the behaviour of people, which accepts that behaviour makes sense (is logical) within a particular culture, but which denies any overall functional rationality of behaviour, could be considered more appropriate. Decisions of individuals must be consistent with their cultural perspective and not necessarily related to an ends-based rational analysis of the appropriate decision. As Long (among many others) has emphasised, culture is constraining as well as empowering. People tend not to engage in behaviour which is outside their cultural framework. Cultures find it difficult or impossible to develop responses that will be useful in situations that the culture has never experienced before. A culture experiencing rapid change -- such as brought about by a rapidly deteriorating environment or by an increased level of contact with other cultures (as in colonialisation), or a new environment in the case of relocated peoples -- may not have the appropriate behavioural responses within their cultural repertoire.

The actor perspective is not opposed to macro analysis, but it chooses to concentrate on actor responses rather than on the macro processes themselves. Obviously, both issues are important, and so the actor perspective does not attempt to be the sociological explanation: rather it must be viewed as providing one explanation forming part of an overall sociological understanding involving structural and non-structural interpretations.

Finally, the actor perspective is not a comprehensive theoretical position, nor does it pretend to be. It does not prescribe a complete theoretical and methodological approach. Nor does it serve as a theoretical worldview. It provides, instead, an orientation -- one which concentrates upon the ways social actors view the world. Because it is not an overarching theoretical framework, it is incapable of becoming a 'dominant paradigm' within the discipline.

FARMING STYLES AND FARMING SUBCULTURES

A potentially more coherent theoretical and methodological position which has developed out of the actor perspective is the notion of 'farming styles', developed by Jan Douwe van der Ploeg (1986, 1989, 1990, 1993; Leeuwis, 1989, 1993b). The farming styles approach is simply the actor perspective applied to an analysis of agrarian change, stressing how farmers themselves shape the patterns of agrarian development.

> Although their choices are often limited by a lack of critical resources, [farmers] should not be seen as the passive recipients of victims of planned change, nor as so routinized that they simply follow laid-down rules or conventions. Like other actors, farmers devise ways of dealing with problematic situations and creatively bring together resources (material and non-material -- especially practical knowledge derived from past experience) in an effort to resolve these (Long and van der Ploeg, 1995: in press).

The key characteristic of this approach is to understand heterogeneity in agriculture. 'The assumption [is] that different farmers ... define and operationalize their objectives and farm management practices on the basis of different criteria, interests, experiences and perspectives', and in the process develop specific conceptualisations of how their farms should be organised, developed and managed. The total composition of these individual strategies of management result in the 'impressive heterogeneity of agriculture, which can be analysed into specific styles of farming' (Long, 1988; Long and van der Ploeg, 1995). Thus:

> farming style refers to a cultural repertoire, a composite of normative and strategic ideas about how farming should be done. A style involves a specific way of organizing the farm enterprise: farmer practice and development are shaped in part by cultural repertoire, which in turn are tested, affirmed and if necessary adjusted through practice. Therefore a style of farming is a concrete form of praxis, a particular unity of thinking and doing, of theory and practice (van der Ploeg, 1993: 241).

The farming styles approach developed because of the failure of other theoretical frameworks to explain satisfactorily the existence of social diversity in otherwise homogenous farming regions. Long and van der Ploeg (1995: in press) argue that 'the articulation of the farm with the politico-economic environment cannot be understood within the framework of methodological individualism or social atomism, nor within a structuralist framework'.

The concept of farming styles differs in many ways from 'farming subcultures' which was introduced in Chapter 5 (and see Vanclay, 1994a). Not only is the farming styles position explicitly based on the actor perspective, it largely rejects analysis of macro processes. The farming styles approach, and the actor perspective generally, attributes much more ability to farmers to act individually and rationally than does the farming subculture approach. The latter approach, like the farming styles approach, assumes farmers develop their own conceptual basis about how their farm ought to be managed. However, the farming styles approach sees this largely as an individual strategy, albeit within a cultural setting, while the farming subculture approach sees such a process being less individually, and more collectively, based.

Both positions see agriculture as a social practice, one taking place within a socially and politically created setting. Yet structure (and its link to history) remain essential to any understanding of the way any particular system of farming has developed. Whereas van der Ploeg (1993: 242) agrees with Timmer (1949: 22) that 'the countryside forms as it were a stage upon which, for the world, a very important play is performed; this play is called agriculture, and the head role is played by the farmer', it would be undeniably lax to ignore the fact that the stage and plot are set by macro political and social forces. The farming subculture approach is more openly accepting of structural influences than is the farming styles approach.

The farming styles approach continuously stresses the empirical rationality of farmers' actions and implicitly accepts the significance and relevance of local culture and local knowledge, which van der Ploeg (1989) calls *art de la localité*. However, van der Ploeg argues that local knowledge has a different cognitive structure than scientific knowledge to farmers -- a cognitive structure to which they relate in a more direct way (Leeuwis, 1993b). The farming subculture approach does not necessarily accept farmers' knowledge as objectively or empirically rational. Rather, it accepts that such knowledge and the behaviour and management activities occurring as a result of such behaviour can be maladaptive, in both an economic sense (as is witnessed by the failure of farmers to continue to survive in a changing political situation) and an environmental sense (via the continuing environmental degradation of farmlands). However, despite arguing that farmer behaviour may be maladaptive, the farming subculture approach accepts that compliance with subcultural behaviour is legitimate human behaviour. All people in all situations are seen as complying to a certain extent with the subcultural expectations of the groups of which they are part -- thus scientists comply with a scientists' subculture (Knorr-Cetina, 1981; Charlesworth *et al.*, 1989), extension workers comply with an extension subculture (Vanclay, 1992d), and academics comply with an academic subculture (see Waters and Crook, 1993). Furthermore, the farming subculture approach -- while accepting that subcultural behaviour may not be environmentally or economically adaptive, and therefore not necessarily objectively rational -- accepts that most behavioural practices within the subculture are logical, understandable, and rational within the worldview of the farmers in that subculture (Vanclay 1992d; Vanclay and Lawrence, 1994a).

The implications of the differences between the 'farming styles' approach and that of 'farming subcultures' for extension are considerable. In the farming styles approach, there is no reason to have an extension at all: farmers have knowledge and experience that is valuable, and extension services are unlikely to be able to assist farmers. More likely, extension may act inappropriately in attempting to alter farm management practices to something inconsistent with the existing farming style. In this model, extension would be, at best, irrelevant and, at worst, an instrument of subordination and domination. However, in the farming subculture view, extension determines its role by the ability of the extension service to respond to the needs of farmers, and to the effectiveness of the extension service to change farm management practices, especially those which contribute to environmental degradation. Extension would be, at best, a valuable source of information for farmers, and, at worst, irrelevant, naive, patronising and therefore ignored by most farmers and a waste of public funds.

Thus, the farming subculture approach provides justification for a continuing role for extension services. Extension services have been criticised, in this book, in terms of the 'at worst' scenario: for failing adequately to address the needs of farmers; for ignoring the worldviews of various groups of farmers; for failing to appreciate and respond to the diversity that exists; and for delivering an agribusiness-oriented style 'industrial agriculture' message. The linkage between state extension agencies and agribusiness, especially with agri-chemical companies, will invariably 'taint' the image of state extension. It may come to be seen as little more than an industry mouthpiece rather than as a provider of 'independent' and 'unbiased' knowledge (to the limited extent that this could ever be achieved) (see Lockie and Vanclay, 1992; Lockie *et al.*, 1993, 1995; Vanclay and Lockie, 1993). Commercial sponsorship of extension is increasing: many extension agencies, and specific activities of extension agencies are accepting commercial sponsorships, as witnessed by agri-chemical sponsorship of recent Australian extension conferences. Extension agencies may be losing credibility by their use of this financial strategy.

There are other problems of the farming styles approach that have been raised by Vanclay (1994a), Leeuwis (1993b), de Bruin and Roex (1994) and others. These relate to how the farming styles are conceived, the methodology for determining them, the number that exist, and whether the number is increasing or decreasing over time. Briefly expressed, both Vanclay and Leeuwis consider that the concept of farming styles is reified. Van der Ploeg regards the farming styles to be empirical objective entities which can be identified through an ethnotaxonomic procedure. However, van der Ploeg tends to confine his classification to market orientation. This contrasts strongly with the farming subculture approach which does not reify the concept, at least no more than do the accepted sociological concepts of culture and subculture. The subculture is not prescriptive, nor empirically objective, but is a heuristic device to explain a process. The subculture approach accepts differences between farmers on a wide range of dimensions, including diversity in terms of social, cultural, economic, agronomic and environmental practices, and not solely on market orientation.

There are problems with the farming subculture approach as well. Most problematic is that there is no definitive statement of the 'farming subculture approach'. There are a number of writers who have considered rural cultural identity in different ways. Even in the way it has been elaborated in this book, the idea of a farming subculture lacks extensive explication. It is likely that, as with any particular approach, the concept highlights some things while potentially ignoring others. It is also likely that the use of the term 'subculture' will tend to make the concept seen to be an extension of functionalist thinking in sociology, and thus will be associated with other ideas from functionalism which we would not support. Further research and articulation of this position are required.

THE APPROACH OF BOURDIEU

Bourdieu (1977) argues that as people do not act by reference to 'rules' set by (sub)cultures, but in terms of the 'shifting possibilities' which are on offer (or perceived to be on offer). Branson and Miller (1991: 40), summarising Bourdieu's position suggest that:

> Once we grasp [that people are] strategic agents operating through and transforming culture, we are on the road to a transcendence of the simplistic schemes that have dominated anthropological and sociological writing. Ideologies are no longer either sets of rules and regulations oriented toward order or reflections of the material conditions of existence; kinship is no longer a clear unambiguous field of rules and terminologies understood through arbitrarily devised concepts; and culture is anything but a field of symbols with clear unambiguous referents.

The notion of 'habitus' is crucial to Bourdieu's system of explanation. It is suggested that people have particular dispositions which, based on their education, wealth, and a host of other social factors, largely contour the strategies which they will adopt in social settings. There is no assumed obedience to rules (which might be implied in the subcultural position) but, rather, a sort of regulated pattern of interaction which occurs, for most people, without a conscious understanding of 'ends' or goals. With unequal opportunities to gain symbolic capital (awards, honours or cultural 'competencies', as defined by those with power to determine what 'counts'), the views of some -- usually the minority with wealth -- will be dominant and be reproduced in society. The task of the sociologist is to understand and expose the meanings which are unknowingly created by people in their day to day lives (Branson and Miller, 1991: 41). This is a necessary first step in overcoming social inequality and other manifestations of domination/subordination in society.

While Bourdieu's approach might appear somewhat esoteric, it nevertheless provides some conceptual tools to extend the subcultural approach. For example, van der Ploeg, (1993) has stated how close Bourdieu's approach is to that of Hofstee (1946) in the latter's path-breaking attempt to understand something called farming 'lifestyle'.

Bourdieu's work does not appear to have received the theoretical attention which it would seem to deserve, despite potentially having useful explanatory value. However, one approach using the framework created by Bourdieu is a study into the intersections of biography, culture and social structure within agriculture. In her ethnographic work among farm families in the Riverina, Emily Phillips (see Phillips and Gray, 1994; Phillips, forthcoming) is attempting to understand what makes a 'good' farmer in terms of the social relations of everyday life -- social relations which invest some farmers (those with symbolic, cultural and economic capital) with the ability to define what is 'good' and to have others accept that definition. Time (how long one has been farming) and space (which land is owned and farmed) considerations are important to the analysis. Importantly, once the social relations of farming are understood, it will provide opportunities for sociologists to understand how sustainability is conceived, discussed, valued and applied. If it does not accord cultural capital to those who practice it, or if joining Landcare is viewed as something which is not condoned, or if catchment management is viewed in a similar manner, it might be predicted that such approaches may be doomed to fail. If they do provide cultural capital, the opposite might be predicted. There would seem to be some useful insights which might be gained from Phillips' research.

TOWARDS AN INTEGRATIVE APPROACH IN EXTENSION PRACTICE

So far, this chapter has concentrated on the theoretical issues of relevance to extension. The points of value that emerge from these issues need to be reflected in an appropriate model of extension practice. Traditional extension based on the Transfer of Technology (ToT) model has been widely discredited. A radical alternative to the ToT model, the Farmer First position (Chambers et al., 1989), has not been widely accepted or endorsed, is internally inconsistent, and is not helpful in the context of an environmental imperative. Somewhere between these two extreme positions, acknowledging the rationality and diversity of farmers, and the social context in which adoption occurs, as well as understanding the contribution extension can make to sustainable agriculture, must lie an appropriate alternative model of extension practice. Such an approach would necessarily be participatory and can be contrasted from the other perspectives as detailed in Table 8.1.

Table 8.1: Three Idealised Agricultural Extension Models

	Technology transfer	Farmer first	Participatory
Strategy	top down	bottom up	interactive
Aim	technology adapta-tion	empower farmers	co-operative action
Precursors	R&D	experienced farmers	participation of key-stakeholders
Key Players	scientists, extension agents	farmers	stakeholders/ facilitators

Source: Foster, Norton and Brough (pers. com.)

The participatory approach conceives of the activities of research, development and extension/education as complementary. They are also seen as 'developing' in a cyclical manner, involving the activities of key stakeholders throughout the process. Active participation in group meetings is encouraged and the 'extension' task is not one of delivering a product, but of facilitating cooperative action in relation to a negotiated and shared agenda.

To overcome the problem that the farmers' agenda may be different from the more pressing environmental agenda, Richard Clark (see Clark and Coffey, 1993) -- among others (eg, Chamala and Mortiss, 1990; Frank and Chamala, 1992) -- has developed an action learning model in which the extension agent forms groups of like-minded farmers (that is, those who will feel comfortable to discuss specific issues about farming with another 7 or 8 producers). The extension agent facilitates group discussion leading to agreement on what is termed Local Best Practice within the district. Local Best Practice is like an 'ideal type' in that it represents the best methods, approaches, and strategies for solving those problems which farmers themselves have identified. However, the process does not end there. Further learning cycles occur. Farmers will, for example, recognise that they do not understand what a particular plant will do to the soil, how to determine a paddock's acidity level, when to mate cattle after dry conditions and so on. At these times, the extension agent facilitates in a different way, and will, on behalf of the group, invite someone with the requisite knowledge to attend the next meeting at which the issue will be discussed. In further meetings, the new knowledge is incorporated into the Local Best Practice model by the farmers, according to their interests and priorities. If further questions/ concerns need to be addressed, these become the focus of further meetings and others may be invited to present to the group.

The actions of the group in trying to follow Local Best Practice is another essential feature of this model. It is not sufficient for the group to have developed what is seen to be desirable by group members. Members are asked to consider the ways in which their own farms and their own farm practices vary from those in the best practice model. More importantly, they seek ways to implement best practice (or best practices) on their own properties and to report back to the group the outcomes of the changes in their management of their properties. The overall outcome, in this sense, is the adoption by farmers of what they have jointly decided is the best means of managing their properties. There has been no 'directive' from an extension agent. There have been suggestions from -- but no imposition of ideas by -- 'experts', and no requirement that any particular activity be undertaken on the farm. Instead, there has been a non threatening environment for producers to become aware of the problems which are being experienced in the district, to have developed a form of strategic plan which is 'owned' by the group, to try new ideas and methods, to report back to the group the results of the implemented changes, and to have had input from those with external knowledge in a way which serves the interests of the group rather than the interests of those providing the knowledge. It is democratic, fosters participation, is -- for the extension service -- a relatively cost effective method of extension service delivery, and appears to lead very quickly to actions by the group which address issues which members of that group have decided are important.

This is not to suggest that the Local Best Practice approach is the answer to the extension needs of the entire Australian farming community. It too would appear to generate its own concerns. First, what of those farmers who do not, cannot, or will not, readily form part of any local group? They will remain, just as with the traditional extension model, as 'outsiders' whose actions may (or may not) be deleterious to the environment. Second, many things will not be revealed about individual on-farm behaviour within group settings. Farmers may not be willing to expose their current practices for fear of being ridiculed, or for fear of having others copy what has taken years of work to achieve. Third, there is a desire to reach a consensus about what constitutes Local Best Practice. What room is there for dissension? What if dissension leads to ostracism? Fourth, the composition of the group will, of necessity, be limited to begin with. Will women have representation? Will older farmers be preferred over younger members of a farm family? This is an important issue when it is considered that younger farm members may have a better formal education than their (male) parent, and be more attuned to environmental issues. Fifth, what if the group's solution to the issue being discussed is one which is out of keeping with what is desired by the authorities? Does the facilitator have a role to inform the state about practices which may well suit the group, but lead to downstream problems which undermine sustainability in those areas? Sixth, if a group fails time and time again to bring about actions which alleviate the problems faced, does the facilitator return to what might be a more familiar role of adviser? Many extension agents receive both status and personal satisfaction from providing expert knowledge. And most have a great deal to give. How is this knowledge to be legitimised within the group setting, and what if a dependency relationship develops between the extension agent and the group which is being facilitated? Seventh, very few existing extension agents have been trained in group processes. What if the agent is unable to move from the older one-to-one paradigm to the group setting? Who should be recruited to undertake the new group-based extension, what training should those people receive and who is to pay? Eighth, when, if at all, should the extension agent leave the group entirely to its own devices -- when the extension agent believes that all has been achieved that is possible, when the state determines that a group has had sufficient of the extension officer's time, or at a time at which the group decides? Ninth, what of the involvement in decision making on farms by others residing in the catchment area? Most farmers would be outraged if it were suggested that the discussion about activities on their properties should include 'outsiders' who might possibly know nothing about agriculture. Yet, this is the very essence of catchment management and Landcare -- two approaches which have been very successful in having farmers understand the relationship of their properties to the wider catchment and the competing interests of those within it (see Campbell and Siepen, 1994; cf Morrisey and Lawrence, 1995). Finally, there is the wider issue of what constitutes Best Practice. What might appear sound at one time, might prove to be economically disastrous, environmentally improper or politically naive, at another. Farmers may interpret the group processes as little more than the latest 'fad' and not be prepared to invest time (and money) into something which places peer group pressure on them to alter their attitudes and behaviour. The only incentive many will have is that they will be conforming with a group decision. They may remain sceptical about the longer term benefits of any group-based decision, particularly one which might lead to changes in practices which reduce output for the sake of the environment.

Clearly, there is a need to research the new methods of extension in a rigorous way before there is any wholesale abandonment of traditional extension methods. Other similar approaches to that of Local Best Practice -- Farm Management 500, Participative Action Management, various ideas about Landcare, and so on -- are also being trialed around Australia (see discussion in Frank and Chamala, 1992; Campbell and Siepen, 1994). They show great promise of being part of a multifaceted approach to extension which is evolving in Australia. As Frank and Chamala (1992: 136) have noted:

> Agricultural extension strategies have shifted from the 'transfer of technology' model with its emphasis on optimal productivity to the management of knowledge systems for sustainable and equitable productivity. This requires a multidimensional perspective involving multiple organisations as partners ... [This requires] individual empowerment and associated freedom of choice. It requires the devolution of power from hierarchical authorities so that common, sustainable benefits may be distributed throughout the community. Extension therefore ... [ought to be] concerned with managing change in complex societies which are dynamic and uncertain. It has grown from agriculture to service the needs of all stakeholders within the community. In order to be effective, it needs to select from a wide range of methodologies generated by new ways of thinking, spread across traditional paradigm boundaries.

CONCLUSION

The 'farming styles' approach of van der Ploeg remains an important (albeit somewhat limited) contribution in terms of increasing the awareness of the existence, and of identifying the different types, of farming styles adopted by farmers in particular settings. Some of the limitations of the farming styles approach would appear to be overcome by developing an approach which focusses upon the ways meanings are negotiated between farmers. Such a 'subcultural' approach would benefit from the theoretical insight provided by Bourdieu. In all cases, the important point is that the different management philosophies of farmers need to be considered in any sociology of agriculture and in any agricultural extension program. They help to explain how diversity in agriculture is created and reproduced -- despite the influence of powerful macro political and economic processes.

Logical contradictions in extension models and theories have been identified. These have become increasingly obvious as environmental degradation in agriculture has become more severe. It is obvious that some sort of participatory model for extension practice is required -- one that recognises not only the heterogeneity and diversity within agriculture, but which also accepts farmers as knowledge generators who make choices based on available information as evaluated by themselves and with reference to their experience both in a practical and cultural sense.

CONCLUSION
THE ENVIRONMENTAL AND SOCIAL IMPERATIVE FOR AUSTRALIAN AGRICULTURE

CHAPTER 9

POLITICAL ECONOMY PERSPECTIVES ON AUSTRALIAN AGRICULTURE

Despite GATT and other attempts to eliminate those trade and other barriers which, if fully successful, would result in benefits flowing to a relatively unprotected Australian agricultural sector, there is little evidence at this stage that the expected advantages are being obtained. The protectionist policies of the European Economic Community and the United States, the impact of drought, and the sluggishness of commodity trade, combined with the economic rationalist policies of the Australian government (manifested in the withdrawal of services and support for farming), have resulted in a continuation of a *crisis in Australian agriculture*. This crisis can be seen in reduced incomes to Australian farmers, the foreclosing by banks on farms considered unviable, governmental moves to strengthen structural adjustment, and a growing social malaise within farming. There had been, as well, a deterioration in the capacity of the farming community to address the economic (and other) problems it faces in the nineties.

It has not always been the marginal farmers who have been forced out of agriculture. The most marginal farmers in an income-generating sense are often the ones who have no debt and who may have the best strategies for surviving in times of financial crisis. They may continue in production by adopting survivalist strategies which include, among other things, minimising their input costs, reducing household expenditures, or by having members undertake off-farm work.

Declining wealth in agriculture, in concert with the rationalisation of government and private sector services, has led to a decline in the financial well-being of many rural towns. The resulting downward spiral in economic activity contributes further to a reduction in services available to rural people and undermines the fabric of social life (Lawrence, 1987; Stone, 1992). In this sense it can be reasonably argued that the crisis in agriculture has lead to a more thoroughgoing *rural crisis*. In Australia, as in the United States, increases in agricultural production are associated with economic and social underdevelopment in rural areas, in particular, to reduced employment opportunities and to population decline in those areas (Lawrence, 1987; Lawrence, 1990).

Concurrent with the crises in agriculture and rural society has been a crisis in *agricultural extension* in Australia. It may be conceived as having four components: *a fiscal crisis* as a response to reduced government funding; *an effectiveness crisis* because it has been adduced that extension practices are not working -- with farmers failing to adopt many practices, particularly environmental management practices; *a legitimation crisis* in that extension services have been criticised by farmers; and *a theoretical crisis,* because outdated traditional extension thinking is yet to be replaced by any cohesive, coherent and widely-accepted alternative.

Of importance in the nation's overall pursuit of economic rationalist policies (Carroll and Manne, 1992; Rees et al., 1993) has been the ways the States have addressed the fiscal problem of financing the infrastructural needs of growing urban populations from a slowly growing tax base. In a crude fashion, what State governments have done is to reduce the level of services available to particular sections of the population -- including, where possible, turning government activities into user pays services. Agricultural extension services -- as with other services that were provided freely (or with subsidy) to farmers -- have been cut, reorganised, 'rationalised' and, where possible, commercialised. At the very time the rural sector has experienced considerable upheaval, State governments have reduced their level of activity in funding its activities in the 'people side' of agriculture. Extension has been one of the main government services to face internal restructuring.

At the same time as Australia has experienced crises in agriculture, rural society and extension, it has also experienced a growing *environmental crisis*. This has been related, in particular, to the practices which Australian farmers have adopted as a means of remaining viable. The extent and scale of these environmental problems -- particularly those associated with land degradation -- are unprecedented. We have suggested that the severity of the environmental crisis has lead to an inescapable environmental imperative to find ways to allow farmers to remain economically viable while moving to more sustainable forms of production and resource management.

An important question we raise in this book is: how will the environmental imperative be addressed without some form of state intervention aimed at supporting farmers in the widely acknowledged task of altering their attitudes to farming and abandoning the (non sustainable) practices upon which many have based their livelihood?

WILL BIOTECHNOLOGY PROVIDE SOLUTIONS TO ENVIRONMENTAL DEGRADATION?

In our coverage of agro-biotechnology, we canvassed the notion of a new 'technical' approach to the problem of degraded farmlands and slow productivity growth. It was suggested that agro-biotechnology -- supported by the state in its desire to increase the international competitiveness of Australian agriculture -- carries with it the promise of improving, in a dramatic fashion, such things as the amount of milk produced per cow, the growth rate of pigs, the ability of fruits to survive long periods after harvesting, the creation of novel plants which have their own capacity to repel insect and fungi attacks, as well as plants which will grow in saline conditions and colder/warmer or drier/wetter locations. Australian biotechnologists and genetic engineers have, for example, recently discovered the 'browning' gene in fruits and vegetables. Its 'neutralisation' would allow consumers to purchase pre-cut vegetables which do not exhibit deterioration, potato growers to reduce the bruising which causes losses during harvesting and packing, cane farmers to have premium quality sugar in an increasingly competitive world marketplace, and wine makers to prevent discolouration, oxidation and flavour loss in wine grapes (*Australian,* 17 December 1994: 46).

There is no denying the great promise that biotechnology holds. In the national survey of agro-biotechnologists described in Chapter 4, the scientists were largely unequivocal about the potential benefits of genetically engineered products. They would -- at one and the same time -- increase agricultural productivity, improve the quality of the environment, increase the sustainability of agriculture and allow for a reduction in the level of inputs, including those agro-industrial inputs which are implicated in environmental pollution. When farmers were asked for their assessment, while largely positive about the development of biotechnologies, they were generally ignorant about what was being developed, by whom and for what purpose. They gave qualified support for the new technology, but rather wondered how they would decrease production costs, improve the quality of the environment, or increase sustainability. They overwhelmingly endorsed the view that agro-biotechnologists should spend more time talking to them about research being conducted and the products resulting from that research.

For their part, the scientists also agreed that more time should be spent with farmers -- the eventual users of the results of their research. Most felt, however, that with the new demands forced upon science by the state, there was little opportunity to do this. In other words, there was evidence that the mistakes of the past -- of not considering the needs of clients in agricultural research from the very beginning -- were being perpetuated. The idea of biotechnology as some sort of technical solution which has merit independently of any social considerations must be seen for what it is -- a modern form of technological determinism. As such, and notwithstanding the important ecosocial concerns about the likelihood for environmental destruction, a reduction in biodiversity and rejection by consumers, biotechnology has the potential to fail for the same reasons other technologies have failed before: it is not likely to be whole-heartedly embraced by those who are expected to use it; it has been developed outside the context of the knowledge and experiences of average farmers and their concerns; and it is consistent with a strategy of agribusiness to patent products for sale as inputs to the agricultural production process. In other words, it conforms to, rather than challenges, the present 'high tech' trajectory in agriculture -- one which has seen Australian producers produce increasing volumes of food and fibre for oversupplied world markets.

At a time when farmers and farming communities could be expected to have a real interest in the development and application of biotechnologies, they have largely been prevented from gaining such knowledge. The scientists have not had time to explain what is happening; and, in the context of pressure on extension services, extension officers have not had the resources, training or the state's imprimatur to explain the 'new' agriculture to potential users. It must be assumed that the older 'trickle down' theories are still in vogue. The discussion of biotechnology, as one of the latest technologies to impact upon Australian agriculture, might lead us to believe that very little has changed in relation to the state's understanding of so-called 'technology transfer' and of the relationship between science and agriculture. It would seem also, given the potential to alleviate (and the potential to create) environmental problems facing Australian farmlands, that an opportunity for the state to elevate biotechnology in the minds of farmers and those concerned with resource depletion is being missed.

THE POTENTIAL FOR AGRICULTURAL EXTENSION

Agricultural extension agencies have tended to respond to reduced government funding in three main ways: by *segmentation of the client base* and only dealing with top-end farmers; by *privatisation* and the adoption of user-pays fees for services; and by the *adoption of group extension approaches and bottom-up philosophies* that reduce the cost of extension services and show farmers how to take responsibility for their own problems. While these strategies may or may not be politically acceptable and/or socially desirable, none is appropriate for dealing with environmental problems. None, that is, has been shown to address successfully the environmental imperative.

In order to protect the agricultural environment, Federal and State governments must consider giving renewed consideration to interventionist strategies. Farmers believe they need more education and support (Reeve and Black, 1993) and even as 'dry' an organisation as the NFF has explicitly stated its support for the continued government funding of extension:

> [The] NFF believes that State agencies should maintain their extension services. Government advisory services are an essential supplement to the publicly funded research effort, and also to support the research which is being undertaken in environment, landcare and catchment management, and that is unlikely to be effectively extended to farmers by private agencies (NFF, 1993: 87).

At the moment, Australian governments are committed to the philosophy of economic rationalism (see Pusey, 1992). Intervention in the agricultural economy, which is needed in order to protect society and the environment from the non-market externalities of the production processes, does not have to take older, less acceptable forms such as fertiliser bounties, development allowances, direct subsidies and product underwriting. But they should, at least, provide incentives for farmers to take up, as a matter of urgency, those approaches to farm management, new types of machinery, and environmentally-proven conservation measures which have been shown unambiguously to improve agricultural sustainability.

ALTERNATIVE SOLUTIONS

Australia may take the lead from governments in other developed nations and 'redefine' the meaning of farming and the role of the farmer. A farmer could very easily become a land manager (or conservation officer) for the state. Why, for example, would it not be appropriate in degraded farming systems, for the state to support (pay) farmers better to manage the land on behalf of the people of Australia? Several things would be accomplished here: a farmer would have the income to remain on the land; the state could, in conjunction with the farmer, decide on a plan of soil and vegetative rehabilitation; commercial agriculture -- which has been the cause of so much of the problem -- may give way to the regeneration of a natural habitat; and the effect of regular wages on farming properties might help to keep others in the district (and thereby contribute to rural community sustainability).

This farmer-as-ranger scenario may seem at first a little far fetched. Does it not act against 'free market' forces which should remove the least efficient producer from agriculture? And, in any case, are not farmers the last people to consider working for a wage provided by government? In answer to the first question, it should be recognised that the great majority of farmers are doing all that they can to remain in agriculture. The free market -- which *should* tell them that their skills and capital could be employed elsewhere for greater economic returns -- fails to convince them to sell up and leave. They remain in agriculture, hoping for better times in the future. Here, the state has an opportunity to harness their skills in a manner which both satisfies their desires to remain on the farm, and society's need to ensure that farming practices are conducive to a more sustainable agriculture. In answer to the second question, while it is acknowledged that farmers have valued their independence, they have sought all variety of means to remain in agriculture. This has, in the past included quite significant state underwriting. While such subsidisation is no longer available, it would seem that the environmental imperative puts a new slant on what the state should do to place agriculture firmly on a sustainable trajectory. In other words, there may be many farmers willing to adopt the role as 'land manager' if it helps them simultaneously to improve their farms and to remain in agriculture. Certainly, social research needs to be undertaken to establish whether such an option is at all feasible.

A radical policy shift such as that suggested above may seem out of place in an era defined by economic rationalism. There is a growing need, however, to confront those policies which are undermining farming and slowing the movement to more sustainable forms of production. Current policies, consistent with economic rationalism, have extended the influence of foreign agribusiness. The deregulation of the banking industry and the airlines, the abolition of the monopoly marketing boards, the very limited control on levels of foreign ownership, the privatisation and deregulation of telecommunications and the mass media, and so on, have facilitated the entry of transnational corporations into the Australian economy. In agriculture, both upstream and downstream sectors exhibit high levels of foreign ownership. The food processing industries, the manufacturers, distributors and retailers of agricultural inputs and equipment, and the distributors and retailers of agricultural commodities are largely foreign owned. Australia's largest stock and station agent (agricultural commodity brokers), Elders -- part of the history of Australian agriculture -- is now owned by ConAgra (a US-based multinational). Other Australian icons, including Vegemite, Coon cheese, Akubra hats, Rosella jam, Arnott's biscuits, RM Williams country wear, most Australian beers, and many other rural based companies are owned by foreign interests. It is something of which few Australians appear to be aware of, or -- if they are aware -- to be concerned about.

It is a moot point whether the policies of the state have improved the position of agriculture in the Australian economy. It is true that they have facilitated the entry of foreign capital, made the Australian economy more dependent on the world market, and linked Australian farmers to global agribusiness. But it is not known at this stage whether the agricultural environment is moving toward any long term sustainability. While there appears to be some interest on the part of government to create, through regional development initiatives, what might be termed rural social sustainability, it is likely that this, too, will be premised upon financial interventions. It has been questioned whether the nation could ever achieve environmental sustainability when it is incapable of solving the problem which most rural people want solved: how to create and maintain a quality of life in rural regions which is commensurate with that in urban Australia (see Stehlik and Lawrence, 1995).

We have termed the tendency for centre nations to 'export' environmentally unfriendly, low value agricultural production to the periphery and semi-periphery, while maintaining high value agricultural production and more environmentally friendly agriculture in the centre, as *environmental imperialism*. Such a strategy not only causes environmental degradation in the periphery and semi-periphery, but restricts the economic potential of those countries as well -- limiting them in the present and future to the production of low value commodities. In an increasingly globalised world, any nation attempting to enact environmental regulation beyond that which the multinational corporations believe is acceptable to them is likely to find that the multinational corporation relocate. Molnar (pers. com.) calls this 'jurisdiction shopping'. Peripheral and semi-peripheral nations -- those whose economic power is circumscribed and which are reliant on export earnings -- are limited in what they can or might do in a policy sense by their links with transnational capital. This aspect of globalisation can occur in the centre as well, as witnessed by the transfer of the tuna fishery away from the United States to South America, and then later to Asia, in response to stringent US regulations about the use of the purse-seine method in tuna fishing (in which large numbers of dolphins are also caught) (Bonanno and Constance, 1993; Constance *et al.*, 1993). While the United States might have been able to afford the loss of the tuna industry, losses of entire industries in peripheral nations which exhibit dependency on one or two export-oriented industries can be devastating.

In fact, the continuation of production of high value agricultural production in the centre (for example pork and dairy products in The Netherlands) is directly dependent on the production of cheap bulk feed in the periphery (cassava and what ever other bulk protein can be produced and transported cheaply), and should be seen as part of the economic exploitation of the periphery.

In Australia (the semi-periphery), beef feedlotting is being undertaken and is expanding, but such activity is highly polluting, and since the feedlots tend to be owned by foreign interests, and much of the profit derived from such value adding activity would appear to be bound for overseas shareholders (Lawrence, 1995). Australia is left with the pollution, and with new -- and not necessarily beneficial -- contractual relations in agriculture as farmers, in entering those new production relations, lose autonomy over farm decision-making processes (see Burch, Rickson and Annels, 1992).

The financial situation in which Australian farmers find themselves means that -- irrespective of any improvement in the mid nineties' drought -- there will continue to be economic reasons for farmers to exploit the environment. The characteristics of the environmental problems which farmers are experiencing means that there is very little financial incentive for farmers to adopt more environmentally friendly management practices.

However, in addition to financial constraints upon the implementation of environmental management practices, there are many other reasons why farmers do not adopt these practices -- something which we have identified as being rational from the viewpoint of farmers. As we have shown in our analyses, however, farmers are not exclusively 'rational' in their actions. They pursue many non-economic goals and objectives including the fulfilment of various social values. Yet, the satisfaction of those values, goals and objectives is rational in the sense that it increases individual well-being. While the above political economic analysis sets the general context of the situation of Australian farming and environmental management, it provides insights at the macro level. We need as well to assess how farmers live and make decisions on their own farms and how they conceive, in their own terms, pollution, degradation and environmental management.

We recognise that what is being suggested in these pages may be construed as little more than 'bandaids' for a increasingly volatile and inequitous system of capitalist production. It has been argued in detail elsewhere (Lawrence, 1987; Hindmarsh, 1994), that incremental change within the structure of the system might serve to ameliorate, but is unlikely -- because of the contradictory and exploitative nature of capitalist development -- to overcome, environmental degradation.

As Pfeffer (1992) has suggested, sustainable agriculture within capitalism may not be sustainable agriculture at all. If farmers simply reduce their fuel requirements, and synthetic chemical and fertiliser applications, yet rely upon agribusiness for the purchase of the new genetically engineered seeds, biopesticides and biofertilisers needed for their growth, all that might have been achieved is the movement from an older form of agribusiness dependence, to a new and potentially more environmentally dangerous one (see also Buttel, 1994; Hindmarsh, 1994).

Other writers have erected elaborate theoretical approaches to, and have provided strident defences for, a number of positions which seek to transcend capitalist relations of production and other systems marked by oppressive social relations. Pepper (1993) for example, has suggested that ecosocialism -- in which capitalism is confronted by an environmentally aware working class and its allies -- is potentially the only hope for fundamental changes to a system of production which is based on continued pollution. Albrecht (1994) has stressed that intra- and inter- generational equity and biodiversity are the keys to any real 'sustainable development', and proposes that left-anarchist thought -- which promotes human freedom and understands the 'self-generated organisation present in ecological systems' -- should be embraced by those seeking alternatives to a market based social order. In contrast to the positions of Pepper and Albrecht, Plumwood (1993) has strongly argued that gender relations must be central to any discussion about the future of the environment and the dismantling of structures of domination. She criticises 'deep ecology' as not having a coherent framework to enable liberation from exploitative systems, explores ecofeminist approaches, and concludes that, in a situation in which women were drawn fully into human culture, many of the structural dualisms (such as culture/nature, male/female, mind/body, reason/emotion, self/other) which prevent our understanding the environment, (and ourselves in the environment) will dissolve. True liberation for people and the environment will only be achieved in a system of 'radical democracy, co-operation and mutuality' (1993: 196).

Approaches such as those above are essential in providing alternative frameworks for argument and for disclosing the range of possibilities in the human struggle for personal and environmental 'liberation'. We have not dealt with these at all in this book. We have taken for granted that the political system (with its social inequalities), agricultural practices and existing belief systems will, for better or worse, remain more or less intact for the foreseeable future. While wanting, like the above authors to bring about change, and while recognising that change within an unjust system does not provide the basis for the dismantling of that system, it was nevertheless decided in constructing this book to focus upon how changes could be made now and at the group (rather than the wider structural) level.

As we have stated throughout the book, sociological approaches accept that groups of people develop certain behavioural practices, ways of thinking, and value judgements that are common to that group. It is our contention that to bring about desirable change in agriculture, there is reason to focus upon the ways people -- in this case farmers -- live their daily lives. Understanding farming subcultures must be part of the solution to the problems of environmental degradation in agriculture. Farmers have preferred ways of conceiving of issues concerning farm management and environmental management. These can be described as 'farming styles'. Is this latest thinking in agricultural extension/rural sociology the way forward in the development of extension theory? How might extension theory lead to improvements in agricultural sustainability?

AGRICULTURAL EXTENSION: THE KEY TO SUSTAINABILITY?

In Australia, agricultural extension services have, for the greater part of this century, promoted various approaches to productivity enhancement and environmental management. The management practices that have been promoted and adopted have, as revealed in this analysis, resulted in widespread environmental degradation. As part of the recent and pervasive ideology of ecologically sustainable development, and as a response to the economic losses which are being experienced as a result of environmental degradation in agriculture, the task of linking productivity enhancement with environmental management has come to be seen as crucial. In the past, and for the most part the present as well, different agencies have been responsible for different tasks -- some for bringing about productivity increases and some for introducing environmental controls. The future requires extension services to be able to meet the task of bringing together the (previously conflicting) productivity and environmental concerns in agriculture and to do so under the banner of 'sustainable agriculture'.

Yet, one would not wish to rely upon the services of traditional extension agencies as the catalyst for environmental improvement. Agricultural extension has come under considerable criticism especially for its reliance on, and the limitations of, the top-down, unilinear model of transfer of technology. Extension has also been criticised for uncritically promoting the products of agricultural science research, for being at the behest of agribusiness (advocating, almost exclusively, pro-agribusiness solutions to the problems of commercial farming) and for marginalising farmers' local knowledge. Some people have used these criticisms of extension to argue that extension services ought to be disbanded and that instead, farmers ought to be encouraged to solve their own problems. The most appropriate role for the state in this conception is that of providing group facilitation. This is partly the rhetoric of Landcare in Australia.

Australian Federal Government support for Landcare may be a partial response to the withdrawal by the States of extension services. It may also be predicated on Landcare being a cheaper form of delivery than traditional extension activities. It is also a response to community demands for both participation in decisions affecting the environment and pressures from green groups to include the so-called 'brown' concerns of agricultural environmental degradation in policies relating to environmental improvement in Australia.

While farmers are critical of traditional extension services, they are also very supportive of them. Farmers complain that the advice given is not practical enough, that the recommendations are not cost effective, that the information given is occasionally wrong, that extension officers do not spend enough time in the field, and that they help certain farmers more than other farmers (usually rich farmers over poor farmers). These complaints have been -- but should not be -- construed to mean that farmers do not value or do not want those services. The evidence suggests that farmers are concerned about the delivery and implementation of extension services -- not their existence. Not surprisingly, farmer surveys consistently reveal considerable concern about the reduction of funding to extension services and about the reduction in the quality of those services.

Farmer support for traditional extension (on-farm visits, field days and literature) does not restrict their support for new approaches to extension such as group extension. Australian farmers are very supportive of Landcare, for example. Considerable benefits have accrued and will continue to accrue because of the activities of Landcare groups in Australia -- as Campbell and Siepen (1994) have so clearly shown in their recent book. But Landcare should not be seen as an alternative to traditional extension. We would suggest it is a complementary approach to existing extension methods in increasing farmers' awareness of certain issues, especially environmental issues. We have noted earlier that Landcare activities have actually led to the increased utilisation of traditional extension services. In circumstances where Landcare increases farmers' motivation for information and awareness about environmental problems, but farmers are still reliant on traditional extension services to implement environmental management practices -- and those services are not provided -- then Landcare will have served only to frustrate the very farmers who might have been relied upon to alter their farming practices. If appropriate safeguards required in all voluntary associations (to ensure, for example, equality of participation, develop leadership, and address the problem of 'burnout') are not implemented within Landcare, it may become little more than a short lived -- albeit creative -- experiment. One of the keys to its likely future success appears to be the injection of more funding (Campbell and Siepen, 1994).

Given the above analysis, there exists a complex problem: an environmental crisis of unprecedented proportion; an economic situation in which farmers and the government have limited resources to invest in environmental management; and Australian governments committed to economic rationalist/de-regulationist ideologies (one result of which is a reduction in agricultural extension services). Continued environmental degradation might be assumed to be an inevitable outcome of this situation. It is not likely that any solution exists without a major change in government philosophy. It is difficult to see how the continued commitment to deregulation and to market-based approaches, together with the predominance of transnational capital in the food and fibre industries, will do anything but hamper attempts to improve environmental management and, *ipso facto,* reduce environmental degradation in agriculture.

It is important, as well, not to overestimate the 'stand alone' possibilities of Landcare-type groupings of farmers and community members. Buttel (1993a) has reported that the momentum behind the drive toward sustainability in US agriculture has slowed. He attributes this to a number of related factors. First, for the wealthier farmers who have survived the farm crisis, there is not the same incentive -- as there might be for poorer farmers -- to embark upon input cost minimisation strategies. Second, the fiscal problems of state governments have largely prevented them from funding new 'sustainable agriculture' programs. Third, there has been a change of interest in the environmental lobby away from agricultural issues to those of biodiversity, rainforests and so forth. Fourth, contradictory views among scientists over the issue of global warming, have thrown into confusion the very basis of other arguments about the likelihood of environmental catastrophe. Finally, there has been very little evidence that the voters in developed nations are keen to support 'green foreign aid' packages designed to address the problem of environmental degradation in developing nations.

Buttel also highlights the internal divisions within the environmental movement in the USA as well as the failure of public policy to encourage 'resource conserving' agricultural production systems. He highlights, in particular, the inherent vulnerability of green- focussed movements:

> Sustainability is essentially an environmental ideology. Accordingly, it faces the dilemma of most extralocal (rather than 'Not In My Back Yard') environmentalism, in that it has no 'natural constituency' or self- evident 'bearers'. By contrast with most other left movements, such as the civil rights movement and feminism, in which each has a clearly identifiable core constituency, extralocal environmentalism does not. Environmentalism is in the interests of everyone, and thus of no one (Buttel, 1993b: 36).

While we might agree that the environmental movement -- as a 'new social movement' -- is becoming relatively more influential in relation to the older working class movements (see Buttel, 1994), this is not to say that agriculture will be high on the agenda. Those environmentalists in Australia who believe that movements, such as Landcare, are the answer to the problems of agriculture, might be a little more reflective. There is no obvious reason to believe that Landcare will continue to grow in a manner which embraces the entire farming community; and it is unlikely that green concerns will come to bear, in some inevitable way, on the practices of farming. One means of ensuring that sufficient state support for sustainable agriculture is to develop an integrated approach to extension. It has, in conjunction with new forms of technology developed to counter the current problems of land degradation, the ability to somehow regularise and legitimatise the new practices which have received the seal of approval from the environmental movement.

AGRICULTURAL EXTENSION: THE NEED FOR AN INTEGRATED PERSPECTIVE

Like Wendell Berry (1977, 1981, 1990) and Rivera (1991), we cannot accept that agriculture means 'agriscience', some inexact 'agribusiness', or simply 'cultivation of the land'. Agriculture means much more than this. Farmers' land management practices have a social, cultural, historical, political, economic, and environmental basis. This implies that the 'cultivation of the land' is more than a technical activity, more than a cultural activity, and more than a response to structural situations. It is a composite activity of enormous social significance to those engaged in it, who consume the products, and who experience the environmental effects of its practices.

In this book, the problems inherent in many of the sociological (and other) theories about contemporary agriculture and agricultural extension have been canvassed. The issue for extension theory is: how is it possible to construct both theory and practice which, at one and the same time, ensures that public interest is considered alongside an entrenched requirement that those with access to the nation's rural resources must succeed in obtaining private profit? If the needs of the public are for clean food, a clean environment (and, of the nation, for export dollars), then this must be given prominence alongside the needs of the farmer to improve output, efficiency and productivity. Two things would seem to be necessary in any adequate analysis: macro processes which allow an understanding of structural constraint, and micro processes which focus upon the subcultural activities of those controlling the nation's resources -- the farmers.

Habermas (1973) challenges researchers, scientists and academics to cater for three elements in the achievement of social praxis:

1. the provision of critical social theories;
2. the organisation of enlightenment, in order to socially validate the theories;
3. the selection of appropriate strategies.

The book has touched upon all three. Our endorsement of an 'actor perspective' -- one which remains conscious of social structure -- is an important start. The point, here, is that it is not appropriate to prescribe specific action for farmers when that action will be based on the decisions made by those who become aware of the problems as it affects them. But it is possible to state that *one* of the appropriate strategies at the level of the state will be to find ways of combining the best of 'one-to-one' extension with the group techniques now being pioneered throughout Australia.

THE VALUE OF A SOCIOLOGICAL CONTRIBUTION

Sociology has not occupied a position of prominence in Australian agricultural research and extension. It is now beginning to make inroads into both, as R&D corporations, governments and local farm and other organisations recognise that the 'people part' of agriculture can no longer be ignored. We have argued that, despite its deficiencies, a modified 'farming styles', or 'subculture of farming' approach needs to be adopted as a means of mapping the variations in farming types, as well as understanding the motivations, interests, concerns, values, desires and actions of farm family members. Sociologists need to do extensive ethnographic fieldwork as a basis for building theories about (and, in more general terms, understanding the basic social relations within) Australian farming systems. They will invariably draw from a variety of theorists and theories.

One strand showing promise at the moment is the application of the work of the French sociologist, Pierre Bourdieu (see Branson and Miller, 1991). Bourdieu has argued that social actors accumulate cultural capital which includes artefacts (such as cars, houses, paintings, gardens and so on) and practices (for example, attending church, speaking in a certain manner, undertaking tertiary studies, or ploughing fields). Such cultural capital links directly with wider social relations of power -- of class, gender, ethnic and racial relations of domination/ subordination. There is a certain logic in the ways cultural capital is accumulated, as well as the way it is valued by social groups. Farmers occupying a particular social field (as part of a farming subculture) have a set of dispositions which attach particular value to (provide cultural capital to) those who achieve in ways sanctioned by others in their social field. In terms of agricultural practices, there will be some farmers who gain community respectability through some practices, or possession of particular knowledge. In the past, cultural capital may have been associated with high levels of output, the quality of output, neat fields, the presence of new machinery, well- kept machinery, the absence of pests, private schooling for children and so on. The task of the sociologist is to find, at the 'subcultural' level, what makes the farming community 'tick': to discover what it values and for what reasons, and how it comes to change its views about what is desirable or undesirable.

People act not according to set rules, but to what they perceive as opportunities and possibilities. They do what they 'sense' is right and which will bring them credit. Bourdieu's approach contains within it the political task of transforming culture through 'subversive revelation' (Branson and Miller, 1991: 38). By exposing taken-for-granted practices as those which often mask inequalities in power, his approach may be employed to *empower* those whose actions on environmental matters will be crucial to Australia's future.

Sociologists would also want to relate the practices of farmer groups to wider structures of power. How do power relations form? Are they organised around gender and class (or other) lines? Are some groups marginalised/dispossessed of power? How does power at the wider level translate to a local system of power relations? It is here that larger macro- sociological concerns reappear: what is the role of the state in fostering certain forms of action at the local level? Is the state's power circumscribed by the nation's relation to global production systems? How are the decisions of transnational capital influencing decisions at the local level? These are at least some of the questions.

The task for rural sociology remains enormous. It would seem desirable for the discipline to learn from the mistakes of extension theory and practice and to ensure that researchers study farmers on farmers' terms. This means spending long periods in the field doing the sorts of observational/ethnographic studies which may appear, to the outsider (and the funding body!), a little too indulgent and/or a waste of time and resources. Van der Ploeg (1993) has gone so far as to suggest that rural sociology should become a 'narrative science' -- one 'recording narrations, documenting those experiences, insights, practices and significant biographies that currently are forgotten, neglected, or deemed irrelevant' (van der Ploeg, 1993: 256). Ethnographic and other 'micro' level studies promise to be some of the most fruitful in rural sociology and have the capacity to contribute greatly to our knowledge of farmer behaviour.

In suggesting this, it is not desirable to abandon sociological survey work among farming populations. In a three state survey, Gray *et al*. (1993) have provided new insights about the ways farmers cope with stress. And in their national survey, Reeve and Black (1993) were able to uncover some of the subtleties of farmer attitudes. Their work provides evidence of the heterogeneity of approaches to farming and resource management and they provide a reminder to those who would overgeneralise about 'Australian farmers'. They found, for example, that:

> in addition to there being financially well off-farmers who are investing in landcare and sustainable practices, and financially-stressed farmers who cannot consider making such

investments ... there (are) ... at least two other groups. These groups are: financially well off farmers with unfavourable conservation attitudes and behaviour, and financially stressed farmers who are probably making considerable personal and family sacrifices to invest in landcare and sustainable practices (Reeve and Black, 1993: 133).

Vanclay and Lockie (1993), and Vanclay and Glyde (1994) have researched the extent of farmers' knowledge about sustainable agriculture, environmental management, and issues involved in farmers' adoption of improved cropping rotations and environmental management strategies. All of these studies have contributed to environmental policy and to the environmental management strategies of various extension agencies. What remains is to undertake further research into the various farming groups and how extension and other policy initiatives can assist in moving these farming groups along a more sustainable trajectory.

Sociology would seem to justify an 'extension of extension' -- the movement of extension toward the understanding of, and the evolution of, new practices based upon, social groups. In proceeding in this direction, there is a need to recognise that farmers are knowledgeable and intelligent and that they interpret information and technology in terms of their own understanding of the world. Research would most likely reveal that they have partial knowledge of many of the issues which they face, and that they desire assistance in formulating, and finding solutions to, the environmental and other problems they face. In assisting farmers, agricultural extension personnel are likely to achieve success by working with them and not against them. Group processes, in which farmers control the agenda, promise to be a forum for the 'reclaiming' of knowledge. In their new group facilitation roles, extension agents should avoid condescension. Neither should extension agents attempt to marginalise or ignore farmers who do not agree with the extension message. Sociology can help to establish which group processes are conducive to change among participants as well as to identify the social limits to group 'performance'. Just as significantly, it has the tools to enable the identification of group 'type', farming 'style' or 'subculture'.

GUIDELINES FOR THE FUTURE
OF AGRICULTURAL EXTENSION

There is a need to recognise that farmers adopt new ideas, not because those ideas have been transferred and disseminated or diffused, but because they are of value, in one form or another. When ideas or technologies are not adopted, it is because the ideas or technologies were of no value, were interpreted (correctly or incorrectly) as being of no value, accorded no cultural capital, or did not fit with the economic or social needs and expectations of the farmers themselves. It is also important to appreciate that ideas and technologies that are adopted are also *adapted* by farmers as they use them in the development of their own farming strategy. Farmers are quite creative with respect to management practices and technological ideas: they will decide upon what they want and under the circumstances which they choose.

There is a need to accept that farmers, like all people in society, are cultural beings who operate in social groups which may, in a sociological sense, be 'subcultures'. The compliance with the subculture is not a conscious activity. Such subcultural behaviour is group behaviour which prescribes certain actions and understandings, and proscribes others. We argue explicitly for a return to a focus, not on some nebulous and homogeneous 'rural society', but on the variety of cultural forms of *different farmer groups* within Australian agriculture.

In our experience, and as suggested above, we recognise it is dangerous to argue that 'farmers' -- as some supposed homogeneous group -- support particular policies, believe certain things, or act in a certain manner. Australian agriculture is extremely varied. A pineapple producer from Central Queensland is linked in structurally different ways to the economy than, say, a grazier from Victoria, or a beef producer in Western Australia. Furthermore, as British researchers Flynn and Lowe (1994) have argued, it is not only the differences in farming practices and attitudes which vary between regions, but the countryside itself varies. They were able to identify four different types: the 'preserved', 'contested', 'paternalistic' and 'clientist' countryside. Such differentiation has occurred as a result of challenges to the dominant local culture by new social groups with their own social and political agendas. The sociologist's task is to discover the variations between groups and what this might mean for sustainable agriculture.

The secret to effective extension is to understand what motivates farmers to do certain things under certain conditions and to see the class, status and gender relations which impinge upon any/every decision. This, in turn, requires an understanding of power relations in society, an appreciation of group processes and a concern for the wider structural imperatives and impediments which confront the farmer. Such an approach might easily be expected to be the task of a sociologically trained extension staff. That staff does not exist at present in Australia.

In a similar vein, the rationality of farmer behaviour needs to be considered in response to the values held by individuals. While, for the reasons above, we would not want to overgeneralise, we can suggest that studies of farmers have revealed that they are not necessarily overly motivated by profit maximisation: they are interested in making a good living, for a certain amount of work, and by employing a certain style of farm management -- one that does not cause too much environmental damage, and does not mean they (or their families) will be exposed daily to unacceptable financial or physical risks. A primary goal in life for Australian farmers is to hand the farm on to the next descendant (usually -- in the context of the entrenched and subordinate place of women in the structure of farming relations -- to the eldest son) in a better condition than it was received from their own parents. While this may simply be farmer ideology talking, it is nevertheless useful to take the statement at face value and, through extension practice, constantly remind farmers that the goal may be one which can be achieved through the adoption of more sustainable practices.

CONCLUSION

Australia is facing a serious environmental crisis of massive land and water degradation. There is an environmental imperative for action to prevent this problem continuing and/or worsening. Land degradation has occurred as a result of the aggregate, everyday, activities of Australian farmers. The management practices of Australian farmers are clearly not environmentally sustainable. Furthermore, because some of these environmental problems are occurring for the first time, or are at an unprecedented level of severity, there may be little in the knowledge or experience of farmers which is especially useful in dealing with these problems. We know, from our -- and others' -- research, that some farmers ignore these problems and may refuse to accept that they are occurring on their own farms. The complexity of these environmental problems means that even if farmers did perceive these problems as occurring, there is little that they could do to ameliorate the longer term effects. The regional basis of the problems means that community-based action for change is required.

The environmental problems in agriculture can be conceived as part of what is known as the social dilemma (prisoners' dilemma, tragedy of the commons, free rider problem) (see Hardin, 1968; Olson, 1965; Vanclay, 1981). To encapsulate, while at the aggregate level the practices of farmers need to change, at the individual farmer level, it may not make economically rational sense to change. Of course, these dilemmas do not adequately reflect the social nature of agriculture; they ignore the subcultural aspects of farming. Nevertheless, the point is *society cannot expect that farmers will act against what they view as their own self interest in order to protect the environment for the future of all Australians.*

New environmentally-friendly management practices need to be developed in conjunction with farmers, and farmers need to be assisted in adoption/adaptation of these new management practices. It is already known, for example, that more sustainable practices include (in different regions and under different conditions): improved crop rotations, weed control, constraints on fertiliser use, minimum tillage, the retention of stubble, regular liming, use of deep rooted perennial pasture species, lower stocking rates, increased vegetative cover, revegetation (especially tree replacement), increased efficiency of water use, and a reduction of the use of toxic pesticides (Standing Committee on Agriculture and Resource Management, 1993). What might the farmers' own interpretations of these strategies be? There is a need for useful and applied agricultural research, new links to be formed between those conducting research and those responsible for its 'extension' and eventual utilisation, and a need for new forms of extension which effectively operate to encourage farmers to adopt environmentally friendly practices. Such research needs to be done in conjunction with farmers to increase the usefulness, validity and effectiveness or the research and extension process.

Finally, we need to consider the economic situation of farmers. Farmers are not able to change management practices when they are financially stressed. Yet changes in the macro-processes of capitalist society are continuing to limit their capacity to harness new, more environmentally sound, farming strategies. The crisis of agriculture in Australia is of an enormous magnitude, partly as a result of global processes over which Australian farmers and Australian governments have little control, and partly because of the responses of Australian governments which, in the name of 'economic rationalism', appear to be exacerbating the situation. If we are at all concerned about the future of the Australian agricultural environment, we must implore Australian governments (State and Federal) to rethink their policies in relation to structural adjustment, rationalisation of services, privatisation of agricultural agencies, funding of extension services, subsidisation and support to farmers, protectionism, as well as a whole array of related policies.

It would be prudent, in the latter years of the 1990s -- when we know that we must change our agricultural strategies, but have not quite found the best means of doing so -- to treat the environment as a non-renewable resource. The soil that is blown across to Aotearoa (New Zealand) can not be replaced; the trees which are bulldozed in the name of 'development' can no longer protect catchment areas against rising watertables; the chemicals which are applied to farmlands must invariably enter the fragile river systems of Australia; and the people who live in environmentally degraded and socially marginal communities will continue to face a deteriorating standard of living. We need to give greater consideration to the protection and rehabilitation of our natural resources and to the improvement in the economic opportunities afforded rural people. Hopefully, a more rational and less ideologically-committed debate can occur in Australia -- with governments recognising their obligations to farmers and to the environment. Strategic interventions aimed at addressing the environmental imperative may be one means of helping to ensure that the lifestyle prospects of rural people, and the sustainability of the countryside, will be enhanced for the benefit of future generations of Australians.

REFERENCES

Ackoff, R. (1979), 'Resurrecting the future of operational research', *Journal of the Operational Research Society* 30 (3): 189-199.

Almås, R. (1992), 'Social consequences of the new biotechnologies in Norway', *Paper delivered at the Fifth Annual Meeting of the Rural Sociological Society,* Pennsylvania State University, 16-19 August.

Alston, M. (1995), *Women on the Land: the Hidden Heart of Rural Australia,* Kensington: University of NSW Press.

Armstrong, W. (1978), 'New Zealand: imperialism, class and uneven development', *Australian and New Zealand Journal of Sociology* 14(3): 297-303.

Arrighi, G. (1990), 'The developmentalist illusion: a reconceptualisation of the semi-periphery', in Martin, W. (ed.), *Semi-Peripheral States in the World Economy,* Westport: Greenwood, 11-44.

Australian   26 June 1991.

Australian   14 November 1992.

Australian   22 May 1993.

Australian   2 February 1994.

Australian   7 December 1994.

Australian   17 December 1994.

Australian   21 December 1994.

Australian Consumers Association and Australian Confederation of Consumer Organisations (1990), *Submission to the Inquiry into Genetically Modified Organisms,* Sydney: Australian Consumers Association.

Australian Farm Journal   May 1991.

Australian Farm Journal   November 1991.

Australian Farm Journal   October 1992.

Australian Farm Journal   November 1992.

Australian Farm Journal   October 1994.

Australian Farm Journal   November 1994.

Australian Farm Journal   December 1994.

Australian Farm Journal   January 1995.

Australian Farm Journal   April 1995.

Australian Science and Technology Council (1990), *Science, Technology and Australia's Future,* Canberra: Australian Government Publishing Service.

Avery, J. (1992), 'Extension methods for sustainable farming in Victorian cropping zones', in Department of Primary Industries and Energy, *Improved Extension Methods Workshop: Proceedings and Papers,* Canberra: Department of Primary Industries and Energy, 20-26.

Ban, A. van den, and Hawkins, S. (1988), *Agricultural Extension,* Harlow: Longman.

Barr, N. and Cary, J. (1984), *Farmer Perceptions of Soil Salting: Appraisal of an Insidious Hazard,* School of Agriculture and Forestry, University of Melbourne.

Barr, N. and Cary, J. (1992a), *Greening a Brown Land: The Search for Sustainable Land Use in Australia,* Melbourne: Macmillan.

Barr, N. and Cary, J. (1992b), 'The dilemma of conservation farming: to use or not use chemicals', in Lawrence, G., Vanclay, F. and Furze, B. (eds), *Agriculture, Environment and Society,* Melbourne: Macmillan, 233-258.

Baumgardt, B. and Martin, M. (eds) (1991), *Agricultural Biotechnology: Issues and Choices,* Purdue University Agricultural Experiment Station, Indiana.

Bawden, R. (1989), *Systems Agriculture: Learning to Deal with Complexity,* Sydney: Wiley.

Beale, B. and Fray, P. (1990), *The Vanishing Continent,* Sydney: Hodder and Stoughton.

Begg, J. and Peacock, J. (1990), 'Modern genetic and management technologies in Australian agriculture', in Williams, D. (ed.), *Agriculture in the Australian Economy* (3rd edn), Melbourne: Sydney University Press, 68-81.

Beilharz, P. (1991), 'Max Weber', in Beilharz, P. (ed.), *Social Theory: A Guide to Central Thinkers,* Sydney: Allen and Unwin, 224-230.

Bell, S. (1994), 'Lies of the land', *Arena Magazine* October-November: 18-21.

Berlan-Darque, M. and Kalaora, B. (1992), 'The ecologization of French agriculture', *Sociologia Ruralis* 32(1): 104-114.

Berry, W. (1977), *The Unsettling of America: Culture and Agriculture,* San Francisco: Sierra Club.

Berry, W. (1981), *The Gift of Good Land,* San Francisco: North Point Press.

Berry, W. (1990), *What Are People For?,* San Francisco: North Point Press.

Bolton, G. (1981), *Spoils and Spoilers: Australians make their Environment 1788-1980,* Sydney: Allen and Unwin.

Bonanno, A. (1987), *Small Farms: Persistence with Legitimation,* Boulder: Westview.

Bonanno, A. and Constance, D. (1993), 'The state and the regulatory process: the case of the global tuna-fish industry', *Paper presented to the workshop on 'Concepts of the State in a Changing Global Agri-Food System',* Wageningen, The Netherlands, July 31- August 2.

Bonanno, A., Busch, L., Friedland, W., Gouveia, L. and Mingione, E. (eds) (1994), *From Columbus to ConAgra: The Globalization of Agriculture and Food,* Kansas: University Press of Kansas.

Boreham, P., Clegg, S., Emmison, J., Marks, G. and Western, J. (1989), 'Semi-peripheries or particular pathways: the case of Australia, New Zealand and Canada as class formations', *International Sociology* 4(1): 67-90.

Bourdieu, P. (1977), *Outline of a Theory of Practice,* London: Cambridge University Press.

Bourdieu, P. (1981), 'Men and machines', in Knorr-Cetina, K. and Cicourel, A. (eds), Advances in *Social Theory and Methodology: Toward an Integration of Micro- and Macro- Sociologies,* London: Routledge and Kegan Paul, 304-317.

Bourdieu, P. (1990), *The Logic of Practice,* Cambridge: Polity.

Bowler, I. (1992), '"Sustainable agriculture" as an alternative path of farm business development', in Bowler, I., Bryant, C. and Nellis, M. (eds), *Contemporary Rural Systems in Transition,* Volume 2, Wallingford, UK: CAB International, 237-258.

Branson, J. and Miller, D. (1991), 'Pierre Bourdieu', in Beilharz, P. (ed.), *Social Theory: a Guide to Central Thinkers,* Sydney: Allen and Unwin, 37-45.

Brokensha, D., Warren, D. and Werner, O. (1980), *Indigenous Knowledge Systems and Development,* Lanham: University Press of America.

Bronowski, J. (1973), *The Ascent of Man,* London: British Broadcasting Service.

Brouwers, J. (1993), *Rural People's Response to Soil Fertility Decline: The Adja Case (Benin),* PhD thesis, Wageningen Agricultural University Papers 93-4.

Bruin de, R. and Roex, J. (1994), 'Farmer initiatives as countervailing power: a new approach to sustainable agricultural development', in Symes, D. and Jansen, A. (eds), *Agricultural Restructuring and Rural Change in Europe,* Wageningen: Wageningen Agricultural University, 195-208.

Bryant, L. (1991), 'Farm family displacement', in Alston, M. (ed.), *Family Farming: Australia and New Zealand,* Wagga Wagga: Centre for Rural Social Research, Charles Sturt University, 77-92.

Bryant, L. (1992), 'Social aspects of the farm financial crisis', in Lawrence, G., Vanclay, F. and Furze, B. (eds), *Agriculture, Environment and Society,* Melbourne: Macmillan, 157-172.

Bulletin 16 July 1991

Bulletin 31 July 1991

Bultena, G., Nowak, P., Hoiberg, E. and Albrecht, D. (1981), 'Farmers' attitudes toward land use planning', *Journal of Soil and Water Conservation* 36(4): 37-41.

Burch, D., Hulsman, K., Hindmarsh, R. and Brownlea, A. (1990), *Biotechnology Policy and Industry Regulation: Some Ecological, Social and Legal Considerations.* Submission to the

House of Representatives Standing Committee on Industry Science and Technology Inquiry into Genetically Modified Organisms, Brisbane: Griffith University.

Burch, D., Rickson, R. and Annels, R. (1992), 'The growth of agribusiness: environmental and social implications of contract farming', in Lawrence, G., Vanclay, F. and Furze, B. (eds), *Agriculture, Environment and Society*, Melbourne: Macmillan, 259-277.

Burdge, R. and Vanclay, F. (1995), 'Social impact assessment', in Vanclay, F. and Bronstein, D. (eds), *Environmental and Social Impact Assessment*, Chichester: Wiley, 31-65.

Bureau of Rural Resources (1991), *Biotechnology in Australia: Perspectives and Issues for Animal Production.* Working Paper WP/16/91, Canberra: Bureau of Rural Resources.

Busch, L., Lacy, W., Burkhardt, J. and Lacy, L. (1991), *Plants, Power, and Profit*, Oxford: Basil Blackwell.

Buttel, F. (1989), 'Social science research on biotechnology and agriculture: a critique', *The Rural Sociologist* 9(3): 5-15.

Buttel, F. (1992), 'Environmentalization: origins, processes and implications for rural social change', *Rural Sociology* 57(1): 1-27.

Buttel, F. (1993a), 'The sociology of agricultural sustainability: some observations on the future of sustainable agriculture', *Agriculture, Ecosystems and Environment*, 46(1-4): 175-186.

Buttel, F. (1993b), 'The production of agricultural sustainability: observations from the sociology of science and technology', in Allen, P. (ed.), *Food for the Future: Conditions and Contradictions of Sustainability*, London: Wiley, 19-45.

Buttel, F. (1994), 'Twentieth Century agricultural-environmental transitions: a preliminary analysis', *Paper presented at the Agrarian Studies Program*, Yale University, September.

Buttel, F. et al. (1981), 'The social bases of agrarian environmentalism: a comparative analysis of New York and Michigan farm operators', *Rural Sociology* 46(3): 391-410.

Buttel, F. and Curry, J. (1991), 'Relationships between industry and Land Grant universities: a survey of agricultural scientists', *unpublished manuscript*, Ithaca: Cornell University.

Buttel, F. and Flinn, W. (1975), 'Sources and consequences of agrarian values in American society', *Rural Sociology* 40(2): 134-151.

Buttel, F. and Flinn, W. (1977), 'Conceptions of rural life and environmental concern', *Rural Sociology* 42(4): 544-555.

Buttel, F. and Gillespie, G. (1991), 'Rural policy in perspective: the rise, fall and uncertain future of the American welfare state', in Pigg, K. (ed.), *The Future of Rural America*, Boulder: Westview, 15-40.

Buttel, F., Larson, O. and Gillespie, G. (1990), *The Sociology of Agriculture*, Westport: Greenwood.

Buttel, F. and Newby, H. (eds) (1980) *The Rural Sociology of the Advanced Societies*, Montclair: Allenheld, Osmun.

Byman, W. (1990), 'New technologies in the agro-food system and US-EC trade relations', in Lowe, P., Marsden, T. and Whatmore, S. (eds), *Technological Change and the Rural Environment,* London: Fulton, 147-167.

Cameron, J. and Elix, J. (1991), *Recovering Ground: A Case Study Approach to Ecologically Sustainable Rural Land Management,* Melbourne: Australian Conservation Foundation.

Campbell, A. (1989), 'Landcare in Australia: an overview', *Australian Journal of Soil and Water Conservation* 2(4): 18-20.

Campbell, A. (1990), *Landcare: Progress across the Nation,* First Annual Report of the National Landcare Facilitator, Canberra: National Soil Conservation Program, Department of Primary Industries and Energy.

Campbell, A. (1991a), *Planning for Sustainable Farming,* Melbourne: Lothian.

Campbell, A. (1991b), *Landcare: Testing Times,* Second Annual Report of the National Landcare Facilitator, Canberra: National Soil Conservation Program, Department of Primary Industries and Energy.

Campbell, A. (1992a), 'Farm and catchment planning: tools for sustainability' in Lawrence, G., Vanclay, F. and Furze, B. (eds), *Agriculture, Environment and Society,* Melbourne: Macmillan, 224-232.

Campbell, A. (1992b), 'Community first: Landcare in Australia', Paper presented at the Beyond Farmer First: Rural People's Knowledge, Agricultural Research and Extension Practice workshop, Institute of Development Studies, University of Sussex, Brighton.

Campbell, A. (1992c), *Landcare in Australia: Taking the Long View in Tough Times,* Third Annual Report of the National Landcare Facilitator, Canberra: National Soil Conservation Program, Department of Primary Industries and Energy.

Campbell, A. and Junor, R. (1992), 'Land management extension in the '90s: evolution or emasculation', *Australian Journal of Soil and Water Conservation* 5(2): 16-23.

Campbell, A. and Siepen, G. (1994), *Landcare: Communities Shaping the Land and the Future,* Allen and Unwin: Sydney.

Campbell, H., Lawrence, G. and Share, P. (1991), 'Rural Restructuring in Australia and New Zealand', *Paper presented at Socialist Scholars Conference* Melbourne, 19 July.

Campbell, H. (1994) *Regulation and Crisis in New Zealand Agriculture,* unpublished doctoral thesis, Wagga Wagga: Charles Sturt University.

Cancian, F. (1979), *The Innovator's Situation,* Stanford: Stanford University Press.

Carlson, J. and McLeod, M. (1978), 'A comparison of agrarianism in Washington, Idaho, and Wisconsin', *Rural Sociology* 43(1): 17-30.

Carroll, J. and Manne, R. (1992), *Shutdown: The Failure of Economic Rationalism and How to Rescue Australia,* Melbourne: Text Publishing Company.

Cary, J. and Barr, N. (1992), 'The semantics of 'forest' cover: how green was Australia?', in Lawrence, G., Vanclay, F. and Furze, B. (eds), *Agriculture, Environment and Society,* Melbourne: Macmillan, 60-76.

Cataife, D. (1989), '"Fordism" and the French regulationist school', *Monthly Review* 41(1): 40-44.

Catley, R. and McFarlane, B. (1981), *Australian Capitalism in Boom and Depression,* Sydney: Alternative Publishing Cooperative.

Chamala, S. and Mortiss P. (1990), *Working Together for Land Care: Group Management Skills and Strategies,* Brisbane: Australian Academic Press.

Chamala, S., Keith, K. and Quinn, P. (1982), *Adoption of Commercial and Soil Conservation Innovations in Queensland: Information Exposure, Attitudes, Decisions and Actions,* Department of Agriculture, University of Queensland, St Lucia.

Chamala, S., Rickson, R. and Singh, D. (1984), *Annotated Bibliography of Socio-economic Studies on Adoption of Soil and Water Conservation Methods in Australia,* Department of Agriculture, University of Queensland, St Lucia.

Chambers, R. (1983), *Rural Development: Putting the Last First,* London: Longman.

Chambers, R. (1993), *Challenging the Professions: Frontiers for Rural Development,* London: Intermediate Technology Publications.

Chambers, R. and Jiggins, J. (1986), *Agricultural Research for Resource-Poor Farmers: A Parsimonious Paradigm,* Discussion Paper 220, Brighton: Institute of Development Studies, University of Sussex.

Chambers, R., Pacey, A. and Thrupp, L. (eds) (1989), *Farmer First: Farmer Innovation and Agricultural Research,* London: Intermediate Technology Publications.

Charlesworth, M., Farrall, L, Stokes, T. and Turnbull, D. (1989), *Life Among the Scientists: An Anthropological Study of an Australian Scientific Community,* Melbourne: Oxford University Press.

Checkland, P. (1981), *Systems Thinking, Systems Practice,* Chitchester: Wiley.

Checkland, P. (1985), 'From optimising to learning: a development of systems thinking for the 1990s', *Journal of the Operational Research Society* 36(9): 757-767.

Checkland, P. and Davies, L. (1986), 'The use of the term 'weltanschauung' in soft systems methodology', *Journal of Applied Systems Analysis* 13: 109-115.

Chisholm, A. (1987), 'Abatement in land degradation: regulations versus economic incentives', in Chisholm, A. and Dumsday, R. (eds), *Land Degradation: Problems and Choices,* Cambridge: Cambridge University Press, 223-247.

Churchman, C. (1971), *The Design of Inquiring Systems,* New York: Basic Books.

Cicourel, A. (1964), *Method and Measurement in Sociology,* New York: Free Press.

Clark, J. and Lowe, P. (1992), 'Cleaning up agriculture: environment, technology and social science', *Sociologia Ruralis* 32(1): 11-29.

Clark, R. and Coffey, S. (1993), 'Best practice, benchmarks or bulldust?: Benchmarking for a sustainable beef production system', in Coutts, J. et al. (eds), *Proceedings of the Australia Pacific Extension Conference,* Surfers Paradise, October 12-14. 1993, Brisbane: Dove Rural Media, 260-264.

Clegg, S. et al. (1980), 'Re-structuring the semi-peripheral labour process: corporatist Australia in the world economy?', in Boreham, P. and Dow, G. (eds), *Work and Inequality: Workers, Economic Crisis and the State,* Melbourne: Macmillan, 2-53.

Cloke, P. and Thrift, N. (1990), 'Class and change in rural Britain', in Marsden, T., Lowe, P. and Whatmore, S. (eds), *Rural Restructuring: Global Processes and their Responses,* London: Fulton, 165-181.

Collins, R. (1981), 'Micro-translation as a theory-building strategy', in Knorr-Cetina, K. and Cicourel, A. (eds), *Advances in Social Theory and Methodology: Toward an Integration of Micro- and Macro- Sociologies,* London: Routledge and Kegan Paul, 81-198.

Commins, P. (1990), 'Restructuring agriculture in advanced societies: transformation, crisis and responses', in Marsden, T., Lowe, P. and Whatmore, S. (eds), *Rural Restructuring,* London: Fulton, 45-76.

Connell, R. (1987), *Gender and Power,* Sydney: Allen and Unwin.

Connell, R. and Irving, T. (1980), *Class Structure in Australia,* Melbourne: Longman.

Constance D., Bonanno, A. and Heffernan, W. (1993), 'Global contested terrain: the case of the tuna-dolphin controversy', *Paper presented at the annual meeting of the Rural Sociological Society,* Orlando, Florida.

Cook, P. (1988), 'Stewardship of our natural resources: a shared responsibility', in Department of Primary Industries and Energy, *Proceedings of the First Community Conference of the Murray-Darling Basin Ministerial Council's Community Advisory Committee,* Canberra: Australian Government Publishing Service, 1-9.

Crabb, P. (1988), *Managing Water and Land Use Inter-State River Basins,* School of Earth Science, Macquarie University, Sydney.

Craig, R. and Phillips, K. (1983), 'Agrarian ideology in Australia and the United States', *Rural Sociology* 48(3): 409-420.

Daily Advertiser, 8 April, 1995.

Davidson, B. (1966), *The Northern Myth* (2nd edn), Sydney: Angus and Robertson.

Davidson, B. (1976), 'History of the Australian rural landscape', in Sneddon, G. and Davis, M. (eds), *Man and Landscape in Australia: Towards an Ecological Vision,* Canberra: Australian Government Publishing Service, 63-81.

Davidson, B. (1981), *European Farming in Australia: An Economic History of Australian Farming,* Amsterdam: Elsevier.

Department of Foreign Affairs and Trade (1994), *Subsistence to Supermarket: Food and Agricultural Transformation in South-East Asia,* Canberra: Australian Government Publishing Service.

Department of Primary Industries and Energy (1989), *International Agribusiness Trends and Their Implications for Australia,* Canberra: Australian Government Publishing Service.

Department of Primary Industries and Energy (1992), *Extension 2000: New Directions in Extension,* Canberra: Department of Primary Industries and Energy.

Department of Prime Minister and Cabinet (1992), *Food Processing,* Canberra: Australian Government Publishing Service.

Department of Trade (1987), *Agribusiness: Structural Developments in Agriculture and the Implications for Australian Trade,* Canberra: Department of Trade.

Dommen, A. (1988), *Innovation in African Agriculture,* Boulder: Westview.

Donald, C. (1982), 'Innovation in Australian agriculture', in Williams, D. (ed.), *Agriculture in the Australian Economy* (2nd edn), Sydney: Sydney University Press, 55-82.

Douglas, J. (1992), 'Extension: from a Landcare perspective', in Department of Primary Industries and Energy, *Improved Extension Methods Workshop: Proceedings and Papers,* Canberra: Department of Primary Industries and Energy.

Dovers, S. (1992), 'The history of natural resource use in rural Australia: practicalities and ideologies', in Lawrence, G., Vanclay, F. and Furze, B. (eds), *Agriculture, Environment and Society,* Melbourne: Macmillan, 1-18.

Dumsday, R., Edwards, G. and Chisholm, D. (1990), 'Resource management', in Williams, D. (ed.), *Agriculture in the Australian Economy* (3rd edn), Melbourne: Sydney University Press, 172-186.

Dunkley, G. and Kulkarni, A. (1990), 'Structural change and industry policy in Australia', *Regional Journal of Social Issues* Number 24: 19-32.

Dunn, T. (1991), 'Family farming extension', in Alston, M. (ed.), *Family Farming: Australia and New Zealand,* Wagga Wagga: Centre for Rural Social Research, 101-119.

Dunn, T. (1994), 'Rapid Rural Appraisal: a description of the methodology and its application in teaching and research at Charles Sturt University', *Rural Society* 4(3/4): 30-36.

Earle T., Brownlea, A. and Rose, C. (1981), 'Beliefs of a community with respect to environmental management: a case study of soil conservation beliefs on the Darling Downs', *Journal of Environmental Management* 12(3): 197-218.

Ecologically Sustainable Development Steering Committee (1992), *Draft National Strategy for Ecologically Sustainable Development,* Canberra: Australian Government Publishing Service.

Engel, P. (1990), 'Knowledge management in agriculture: building upon diversity', *Knowledge in Society: The International Journal of Knowledge Transfer* 3(3): 28-35.

Engel, P., De Groot, A. and Seegers, S. (1992), *RAAKS, Rapid Appraisal of Agricultural Knowledge Systems,* Department of Communication and Innovation Systems, Wageningen Agricultural University.

Fagan, R. and Bryan, D. (1991), 'Australia and the changing global economy: background to social inequality in the 1990s', in *Social Justice Collective, Inequality in Australia: Slicing the Cake,* Melbourne: Heinemann, 7-31.

Fagan, R. and Webber, M. (1994), *Global Restructuring: the Australian Experience,* Melbourne: Oxford University Press.

Fairweather, J. (1989), *Some Recent Changes in Rural Society in New Zealand,* Agribusiness and Economics Research Unit, Discussion Paper No 124, Lincoln University, Canterbury, New Zealand.

Financial Review 5 March 1988.

Fishbein, M. and Ajzen, I. (1975), *Belief, Attitude Intention and Behaviour,* Reading: Addison Wesley.

Fliegel, F. and van Es, J.C. (1983), 'The diffusion-adoption process in agriculture: changes in technology and changing paradigms', in Summers, G. (ed.), *Technology and Social Change in Rural Areas,* Boulder: Westview, 13-28.

Flinn, W. and Johnson, D. (1974), 'Agrarianism Amongst Wisconsin Farmers', *Rural Sociology* 39(2): 187-204.

Flora, C., (1992), 'Reconstructing agriculture: the case for local knowledge', *Rural Sociology* 57(1): 92-97.

Foster, J. (1988), 'The Fetish of Fordism', *Monthly Review* 39(10): 14-33.

Frank, B. (1995a) 'Constraints limiting innovation adoption in the North Queensland beef industry. I: A socio-economic means of maintaining a balanced lifestyle', *Agricultural Systems* 47(3), 291-321.

Frank, B. (1995b) 'Constraints limiting innovation adoption in the North Queensland beef industry. II: Non-adoption is an intelligent response to environmental circumstances', *Agricultural Systems* 47(3), 323-346.

Frank, B. and Chamala, S. (1992), 'Effectiveness of extension strategies', in Lawrence, G., Vanclay, F. and Furze, B. (eds), *Agriculture, Environment and Society,* Melbourne: Macmillan, 122-140.

Fray, P. (1991), 'On Fertile Ground?', *Habitat Australia* 19(2): 5-8.

Friedmann, H. (1991), 'Changes in the international division of labor: agrifood complexes and export agriculture', in Friedland, W., Busch, L., Buttel, F. and Rudy, A. (eds), *Towards a New Political Economy of Agriculture*, Boulder: Westview, 65-93.

Friedmann, H. and McMichael, P. (1989), 'Agriculture and the state system: the rise and decline of national agricultures, 1870 to present', *Sociologia Ruralis* 29(2): 93-117.

Fuenmayor, R. and López-Garay, H. (1991), 'The scene for interpretative systemology', *Systems Practice* 4(5): 401-418.

Garnaut, R. (1989), *Australia and the North East Asian Ascendancy:* Report to the Prime Minister and the Minister for Foreign Affairs and Trade, Canberra: Australian Government Publishing Service.

Gartman, D. (1991), 'The aesthetics of fordism', *Paper presented at the Annual Meeting of the American Sociological Association*, 23-27 August, Cincinnati, Ohio.

Geertz, C. (1963), *Agricultural Involution*, Berkeley: University of California Press.

Geertz, C. (1973), *The Interpretation of Cultures*, New York: Basic Books.

Geertz, C. (1983), *Local Knowledge: Further Essays in Interpretative Anthropology*, New York: Basic Books.

Geisler, C. and Lyson, T. (1993), 'Bio-technology: rural policy implications of bovine growth hormone adoption in the USA', in Harper, S. (ed.), *The Greening of Rural Policy*, Boulder: Westview, 119-132.

Giddens, A. (1976), *New Rules of Sociological Method: A Positive Critique of Interpretative Sociologies*, London: Hutchinson.

Giddens, A. (1979), *Central Problems in Social Theory: Action, Structure and Contradiction in Social Analysis*, London: Macmillan.

Giddens, A. (1981), 'Agency, institution and time-space analysis', in Knorr-Cetina, K. and Cicourel, A. (eds), *Advances in Social Theory and Methodology: Toward an Integration of Micro- and Macro- Sociologies*, London: Routledge and Kegan Paul, 161-174.

Giddens, A. (1984), *The Constitution of Society: An Outline of the Theory of Structuration*, Cambridge: Polity.

Giddens, A. (1987), *Social Theory and Modern Sociology*, Oxford: Polity.

Glasbergen, P. (1992), 'Agro-environmental policy: trapped in an iron law?', *Sociologia Ruralis* 32(1): 30-48.

Goe, W. and Kenney, M. (1991), 'The restructuring of the global economy and the future of US agriculture', in Pigg, K. (ed.), *The Future of Rural America*, Boulder: Westview, 135-156.

Goldschmidt, W. (1947), *As you Sow: Three Studies in the Social Consequences of Agribusiness*, Glencoe: The Free Press.

Goodman, D. and Redclift, M. (1989), 'Introduction: the international farm crisis', in Goodman, D. and Redclift, M. (eds), *The International Farm Crisis*, London: Macmillan, 1-22.

Goodman, D. and Redclift, M. (1991), *Refashioning Nature: Food, Ecology and Culture*, London: Routledge.

Goodman, D., Sorj, B. and Wilkinson, J. (1987), *From Farming to Biotechnology*, Oxford: Basil Blackwell.

Goss, K. (1979), 'Consequences of diffusion of innovations', *Rural Sociology* 44(4): 754-772.

Gould, S. (1982), 'The meaning of punctuated equilibrium and its role in validating a hierarchical approach to macroevolution', in Milkman, R. (ed), *Perspectives on Evolution*, Sunderland: Sinauer, 83-104.

Gray, I. (1991a), *Politics in Place: Social Power Relations in an Australian Country Town*. Cambridge: Cambridge University Press.

Gray, I. (1991b) 'Family farming and ideology: some preliminary exploration', in Alston, M. (ed.), *Family Farming: Australia and New Zealand*, Wagga Wagga: Centre for Rural Social Research, Charles Sturt University, 52-65.

Gray, I. (1992), 'Power relations in rural communities: implications for environmental management', in Lawrence, G., Vanclay, F. and Furze, B. (eds), *Agriculture, Environment and Society*, Melbourne: Macmillan, 141-156.

Gray, I., Dunn, T. and Lawrence, G. (1993), *Coping with Change: Australian Farmers in the 1990s*, Wagga Wagga, NSW: Centre for Rural Social Research.

Gray, I. and Lawrence, G. (forthcoming) 'Predictors of Stress Among Australian Farmers', *Australian Journal of Social Issues*.

Green, G. (1988), Finance Capital and Uneven Development, Boulder: Westview.

Grierson, I., Bull, B. and Graham, R. (1991), 'Soil Management and Fertilizer Strategies', in Squires, V. and Tow, P.(eds), *Dryland Farming: A Systems Approach*. Melbourne, Sydney University Press, 134-145.

Gruen, F. (1990), 'Economic development and agriculture since 1945', in Williams, D. (ed.), *Agriculture in the Australian Economy* (3rd edn), Melbourne: Sydney University Press, 19-26.

Guerin, L.J. and Guerin, T.F. (1994), 'Constraints to the adoption of innovations in agricultural research and environmental management: a review', *Australian Journal of Experimental Agriculture*, 34(4), 549-571.

Habermas, J. (1981), *Toward a Rational Society*, London: Heinemann.

Hadwiger, D. (1982), *The Politics of Agricultural Research*, Lincoln: University of Nebraska Press.

Hampson, I. (1991), 'Post-fordism, the French regulation school, and the work of John Mathews', *Journal of Australian Political Economy Number* 28: 92-130.

Hardin, G. (1968) 'The tragedy of the commons' *Science* 162 (Dec), 1243-1248.

Harlander, S., BeMiller, J. and Steenson, L. (1991), 'Impact of biotechnology on food and non-food uses of agricultural products', in Baumgardt, B. and Martin, M. (eds), *Agricultural Biotechnology: Issues and Choices*, Indiana: Purdue University Agricultural Experiment Station, 41-54.

Harper, S. (1993), 'The greening of rural discourse', in Harper, S. (ed.) *The Greening of Rural Policy,* Belhaven Press: London, 3-11.

Harris, M. (1968), *The Rise of Anthropological Theory,* New York: Crowell.

Harris, M. (1975), *Cows, Pigs, Wars and Witches: The Riddles of Culture,* Glasgow: Fontana Collins.

Harris, M. (1977), *Cannibals and Kings,* Glasgow: Fontana Collins.

Haverkort, B., van der Kamp, J. and Waters-Bayer, A. (eds) (1991), *Joining Farmers' Experiments: Experiences in Participatory Technology Development*, London: Intermediate Technology Publications.

Hawke, R. (1989), *Our Country Our Future: Statement on the Environment,* Canberra: Australian Government Publishing Service.

Healy, M. (1991), *Strategic Technologies for Maximising the Competitiveness of Australia's Agriculture-based Exports.* IP/2/91, Canberra: Bureau of Rural Resources.

Heathcote, R. and Mabbutt, J. (eds) (1988), *Land Water and People,* Sydney: Allen and Unwin.

Higgott, R. (1987), *The World Economic Order,* Canberra: Australian Institute of International Affairs.

Hightower, J. (1973), *Hard Tomatoes, Hard Times,* Cambridge (MA): Schenckman.

Hindess, B. (1986), 'Actors and social relations', in Wardell, M. and Turner, S. (eds), *Sociological Theory in Transition,* Boston: Allen and Unwin, 113-126.

Hindmarsh, R. (1990), 'Biotechnology: is the green movement meeting the challenge', *Habitat Australia* 18(5): 9-12.

Hindmarsh, R. (1992), 'Agricultural biotechnologies: ecosocial concerns for a sustainable agriculture', in Lawrence, G., Vanclay, F. and Furze, B. (eds), *Agriculture, Environment and Society,* Melbourne: Macmillan, 278-303.

Hindmarsh, R. (1994), *Power Relations, Social-Ecocentrism, and Genetic Engineering: Agrobiotechnology in the Australian Context,* Unpublished PhD thesis: Griffith University, Brisbane.

Hindmarsh, R., Burch, D. and Hulsman, K. (1991) 'Agrobiotechnology in Australia: issues of control, collaboration and sustainability', *Prometheus* 9(2): 221-248.

Hoban, T. (1989), 'Anticipating public response to biotechnology', *The Rural Sociologist* 9(3): 20-24.

Hoban, T., Woodrum, E. and Czaja, R. (1992), 'Public Opposition to Genetic Engineering', *Rural Sociology* 57(4): 476-493.

Hodge, I. (1982), 'Rights to cleared land and the control of dryland salinity', *Australian Journal of Agricultural Economics* 26(3): 185-201.

Hofstee, E.W. (1946), *Over de oorzaken van de verscheidenheid in de Nederlandse landbouwgebieden* (The Causes of Diversity in Dutch Agriculture), Rede uitgesproken bij de aanvaarding van het ambt van hoogleraar aan de Landbouwhogeschool te Wageningen (inaugural professorial address), Wageningen Agricultural University.

House of Representatives Standing Committee on Industry, Science and Technology (1992), *Genetic Manipulation: the Threat or the Glory?* Canberra: Australian Government Publishing Service.

Hurtubise, R. (1984), *Managing Information Systems: Concepts and Tools,* West Hartford: Kumarian.

INRA (1991), *Opinions of Europeans on Biotechnology in 1991* (nd).

Instate (1993), *Agribusiness and Processed Food Development in South-East Asia,* Canberra: Rural Industries Research and Development Corporation.

Jackson, M. (1982), 'The nature of 'soft' systems thinking: the work of Churchman, Ackoff and Checkland', *Journal of Applied Systems Analysis* 9: 17-29.

Jackson, M. (1985), 'Social systems theory and practice: the need for a critical approach', *International Journal of General Systems* 10: 135-151.

Jackson, M. (1991), 'The origins and nature of critical systems thinking', *Systems Practice* 4(2): 131-149.

Jarvie, I. (1984), *Rationality and Relativism: In Search of a Philosophy and History of Anthropology,* London: Routledge and Kegan Paul.

Jenkin, J. and Morris, J. (1982), 'Salinity problems outside the irrigation areas', Conference Proceedings of the AIAS and AAES, *Salinity in Victoria,* La Trobe University, October.

Jensen, R. (1993), 'Some observations on the past and future directions of agricultural extension', *Submission to the Strategic Policy Unit of the Queensland Department of Primary Industries,* May.

Jiggins, J. (1982), 'Farming systems research: a critical appraisal', *Rural Development Participation Review* 3(1): 22-25.

Jiggins, J. (1995), 'Development impact assessment: impact assessment of development projects in non-western countries', in Vanclay, F. and Bronstein, D. (eds), *Environmental and Social Impact Assessment,* Chichester: Wiley, 265-281.

Jiggins, J. and de Zeeuw, H. (1992), 'Participatory technology development in practice: process and methods', in Reijntjes, C., Haverkort, B. and Waters-Bayer, A (eds), *Farming for the Future: An Introduction to Low-External-Input and Sustainable Agriculture,* London: Macmillan, 135-162.

Johnson, M. and Rix, S. (eds) (1993) *Water in Australia: Managing Economic, Environmental and Community Reform,* Sydney: Pluto.

Jones, E. (1988), 'Managing market meltdown: lessons from the crash', *Journal of Australian Political Economy* 23: 14-24.

Jones, E. (1989), 'Australia's Balance of Payments: recent trends', *Journal of Australian Political Economy* 24: 39-55.

Jones, E. (1992), 'Multi-national companies and the balance on current account', *Journal of Australian Political Economy* 30: 61-90.

Jones, J. and Wallace, B. (eds) (1986), *Social Sciences and Farming Systems Research: Methodological Perspectives on Agricultural Development*, Boulder: Westview.

Jussaume, R. and Judson, D.(1992), 'Public perceptions about food safety in the United States and Japan', *Rural Sociology* 57(2): 235-249.

Keesing, R. (1976), *Cultural Anthropology: A Contemporary Perspective*, New York: Holt Rinehart and Winston.

Kenney, M. (1986), *Biotechnology: the University-Industrial Complex*, New Haven: Yale University Press.

Kenney, M., Lobao, L., Curry, J. and Goe, R. (1989), 'Midwestern agriculture in US fordism: from the new deal to economic restructuring', *Sociologia Ruralis* 29(2): 131-148.

Kenney, M., Lobao, L., Curry, J. and Goe, R. (1991), 'Agriculture in US fordism: the integration of the productive consumer', in Friedland, W. et al., (eds), *Towards a New Political Economy of Agriculture*, Boulder: Westview, 173-188.

Kerin, J. (1984), 'Restoring the balance of conservation and agriculture', *Habitat Australia* 12(6): 12-14.

Kidman, M. (1991), 'New town: belonging, believing and bearing down', in Alston, M. (ed.), *Family Farming: Australia and New Zealand*, Wagga Wagga: Centre for Rural Social Research, Charles Sturt University, 33-51.

Kloppenburg, J. (1988), *First the Seed*, New York: Cambridge University Press.

Kloppenburg, J. (1991), 'Social theory and the de/reconstruction of agricultural science: local knowledge for an alternative agriculture', *Rural Sociology* 56(4): 519-548.

Kloppenburg, J. (1992), 'Science in agriculture: a reply to Molnar, Duffy, Cummins and van Santen and to Flora', *Rural Sociology* 57(1): 98-107.

Knorr-Cetina, K. (1981), *The Manufacture of Knowledge: Towards a Constructivist and Contextual Theory of Science*, Oxford: Pergamon.

Korzeniewicz, R. (1990), 'The limits to semi-peripheral development: Argentina in the twentieth century', in Martin, W. (ed.), *Semiperipheral States in the World Economy*, Westport: Greenwood, 97-124.

Kotler, P. (1975), *Marketing for Non-Profit Organisations*, Englewood Cliffs: Prentice Hall.

Kulkarni, A. (1991), 'Networking and industry development', in Costa, M. and Easson, M. (eds), *Australian Industry: What Policy?*, Sydney: Pluto, 357-372.

Lacy, W. and Busch, L. (1991), 'The fourth criterion: social and economic impacts of agricultural biotechnology', *Paper presented to the Third Annual Meeting of the National Agricultural Biotechnology Council,* Sacramento, California, May.

Lacy, W., Busch, L. and Lacy, L. (1991), 'Public perceptions of agricultural biotechnology', in Baumgardt, B. and Martin, M. (eds) *Agricultural Biotechnology: Issues and Choices,* Indiana: Purdue University Agricultural Experiment Station, 139-162

Lacy, W., Lacy, L. and Busch, L. (1988), 'Agricultural biotechnology research: practices, consequences, and policy recommendations', *Agriculture and Human Values* 5(3): 3-14.

Lake, M. (1987) *The Limits of Hope,* Cambridge University Press: Cambridge.

Land   15 January 1989

Land   17 January 1991

Land   31 January 1991

Lash, S. and Urry, J. (1994), *Economies of Signs and Space,* London: Sage.

Latour, B. (1987), *Science in Action,* Milton Keynes: Open University.

Lawrence, G. (1987), *Capitalism and the Countryside: The Rural Crisis in Australia,* Sydney: Pluto.

Lawrence, G. (1990), 'Agricultural restructuring and rural social change in Australia', in Marsden, T., Lowe, P., and Whatmore, S. (eds), *Rural Restructuring: Global Processes and their Responses,* London: Fulton, 101-128.

Lawrence, G. (1992), 'Farm structural adjustment', *Rural Society* 2(4): 5-7.

Lawrence, G. (1994), 'Rural adjustment revisited: in defence of a sociological approach,' *Rural Society* 4(3/4): 11-16.

Lawrence, G. (1995) 'Contemporary Agrifood Restructuring: Australian and New Zealand', *Paper presented to the Conference of the Agri-food Research Network,* Brisbane, Griffith University, 7-9 July.

Lawrence, G. and Campbell, H. (1991), 'The crisis of agriculture', *Arena* 94: 103-117.

Lawrence, G., McKenzie, H. and Vanclay, F. (1992) 'Rural restructuring, genetic engineering and Australian agriculture: some preliminary observations', *Rural Society* 2(2): 2-6.

Lawrence, G., McKenzie, H, and. Vanclay, F. (1993) 'Biotechnology in Australian Agriculture: The views of farmer representatives' *Prometheus* 11(2): 234-251

Lawrence, G. and Norton, J. (1994), 'Industry involvement in Australian biotechnology: the views of scientists', *Australasian Biotechnology* 4(6): 362-368.

Lawrence, G., Share, P. and Campbell, H. (1992), 'The restructuring of agriculture and rural society: evidence from Australia and New Zealand', *Journal of Australian Political Economy* 30: 1-23.

Lawrence, G. and Vanclay, F. (1992), 'Agricultural production and environmental degradation in the Murray-Darling Basin', in Lawrence, G., Vanclay, F. and Furze, B. (eds), *Agriculture, Environment and Society*, Melbourne: Macmillan, 33-59.

Lawrence, G. and Vanclay, F. (1994), 'Agricultural Change in the Semi-Periphery: The Murray-Darling Basin, Australia', in McMichael P (ed.), *The Global Restructuring of Agro-Food Systems*, Ithaca: Cornell University Press, 76-103.

Lawrence, G., Vanclay, F., Gray, I. and Lockie, S. (1992), 'A sociological approach to the improvement of extension methods in agriculture', *Paper prepared for the National Soil Conservation Program Workshop on Improved Extension Methods*, Bendigo, 26 - 27 May.

Lawrence, G. and Williams, C. (1990), 'The dynamics of decline: implications for social welfare delivery in rural Australia', in Cullen, T., Dunn, P. and Lawrence, G. (eds), *Rural Health and Welfare in Australia*, Melbourne: Arena, 38-59.

Le Heron, R. (1991), 'Perspectives on pluriactivity', in Alston, M. (ed.), *Family Farming: Australia and New Zealand*, Wagga Wagga: Centre for Rural Social Research, Charles Sturt University, 24-32.

Leeuwis, C. (1989), *Marginalisation Misunderstood: Different Patterns of Farm Development in the West of Ireland*, Wageningen Studies in Sociology 26, Wageningen Agricultural University.

Leeuwis, C. (1993a), 'Towards a sociological conceptualization of communication in extension science: On Giddens, Habermas and computer-based communication technologies in Dutch agriculture', *Sociologia Ruralis* 33(2): 281-305.

Leeuwis, C. (1993b), *Of Computers, Myths and Modelling: The Social Construction of Diversity, Knowledge, Information and Communication Technologies in Dutch Horticulture and Agricultural Extension*, PhD thesis, Department of Communication and Innovation Studies, Wageningen Agricultural University.

Lipietz, A. (1987), *Miracles and Mirages: The Crisis in Global Fordism*, London: Pluto.

Lipton, M., and Longhurst, R. (1989), *New Seeds and Poor People*, London: Unwin Hyman.

Lockie, S. (1994a), 'Farmers and the State: Local knowledge and self help in rural environmental management', *Regional Journal of Social Issues* 28, 24-36.

Lockie, S. (1994b), 'Community Landcare groups: changing social relations at the local level', *Paper presented at the Issues Affecting Rural Communities Conference*, Townsville, July.

Lockie, S, (1994c) 'Landcare in the balance: Wherefore art thou Landcareman?', *Rural Society* 4 (3/4): 48-49.

Lockie, S. (1995), 'Rural gender relations and Landcare' in Vanclay, F. (ed.) *Rural Issues: Proceedings of TASA94, the Annual Conference of The Australian Sociological Association*, Wagga Wagga: Centre for Rural Social Research, Charles Sturt University, in press.

Lockie, S. (forthcoming), *Social Structure, Community Dynamics and the Development of the Landcare Movement in Australia,* Doctoral Thesis, Charles Sturt University, Wagga Wagga.

Lockie, S., Butler, B., Vanclay, F. and Mead, A. (1993), 'Acceptance and Adoption of broadleaf cropping systems in central and southern NSW', in Coutts, J. et al. (eds), *Proceedings of the Australia Pacific Extension Conference,* Surfers Paradise, October 12-14. 1993, Brisbane: Dove Rural Media, 265-267.

Lockie, S., Mead, A., Vanclay, F., and Butler, B. (1995) 'Factors Encouraging the Adoption of More Sustainable Crop Rotations in South East Australia: Profit: Sustainability, Risk, and Stability', *Journal of Sustainable Agriculture,* in press.

Lockie, S. and Vanclay, F. (1992), *Barriers to the Adoption of Sustainable Crop Rotations: Focus Group Report,* Report to the NSW Department of Agriculture, Wagga Wagga: Centre for Rural Social Research, Charles Sturt University, November, 1992.

Long, N. (1968), *Social Change and the Individual: Social and Religious Responses to Innovation in a Zambian Rural Community,* Manchester: Manchester University Press.

Long, N. (1977), *An Introduction to the Sociology of Rural Development,* London: Tavistock.

Long, N. (1984), 'Creating space for change: a perspective on the sociology of development', *Sociologia Ruralis* 24(3/4): 168-184.

Long, N. (1988), 'Sociological perspectives on agrarian development and state intervention', in Hall, A. and Midgley, J. (eds), *Development Policies: Sociological Perspectives,* Manchester: Manchester University Press, 108-133.

Long, N. (1989), 'Conclusion: theoretical reflections on actor, structure and interface', in Long, N. (ed.), *Encounters at the Interface: A Perspective on Social Discontinuities in Rural Development,* Wageningen Studies in Sociology 27, Wageningen Agricultural University, 221-243.

Long, N. (1990), 'From paradigm lost to paradigm regained?: The case for an actor-oriented sociology of development', *European Review of Latin American and Caribbean Studies* 49: 3-24.

Long, N. (1992), 'From paradigm lost to paradigm regained?: The case for an actor-oriented sociology of development', in Long, N. and Long, A. (eds), *Battlefields of Knowledge: The Interlocking of Theory and Practice in Social Research and Development,* London: Routledge, 16-43.

Long, N. and Long, A. (eds) (1992), *Battlefields of Knowledge: The Interlocking of Theory and Practice in Social Research and Development,* London: Routledge.

Long, N. and van der Ploeg, J.D. (1988), 'New challenges in the sociology of rural development', *Sociologia Ruralis* 28(1): 30-41.

Long, N. and van der Ploeg, J.D. (1989), 'Demythologizing planned intervention: an actor perspective', *Sociologia Ruralis* 29(3/4): 226-249.

Long, N. and van der Ploeg, J.D. (1995), 'Heterogeneity, actor and structure: towards a reconstitution of the concept of structure', in Booth, D. (ed.), *Rethinking Social Development: Theory, Research and Practice,* Harlow: Longman, in press.

Long, N., van der Ploeg, J.D., Curtin, C., Box, L. (eds) (1986), *The Commoditization Debate: Labour Process, Strategy and Social Network,* Wageningen Studies in Sociology 17, Wageningen Agricultural University.

Lowe, P. (1992), 'Industrial agriculture and environmental regulation: a new agenda for rural sociology', *Sociologia Ruralis* 32(1): 4-29.

Lowe, P., Cox, G., Goodman, D., Munton, R. and Winter, M. (1990), 'Technological change, farm management and pollution regulation: the example of Britain', in Lowe, P., Marsden, T. and Whatmore, S. (eds), *Technological Change and the Rural Environment,* London: Fulton, 53-80.

Lowe, P., Marsden, T. and Whatmore, S. (eds) (1990), *Technological Change and the Rural Environment.* London: Fulton.

Lyytinen, K. and Klein, H. (1985), 'The critical social theory of Jurgen Habermas (CST) as a basis for the theory of information systems', in Mumford, E., Hirschheim, R., Fitzgerald, G. and Wood-Harper, A. (eds), *Research Methods in Information Systems,* Amsterdam: North Holland Publishing Company, 219-236.

Mackay, N. and Eastburn, D. (eds) (1990), *The Murray,* Canberra: Murray-Darling Basin Commission.

Marsden, T. (1992), 'Exploring a rural sociology for a fordist transition', *Sociologia Ruralis* 32(2/3): 209-230.

Marsden, T. and Murdoch, J. (1990), *Restructuring Rurality: Key Areas for Development in Assessing Social Change,* Working Paper 4, ESRC Countryside Change Working Papers. Newcastle-upon-Tyne University.

Marsden, T., Lowe, P. and Whatmore, S. (1990), 'Introduction: questions of rurality', in Marsden, T., Lowe, P. and Whatmore, S. (eds), *Rural Restructuring,* London: Fulton, 1-20.

Marsden, T., Murdoch, J., Lowe, P., Munton, R. and Flynn, A. (1993), *Constructing the Countryside,* London: UCL Press.

Martin, P. (1991), 'Environmental care in agricultural catchments: toward the communicative catchment', *Environmental Management* 15(6): 773-783.

Martin, P., Tarr, S. and Lockie, S. (1992), 'Participatory environmental management in New South Wales: policy and practice', in Lawrence, G., Vanclay, F. and Furze, B. (eds), *Agriculture, Environment and Society,* Melbourne: Macmillan, 184-207.

Martin, W. (1990), 'Introduction: the challenge of the semiperiphery', in Martin, W. (ed.), *Semiperipheral States in the World Economy,* Westport: Greenwood, 3-10.

Massey, D. (1984), *Spatial Divisions of Labour,* London: Macmillan.

Mathews, J. (1989), *Age of Democracy: The Politics of Post-Fordism,* Melbourne: Oxford University Press.

Mathews, J. (1989), *Tools of Change,* Melbourne: Pluto.

Mathews, J. (1992), 'New Production Systems: A Response to Critics and a Re-evaluation', *Journal of Australian Political Economy* 30: 91-128.

McMichael, P. (1984), *Settlers and the Agrarian Question,* New York: Cambridge University Press.

McMichael, P. (1987), 'State formation and the construction of the world market', *Political Power and Social Theory* 6: 187-237.

McMichael, P. (ed.) (1994) *The Global Restructuring of Agro-food Systems,* Ithaca: Cornell University Press.

Messer, J. (1987), 'The sociology and politics of land degradation in Australia', in Blaikie, P. and Brookfield, H. (eds), *Land Degradation and Society,* London: Methuen, 232-238.

Metcalf, W. and Vanclay, F. (1987), *Social Characteristics of Alternative Lifestyle Participants in Australia* (2nd edn), Nathan: Institute of Applied Environmental Research, Griffith University.

Molnar, J. and Wu, L. (1989), 'Agrarianism, family farming, and support for state intervention in agriculture', *Rural Sociology* 54(2): 227-245.

Molnar, J., Duffy, P., Cummins, K. and Van Santen, E. (1992), 'Agricultural science and agricultural counterculture: paradigms in search of a future', *Rural Sociology* 57(1): 83-91.

Mooney, P. (1988), *My Own Boss,* Boulder: Westview.

Morrisey, P. and Lawrence, G. (1995), 'A critical assessment of Landcare: evidence from Central Queensland', in Vanclay, F. (ed) *Rural Issues: Proceedings of TASA94, the Annual Conference of The Australian Sociological Association,* Wagga Wagga: Centre for Rural Social Research, Charles Sturt University, in press.

Mormont, M. (1990), 'Who is rural? or, how to be rural: towards a sociology of the rural', in Marsden, T., Lowe, P. and Whatmore, S. (eds), *Rural Restructuring,* London: Fulton, 21-44.

Munro-Clark, M. (1986), *Communes in Rural Australia,* Sydney: Hale and Iremonger.

Munton, R., Marsden, T. and Whatmore, S. (1990), 'Technological change in a period of agricultural adjustment', in Lowe, P., Marsden, T. and Whatmore, S. (eds), *Technological Change and the Rural Environment,* London: Fulton, 104-126.

Murray-Darling Basin Community Advisory Committee. (1991), *Surviving Change: Chance or Choice?,* Canberra: Murray-Darling Basin Ministerial Council.

Murray-Darling Basin Ministerial Council. (1990), *Natural Resources Management Strategy: Towards a Sustainable Future,* Canberra: Murray-Darling Basin Ministerial Council.

Murrumbidgee Irrigator 22 February 1991.

Myers, D. (1989), *Psychology* (2nd edn), New York: Worth.

Nancarrow, C., Ward, K. and Murray, J. (1988) 'The future of Transgenic Livestock in Australian Agriculture', *Australian Journal of Biotechnology* 2(1): 39-44.

Narrandera Argus   21 August 1990.

National Farmers' Federation (1993), *New Horizons: A Strategy for Australia's Agrifood Industries,* Canberra: National Farmers' Federation.

National Research Council (1989), *Alternative Agriculture,* Washington: National Academy Press.

Niosi, J. (1990), 'Periphery in the center: Canada in the North American economy', in Martin, W. (ed.), *Semiperipheral States in the World Economy,* Westport: Greenwood, 141-160.

O'Connor, J. (1971), 'The meaning of economic imperialism', in Fann, K. and Hodges, D. (eds), *Readings in US Imperialism*, Boston: Porter Sargent, 23-68.

O'Connor, J. (1990), 'The second contradiction of capitalism: causes and consequences', *Paper Delivered at the Conference on New Economic Analysis,* Barcelona, Spain, 30 November -- 2 December.

O'Reilly, D. (1988), 'Save Our Land!', *Bulletin,* 2 August: 83-87.

Oates, N. and Campbell, A. (1992), *Working with Landcare Groups: A Handbook for Landcare Facilitators and Coordinators,* Canberra: National Soil Conservation Program.

Ockwell, A. (1990), 'The economic structure of Australian agriculture', in Williams, D. (ed.), *Agriculture in the Australian Economy* (3rd edn), Melbourne: Sydney University Press, 27-49.

Olson, M. (1965), *The Logic of Collective Action,* Cambridge: Harvard University Press.

Oram, D. (1987), *The Economics of Dryland Salinity and its Control in the Murray River Basin of Victoria: A Farm Level Approach,* Occasional Paper No 11, School of Agriculture, La Trobe University, Bundoora.

Otero, G. (1991), 'Biotechnology and economic restructuring: toward a new technological paradigm in agriculture?', *Paper presented to the Annual Meeting of the American Sociological Association,* Cincinnati, Ohio, 23-27 August.

Packham, R., Ison, R. and Roberts, R. (1988), 'Soft systems methodology for action research: The role of a college farm in an education institution', *Agricultural Administration and Extension* 38(2): 109-126.

Packham, R., Roberts, R. and Bawden, R. (1989), 'Our faculty goes experiential', in Weil, S. and McGill, I. (eds), *Diversity in Experiential Learning: Making Sense of Theory and Practice,* Milton Keynes: Open University Press, 130-149.

Pampel, F. and Van Es, J.C. (1977), 'Environmental quality and issues of adoption research', *Rural Sociology* 42(1): 57-71.

Peacock, J. (1993), 'Gene technology in research and commercialisation', *Australasian Biotechnology* 3(5): 278-281.

Pepper, D. (1993), *Eco-socialism: From Deep Ecology to Social Justice*, London: Routledge.

Pfeffer, M. (1992), 'Sustainable agriculture in historical perspective', *Agriculture and Human Values*, 9(4): 4-11.

Phelps, B. (1992), 'A blueprint for the fast track', *The Gene Report*, September: 2-3.

Phillips, E. and Gray, I. (1994), 'Farming "Practice" as Temporally and Spatially Situated Intersections of Biography, Culture and Social Structure', *unpublished paper, School of Humanities and Social Sciences*, CSU, Wagga Wagga.

Piore, M. and Sabel, C. (1984), *The Second Industrial Divide*, New York: Basic Books.

Ploeg, J.D. van der (1986), 'The agricultural labour process and commoditization', in Long, N. et al., (eds), *The Commoditization Debate: Labour Process, Strategy and Social Network*, Wageningen Studies in Sociology 17, Wageningen Agricultural University, 24-57.

Ploeg, J.D. van der (1989), 'Knowledge systems, metaphor and interface: the case of potatoes in the Peruvian highlands', in Long, N. (ed.), *Encounters at the Interface: A Perspective on Social Discontinuities in Rural Development*, Wageningen Studies in Sociology 27, Wageningen Agricultural University, 145-163.

Ploeg, J.D. van der (1990), *Labor, Markets and Agricultural Production*, Boulder: Westview.

Ploeg, J.D. van der (1993), 'Rural sociology and the new agrarian question: a perspective from the Netherlands', *Sociologia Ruralis* 33(2): 240-260.

Plumwood, V. (1993), *Feminism and the Mastery of Nature*, London: Routledge.

Porter, A. (1995), 'Technology assessment', in Vanclay, F. and Bronstein, D. (eds), *Environmental and Social Impact Assessment*, Chichester: Wiley, 67-81.

Poulter, D. and Chaffer, L. (1992), 'Dryland salinity: some economic issues', in Wallace, N. (ed.), *Natural Resource Management: An Economic Perspective*, Canberra: Australian Bureau of Agricultural and Resource Economics, 155-171.

Powell, D. and Pratley, J. (1991), *Sustainability Kit Manual*, Wagga Wagga: Centre for Conservation Farming, Charles Sturt University.

Prime Ministers' Science Council (1991), *Food Processing*, Canberra: Australian Government Publishing Service.

Pusey, M. (1992), 'Canberra changes its mind - the new mandarins', in Carroll, J. and Manne, R. (eds) *Shutdown: the Failure of Economic Rationalism and How to Rescue Australia*, Melbourne: Text Publishing.

Quiggin, J. (1987), 'Land degradation: behavioural causes', in Chisholm, A. and Dumsday, R. (eds), *Land Degradation: Problems and Policies*, Cambridge: Cambridge University Press, 203-212.

Redclift, M. (1987), *Sustainable Development: Exploring the Contradictions*, London: Methuen.

Redclift, M. (1990), 'The role of agricultural technology in sustainable development', in Lowe, P., Marsden, T. and Whatmore, S. (eds), *Technological Change and the Rural Environment*, London: Fulton, 81-103.

Redclift, N. and Whatmore, S. (1990), 'Household, consumption and livelihood: ideologies and issues in rural research', in Marsden, T., Lowe, P. and Whatmore, S. (eds), *Rural Restructuring: Global Processes and their Responses*, London: Fulton, 182-197.

Rees, S., Rodley, G. and Stilwell, F. (eds) (1993), *Beyond the Market: Alternatives to Economic Rationalism*, Sydney: Pluto.

Reeve, I. (1988), *A Squandered Land: 200 Years of Land Degradation in Australia*, Armidale: The Rural Development Centre, University of New England.

Reeve, I. (1992), 'Sustainable agriculture: problems, prospects and policies', in Lawrence, G., Vanclay, F. and Furze, B. (eds) *Agriculture, Environment and Society*, Melbourne: Macmillan.

Reeve, I. and Black, A. (1993), *Australian Farmers' Attitudes to Rural Environmental Issues*, Armidale: The Rural Development Centre, University of New England.

Reijntjes, C., Haverkort, B. and Waters-Bayer, A. (eds) (1992), *Farming for the Future: An Introduction to Low-External-Input and Sustainable Agriculture*, London: Macmillan.

Richards, P. (1985), *Indigenous Agricultural Revolution*, London: Hutchinson.

Rickson, R. and Stabler, P. (1985), 'Community responses to non point pollution from agriculture', *Journal of Environmental Management* 20(3): 281-294.

Rickson, R., Saffigna, P., Vanclay, F. and McTainsh, G. (1987), 'Social bases of farmers' responses to land degradation', in Chisholm, A. and Dumsday, R. (eds), *Land Degradation: Problems and Policies*, Cambridge: Cambridge University Press, 187-200.

Rivera, W. (1991), 'Sustainable agriculture: a unifying concept for agriculture and a central strategy for extension', in Rivera, W. and Gustafson, D. (eds), *Agricultural Extension: Worldwide Institutional Evolution and Forces for Change*, Amsterdam: Elsevier, 189-201.

Roberts, B. (1990), *The Birth of Landcare*, Toowoomba: University College of Southern Queensland Press.

Roberts, B. (1991), 'The big shift: from me now to them later', *Paper presented to the Hawkesbury Centenary Conference on Agriculture, the Environment and Human Values*, University of Western Sydney, Hawkesbury, October.

Roberts, R. (1995), 'Public involvement: from consultation to participation', in Vanclay, F. and Bronstein, D. (eds), *Environmental and Social Impact Assessment*, Chichester: Wiley, 221-246.

Robertson, I. (1987), *Sociology* (3rd edn), New York: Worth.

Rogers, E.M. (1962), *The Diffusion of Innovations*, New York: Free Press.

Rogers, E.M. (1983), *Diffusion of Innovations* (3rd edn), New York: Free Press.

Rogers, E.M. and Shoemaker, F.F. (1971), *Communication of Innovations: A Cross-Cultural Approach,* New York: Free Press.

Rogers, S.C. (1987), 'Mixing paradigms on mixed farming: Anthropological and economic views of specialization in Illinios agriculture', in Chibnik, M. (ed.), *Farm Work and Field Work: American Agriculture in Anthropological Perspective,* Ithaca: Cornell University Press, 58-89.

Röling, N. (1985), 'Extension science: increasingly pre-occupied with knowledge systems', *Sociologia Ruralis* 25(4/5): 269-290.

Röling, N. (1988), *Extension Science: Information Systems in Agricultural Development,* Cambridge: Cambridge University Press.

Röling, N. (1990), 'The agricultural research-technology transfer interface: A knowledge systems perspective', in Kaimowitz, D. (ed.), *Making the Link: Agricultural Research and Technology Transfer in Developing Countries,* Boulder: Westview, 1-42.

Röling, N. (1992a), 'The emergence of knowledge systems thinking: A changing perception of relationships among innovation, knowledge process and configuration', *Knowledge and Policy: The International Journal of Knowledge Transfer and Utilization* 5(1): 42-64.

Röling, N. (1992b). 'Facilitating sustainable agriculture: Turning policy models upside down', *Paper presented at the Beyond Farmer First: Rural People's Knowledge,* Agricultural Research and Extension Practice workshop, Institute of Development Studies, University of Sussex, Brighton.

Röling, N. (1993a), 'Agricultural knowledge and environmental regulation in the Netherlands', *Sociologia Ruralis* 33(2): 261-280.

Röling, N. (1993b), 'Platforms for decision making about eco-systems', *Keynote address for the 75-year Anniversary Conference of Wageningen Agricultural University,* "The Future of the Land: Mobilising and Integrating Knowledge for Land Use Options", August 22-25, held in Wageningen (to be published in the Proceedings).

Röling, N., Ashcroft J. and Chege F. (1976), 'The diffusion of innovations and the issue of equity in rural development', *Communication Research* 3(2): 155-170.

Röling, N. and Engel, P. (1990), 'Information Technology from a knowledge system perspective: concepts and issues', *Knowledge in Society: The International Journal of Knowledge Transfer* 3(3): 6-18.

Röling, N. and Engel, P. (1991), 'The development of the concept of Agricultural Knowledge Information Systems (AKIS): Implications for extension', in Rivera, W. and Gustafson, D. (eds), *Agricultural Extension: Worldwide Institutional Evolution and Forces for Change,* Amsterdam: Elsevier, 125-137.

Röling, N. and Jiggins, J. (1994), 'Policy paradigm for sustainable farming', *European Journal of Agricultural Education and Extension* 1(1): 23-43.

Roobeek, A. (1987), *'The Crisis in Fordism and the Rise of a New Technological Paradigm',* *Futures* 19: 129-154.

Rose, R. (1992), 'Economics of a Sustainable Agriculture', in Wallace, N. (ed.), *Natural Resource Management: An Economic Perspective,* Canberra: Australian Bureau of Agricultural and Resource Economics, 127-135.

Russell, D., Ison, R., Gamble, D. and Williams, R. (1989), *A Critical Review of Rural Extension Theory and Practice,* Report to the Australian Wool Corporation, available from: The Social Ecology Centre, University of Western Sydney - Hawkesbury.

Ruthenberg, H. (1983), *Farming Systems in the Tropics* (3rd edn), Oxford: Clarendon.

Salamon, S. (1985), 'Ethnic differences and the structure of agriculture', *Rural Sociology* 50(3): 323-340.

Sanderson, S. (1989), 'Mexican agricultural policy in the shadow of the US farm crisis', in Goodman, D. and Redclift, M. (eds), *The International Farm Crisis,* Houndmills: Macmillan, 205-233.

Sauer, M. (1990), 'Fordist modernization of German agriculture and the future of family farms', *Sociologia Ruralis* 30(3/4): 260-279.

Sayer, A. (1989), 'Post-fordism in question', *International Journal of Urban and Regional Research* 13(4): 666-695.

Shaner, W. Philipp, P. and Schmehl, W. (1982), *Farming Systems Research and Development: Guidelines for Developing Countries,* Boulder: Westview.

Share, P. (1994) 'Tickle it with a Hoe and it Will Laugh with a Harvest: Discourses of Closer Settlement in Australia 1898-1988' *Unpublished Doctoral Thesis,* Melbourne: La Trobe University.

Share, P., Campbell, H. and Lawrence, G. (1991), 'The vertical and horizontal restructuring of rural regions: Australia and New Zealand', in Alston, M. (ed.), *Family Farming: Australia and New Zealand, Wagga Wagga: Centre for Rural Social Research,* Charles Sturt University, 1-23.

Shaw, A. (1990), 'Colonial settlement 1788-1945', in Williams, D. (ed.), *Agriculture in the Australian Economy* (3rd edn), Melbourne: Sydney University Press, 1-18.

Simmons, P. (1992), 'Soil management: public versus private interest', in Wallace, N. (ed.), *Natural Resource Management: An Economic Perspective,* Canberra: Australian Bureau of Agricultural and Resource Economics, 136-149.

Simmons, P., Poulter, D. and Hall, N. (1992), 'Management of irrigation water in the Murray-Darling Basin', in Wallace, N. (ed.), *Natural Resource Management: An Economic Perspective,* Canberra: Australian Bureau of Agricultural and Resource Economics, 150-154.

Singer, E. and Freire-de-Sousa, I. (1983), 'The sociopolitical consequences of agrarianism reconsidered', *Rural Sociology* 48(2): 291-307.

Smiles, D. (1989), 'Technological developments and opportunities in Australian farm management', in Hampson R.J. (ed.), *Management for Sustainable Farming, Proceedings of the 16th National Conference of the Australian Farm Management Society* held at Queensland Agricultural College March 1989, 123-132.

Smith, D. and Finlayson, B. (1988), 'Water in Australia: its role in environmental degradation', in Heathcote, R. and Mabbutt, J. (eds), *Land, Water and People,* Sydney: Allen and Unwin, 7-48.

Squires, V. and Tow, P. (1991), *Dryland Farming: A Systems Approach*. Melbourne: Sydney University Press.

Standing Committee on Agriculture and Resource Management (1993), *Sustainable Agriculture: Tracking the Indicators for Australia and New Zealand,* East Melbourne: CSIRO.

Standing Committee on Environment, Recreation and the Arts (SCERA) (1989), *The Effectiveness of Land Degradation Policies and Programs,* Report of the House of Representatives Standing Committee on Environment, Recreation and the Arts, Canberra: Australian Government Publishing Service.

Stehlik, D. and Lawrence, G. (1995) 'A Direction for Sustainability? Australian Regional Communities and Care for the Aged', *Paper Presented at the 27th Annual International Conference of the Community Development,* Fayetteville, Arkansas, 23-26 July.

Stilwell, F. (1986), *The Accord ... And Beyond,* Sydney: Pluto.

Stilwell, F. (1992), *Understanding Cities and Regions,* Sydney: Pluto.

Stilwell, F. (1993), 'Economic rationalism: sound foundations for policy?', in Rees, S., Rodley, G. and Stilwell, F. (eds), *Beyond the Market: Alternatives to Economic Rationalism,* Sydney: Pluto, 27-37.

Stock and Land   5 September 1991.

Stockdale, J.D. (1977), 'Technology and change in US agriculture: model or warning?', *Sociologia Ruralis* 17(1): 43-58.

Stone, S. (1992), 'Land degradation and rural communities in Victoria: experience and response', in Lawrence, G., Vanclay, F. and Furze, B. (eds), *Agriculture, Environment and Society,* Melbourne: Macmillan, 173-183.

Strange, M. (1989), *Family Farming: A New Economic Vision,* Lincoln: University of Nebraska Press.

Strathern, M. (1985), 'Knowing power and being equivocal: three Melanesian contexts', in Fardon, R. (ed.), *Power and Knowledge: Anthropological and Sociological Approaches,* Edinburgh: Scottish Academic Press, 61-81.

Summers, G., Horton, F. and Gringeri, C. (1990), 'Rural labour - market changes in the United States', in Marsden, T., Lowe, P. and Whatmore, S. (eds), *Rural Restructuring,* London: Fulton, 129-164.

Sunday Telegraph   25 September 1994

Swanson, L. (ed.) (1988), *Agriculture and Community Change in the US*, Boulder: Westview.

Sydney Morning Herald   17 July 1991

Sydney Morning Herald   20 November 1989

Sydney Morning Herald   23 October 1989

Sydney Morning Herald   1 April 1993

Sydney Morning Herald   31 December 1994

Tait, J. (1990) 'Environmental risks and the regulation of biotechnology', in Lowe, P., Marsden, T. and Whatmore, S. (eds) *Technological Change and the Rural Environment*, London: Fulton.

Taylor, D.L. and Miller, W.L. (1978), 'The adoption process and environmental innovations', *Rural Sociology* 43(4): 634-648.

Thomas, R. (1991), 'Inequality and industrial relations', in *Social Justice Collective, Inequality in Australia: Slicing the Cake*, Melbourne: Heinemann, 32-56.

Thorne, P. (1991), 'Perennial pastures that pay', *Landcare News* 8: 1-3.

Thrupp, L. (1989), 'Legitimizing local knowledge: from displacement to empowerment for third world people', *Agriculture and Human Values* 6(3): 13-24.

Timmer, W.J. (1949), *Totale Landbouwwetenschap* (the science of holistic agriculture), Groningen: Wolters.

Ulrich, W. (1988), 'Systems thinking, systems practice and practical philosophy: a program of research', *Systems Practice* 1(2): 137-163.

Urry, J. (1984), 'Capitalist restructuring, recomposition and the regions', in Bradley, T. and Lowe, P. (eds), *Locality and Rurality*, Norwich: Geobooks, 45-64.

Vail, D. (1991), 'Economic and ecological crises: transforming Swedish agricultural policy', in Friedland, W., Busch, L., Buttel, F. and Rudy, A. (eds), *Towards a New Political Economy of Agriculture*, Boulder: Westview, 256-274.

Vanclay, F. (1981), *A Criticism of the NeoScarcity School in Political Ecology*, Unpublished B.Sc.(Hon) dissertation, School of Australian Environmental Studies, Griffith University.

Vanclay, F. (1986), *Socio-Economic Correlates of Adoption of Soil Conservation Technology*, Unpublished M.Soc.Sci. thesis, Department of Anthropology and Sociology, University of Queensland, St Lucia.

Vanclay, F. (1991) 'Land Degradation: A Social rather than Technical Issue', *Conference Summary Papers*, Third National Conference of the Environment Institute of Australia, 23-25 October 1991, Canberra, Australia.

Vanclay, F. (1992a), 'The social context of farmers' adoption of environmentally-sound farming practices', in Lawrence, G., Vanclay, F. and Furze, B. (eds), *Agriculture, Environment and Society,* Melbourne: Macmillan, 94-121.

Vanclay, F. (1992b), Farmer attitudes or media depiction of land degradation: which is the barrier to adoption?, *Regional Journal of Social Issues* 26: 41-50.

Vanclay, F. (1992c), *Landcare News Reader Survey.* Report to the Soil Conservation Service of NSW, Wagga Wagga: Centre for Rural Social Research, Charles Sturt University.

Vanclay, F. (1992d), The barriers to adoption often have a rational basis', People Protecting their Land, Volume 2, *Proceedings of the 7th International Soil Conservation Organisation Conference,* Sydney, September 1992, 452-458.

Vanclay, F. (1992e) 'Barriers to Adoption: A General Overview of the Issues', *Rural Society* 2(2), 10-12.

Vanclay, F. (1993a) *Salt Awareness of Farmers in Junee and Cootamundra Shires, Report to the Department of Conservation and Land Management,* Wagga Wagga: Centre for Rural Social Research, Charles Sturt University, January.

Vanclay, F. (1993b) 'Utilising Farmer Knowledge in the State Promotion of Sustainable Agriculture', *Paper presented to the European Society for Rural Sociology Conference,* Wageningen Agricultural University, The Netherlands, August 1993.

Vanclay, F. (1994a) *The Sociology of the Australian Agricultural Environment,* Wageningen Agricultural University, (published PhD thesis).

Vanclay, F. (1994b) 'A Crisis in Agricultural Extension', *Rural Society* 4(1), 10-13.

Vanclay F. (1994c) 'Hegemonic Landcare', *Rural Society* 4(3/4), 45-47.

Vanclay, F. and Bronstein, D. (eds) (1995) *Environmental and Social Impact Assessment,* Chichester: Wiley.

Vanclay, F. and Cary, J. (1989), *Farmer Perceptions of Dryland Soil Salinity,* School of Agriculture and Forestry, University of Melbourne.

Vanclay, F. and Glyde, S. (1994) *Land Degradation and Land Management in Central NSW,* Report to NSW Agriculture, Wagga Wagga: Centre for Rural Social Research, Charles Sturt University.

Vanclay, F. and Lawrence, G. (1992) 'A Blue-Green Politics?', *Arena* No 98, 10-14.

Vanclay, F. and Lawrence, G. (1993), 'Environmental and social consequences of economic restructuring in Australian agriculture', *International Journal of Sociology of Agriculture and Food,* No 3: 97-118.

Vanclay, F. and Lawrence, G. (1994a), 'Farmer rationality and the adoption of environmentally sound practices: a critique of the assumptions of traditional agricultural extension', *European Journal of Agricultural Education and Extension* 1(1): 59-90.

Vanclay, F. and Lawrence, G. (1994b), 'Scientists, Science and Agricultural Biotechnology: Public Sector and Private Sector Research Agencies', *Paper Presented to the Sociology of Agriculture Working Group,* World Congress of Sociology, Bielefeld, Germany, 21 July 1994

Vanclay, F. and Lockie, S. (1993), *Barriers to the Adoption of Sustainable Crop Rotations: Final Report,* Report to the NSW Department of Agriculture, Wagga Wagga: Centre for Rural Social Research, Charles Sturt University.

Walker, K. (1992), 'Introduction', in Walker, K. (ed.), *Australian Environmental Policy,* Kensington: University of New South Wales Press, 1-18.

Warren, D., Brokensha, D., Slikkerveer, L. (eds) (1991), *Indigenous Knowledge Systems: The Cultural Dimensions of Development,* London: Kegan Paul.

Waters, M. and Crook, R. (1993), *Sociology One,* Third Edition, Melbourne: Longman Cheshire.

Watson, C. (1992), 'An ecologically unsustainable agriculture', in Lawrence, G., Vanclay, F. and Furze, B. (eds), *Agriculture, Environment and Society,* Melbourne: Macmillan, 19-32.

Weber, M. (1976), *The Agrarian Sociology of Ancient Civilizations,* London: New Left Books.

Wettenhall, G. (1991), 'Selling off the farm: the second green revolution', *Australian Society* June: 14-17.

Wilkinson, R. and Barr, N. (1993) *Community Involvement in Catchment Management.* Victorian Department of Agriculture: Melbourne.

Williams, D. (ed.) (1990), *Agriculture in the Australian Economy* (3rd edn), Melbourne: Sydney University Press.

Williams, K., Cutler, T., Williams, J. and Haslam, C. (1987), 'The end of mass production?', *Economy and Society,* 16(3): 405-439.

Williams, M. (1979), 'The perception of the hazard of soil degradation in South Australia: a review', in Heathcote, R. and Thom, B. (eds), *Natural Hazards in Australia,* Canberra: Australian Academy of Science, 275-289.

Woerkum, C. van (1989), Extension and persuasion in environmental and agricultural policy', in Andersson, M. and Nitsch, U. (eds), *The Role of Agricultural Extension: Proceedings of the 9th European Seminar on Extension Education in Sweden,* Uppsala: Department of Extension Education, Swedish University of Agricultural Sciences, 6-14.

Woerkum, C. van (1991), 'Extension science: to broaden the scope', in Koehnen, T. and Cristovao, A. (eds), *New Focuses on European Extension Education: The Issues,* Villa Real, September, 7-12.

Woerkum, C. van (1992), 'The contribution of communication to the solution of environmental problems in agriculture', in Meulenbroek, J.L. et al. (eds), *Agriculture and Environment in Eastern Europe and the Netherlands,* Proceeding of a Congress to celebrate the opening of a new administration building of the Wageningen Agricultural University, Sept 5-6, 1990, Wageningen: Wageningen Agricultural University, 39-48.

Woerkum, C. van, and van Meegeren, P. (1990), 'Environmental problems and the use of information: The Importance of the Policy Context', *Knowledge in Society: The International Journal of Knowledge Transfer* 3(3): 44-49.

Woerkum, C. van, and van Meegeren, P. (1991), 'Environmental problems and the use of information: The Importance of the Policy Context', in Kuiper, D. and Röling, N. (eds), *The Edited Proceedings of the European Seminar on Knowledge Management and Information Technology,* Wageningen: Department of Extension Science, Wageningen Agricultural University, 231-236.

Woodhill, J. (1991), 'Landcare - Who cares? current issues and future directions for Landcare in NSW', *Discussion Paper from the 1990 Review of Landcare in NSW,* Landcare and Environment Program, Centre for Rural Development, University of Western Sydney - Hawkesbury.

Woods, E., Moll, G., Coutts, J., Clark, J. and Ivin, C. (1993), *Information Exchange: A Report Commissioned by Australia's Rural Research and Development Corporations,* Canberra: Land and Water Resources Research and Development Corporation.

Working Group on Sustainable Agriculture (1991), *Sustainable Agriculture,* Melbourne: CSIRO.

Wormwell, G. (1990), 'Cotton grows glamorous', *AIM* 10, November, 3.

INDEX